Constructions at work

To my family: Ali, Aliza, and Zach, with love

Constructions at work

The nature of generalization in language

ADELE E. GOLDBERG

OXFORD
UNIVERSITY PRESS

OXFORD
UNIVERSITY PRESS

Great Clarendon Street, Oxford OX2 6DP

Oxford University Press is a department of the University of Oxford.
It furthers the University's objective of excellence in research, scholarship,
and education by publishing worldwide in

Oxford New York

Auckland Cape Town Dar es Salaam Hong Kong Karachi
Kuala Lumpur Madrid Melbourne Mexico City Nairobi
New Delhi Shanghai Taipei Toronto

With offices in

Argentina Austria Brazil Chile Czech Republic France Greece
Guatemala Hungary Italy Japan Poland Portugal Singapore
South Korea Switzerland Thailand Turkey Ukraine Vietnam

Oxford is a registered trade mark of Oxford University Press
in the UK and in certain other countries

Published in the United States
by Oxford University Press Inc., New York

British Library Cataloguing in Publication Data

Data available

Library of Congress Cataloguing in Publication Data

Data available

Typeset by SPI Publisher Services, Pondicherry, India
Printed in Great Britain
on acid-free paper by
Biddles Ltd., King's Lynn

ISBN 0-19-9-268517   978-0-19-9268511
ISBN 0-19-9-268525 (pbk)   978-0-199268528 (pbk)

3 5 7 9 10 8 6 4 2

Contents

Acknowledgements

My graduate students have become some of my closest colleagues. Devin Casenhiser, Giulia Bencini, Nitya Sethuraman, and Theeraporn Ratitamkul have all collaborated in the experimental work discussed here. Devin in particular took the lead in the learning experiments, and also acted as an initial copy-editor for the manuscript. Working with them has made working a pleasure.

I owe a huge debt to several mentors, particularly Ray Jackendoff, George Lakoff, Ron Langacker, and Mike Tomasello for their inspiration, encouragement, advice, and friendship. Mike has been especially instrumental in encouraging my forays into experimental work, generously offering his advice. I also owe a special debt to my dear old friends and colleagues Laura Michaelis and Hana Filip for always being willing to confer on ideas, data, references, and Life.

John Davey and Lyndsey Rice have been very responsive and helpful editors, and John Taylor and Ad Foolen graciously provided excellent comments and suggestions on an earlier version of this manuscript. I'm sure I will regret any advice I failed to heed. I am also grateful to Rachel Ezra for her excellent work on the index.

I spent six wonderful years at the University of Illinois, Urbana-Champaign, and I am indebted to the university for affording me a wonderful working environment. I also learned a great deal from Abbas Benmamoun, Kay Bock, Gary Dell, Cindy Fisher, Susan Garnsey, Silvina Montrul, Greg Murphy, and Brian Ross. Many good friends made living in Urbana exciting and fun.

I was also fortunate to spend a year at the Center for Advanced Study in the Behavioral Sciences at Stanford putting these ideas to paper. I am grateful to many there, but especially to Bill Croft and Ivan Sag for many helpful discussions, and to Adela Pinch for the therapeutic walks through the hills.

I am also indebted to my new colleagues at Princeton, having finally made my way back East, where I grew up. The New Jersey accent is music to my ears. In particular I'm grateful to Len Babby, Bill Bialek, Christiane Fellbaum, Mirjam Fried, Bob Freidin, Sam Glucksberg, Phil Johnson-Laird, Danny Oppenheimer, Dan Osherson, Rob Shapire, and Edwin Williams for sharing their insights. Gay Eggers and the psychology staff have been ever ready to help with good cheer.

Over the years, I have also been grateful for enlightening discussions with Farrell Ackerman, Kathleen Ahrens, Ben Ambridge, Eric Besson, John Bryant,

Liz Bates, Cedric Boeckx, Peter Culicover, Jeff Elman, Chuck Fillmore, Paco Gonzálvez García, Lila Gleitman, Mary Hare, Michael Israel, Beth Levin, Tsuguro Nakamuro, Ira Noveck, Malka Rappaport Hovav, Bruno Estigarribia, Paul Kay, Jim Lavine, Alec Marantz, Bill Morris, Anat Ninio, Norvin Richards, Valeria Quochi, Matt Shibatani, Eve Sweetser, Mark Turner, and Annie Zaenen.

I have been fortunate beyond words to have enjoyed the love, support, wisdom, and laughter of my mother, sister, and brother, Ann, Elena, and Ken. Other beloved family members include Harry and Birdie, Tiffany, Dave, Herb, Babak, Lisa, Azita, Parivash, Faizallah, Nina, Marilyn, and all my wonderful cousins, nieces, and nephews.

Finally, my deepest gratitude goes to my own family, who managed to take pride and pleasure in my work even though it has meant time away from them. I am grateful to Aliza for being a blast of sunshine and to Zach for making me laugh. I can't imagine two more wonderful smiles. My husband Ali, a finer person I've never known, has encouraged me from my first day in linguistics, and has made all my dreams come true.

Part I
Constructions

1

Overview

1.1 Introduction

Constructions—form and meaning pairings—have been the basis of major advances in the study of grammar since the days of the ancient Stoics. Observations about particular linguistic constructions have shaped our understanding of both particular languages and the nature of language itself. But only recently has a new theoretical approach emerged that allows observations about constructions to be stated directly, providing long-standing traditions with a framework that allows both broad generalizations and more limited patterns to be analyzed and accounted for fully. Many linguists with varying backgrounds have converged on several key insights that have given rise to a family of approaches, here referred to as *constructionist approaches.*

The term *constructionist* has more than one intended association. The primary motivation for the term is that constructionist approaches emphasize the role of grammatical CONSTRUCTIONS: conventionalized pairings of form and function. In addition, constructionist approaches generally emphasize that languages are learned—that they are CONSTRUCTED on the basis of the input together with general cognitive, pragmatic, and processing constraints.

In an earlier book, *Constructions,* I focused primarily on arguments for adopting a constructionist approach to argument structure and an analysis of several argument structure constructions (Goldberg 1995). The goal of the present book is to investigate the nature of generalization in language: both in adults' knowledge of language and in the child's learning of language. That is, *Constructions at Work* addresses how and why constructions can be learned and how cross-linguistic and language-internal generalizations can be accounted for. Throughout, the function of constructions is emphasized. The present work consists of three parts:

Part I: Constructions: The chapters in Part I combine to provide the theoretical context, including an overview of constructionist approaches (this chapter), arguments in favor of adopting a constructionist approach to argument structure and clarification of what the approach involves (Chapter 2), and an overview of evidence in favor of a *usage-based* model of grammar that includes both item-specific information and generalizations (Chapter 3). Parts II and III are aimed at accounting for how and why constructions are learned, and why the generalizations that exist take the form that they do.

Part II: Learning Constructions: After investigating what is learned (Chapter 3), Chapters 4–6 address issues surrounding how it is learned (Chapter 4), how generalizations are constrained (Chapter 5), and why constructional generalizations are learned (Chapter 6).

Part III: Generalizations: Chapters 7–9 aim to redress a perceived failure of constructionist approaches to account for language-internal and cross-linguistic generalizations without stipulation. "Island" and scope phenomena are investigated in Chapter 7, and it is argued that a combination of the function of constructions and processing demands accounts for a wide range of facts. Chapter 8 argues that recognizing the function of constructions is essential to accounting for their distribution—the focus of this chapter is English subject–auxiliary inversion. Chapter 9 investigates several cross-linguistic tendencies in argument realization and demonstrates that attention to independently needed pragmatic, processing, and cognitive processes accounts for the data without appeal to stipulations that are specific to language.

Constructionist approaches share certain foundational ideas with the mainstream "generative" approach that has held sway for the past several decades (Chomsky 1957, 1965, 1981). Both approaches agree that it is essential to consider language as a cognitive (mental) system; both approaches acknowledge that there must be a way to combine structures to create novel utterances, and both approaches recognize that a non-trivial theory of language learning is needed.

In other ways, constructionist approaches contrast sharply with the generative approach. The latter has held that the nature of language can best be revealed by studying formal structures independently of their semantic or discourse functions. Ever-increasing layers of abstractness have characterized the formal representations. Meaning is claimed to derive from the mental dictionary of words, with functional differences between formal patterns being largely ignored. Semi-regular patterns and cross-linguistically unusual patterns are generally viewed as "peripheral," with a narrowing band of data seen as relevant to the "core" of language. Mainstream generative theory argues further that the complexity of core language cannot be learned induct-ively by general cognitive processes and therefore learners must be hard-wired with knowledge that is specific to language ("universal grammar").

Several basic tenets of constructionist approaches are discussed below. Each represents a major divergence from the mainstream generative approach, and a return in many ways to a more traditional view of language.

Constructions: what they are

ALL LEVELS OF GRAMMATICAL ANALYSIS INVOLVE CONSTRUCTIONS: LEARNED PAIRINGS OF FORM WITH SEMANTIC OR DISCOURSE FUNC-TION, including morphemes or words, idioms, partially lexically filled and fully general phrasal patterns.[1] Examples are given in Table 1.1.

Any linguistic pattern is recognized as a construction as long as some aspect of its form or function is not strictly predictable from its component parts or from other constructions recognized to exist. In addition, patterns are stored as constructions even if they are fully predictable as long as they occur with sufficient frequency (see Chapter 3 for discussion).

Unlike mainstream generative grammar, constructionist approaches tend to emphasize the detailed semantics and distribution of particular words, grammatical morphemes, and cross-linguistically unusual phrasal patterns; the hypothesis behind this methodology is that an account of the rich semantic/pragmatic and complex formal constraints on these patterns readily extends to more general, simple, or regular patterns.

TABLE 1.1. Examples of constructions, varying in size and complexity

Morpheme	e.g. *pre-, -ing*
Word	e.g. *avocado, anaconda, and*
Complex word	e.g. *daredevil, shoo-in*
Complex word (partially filled)	e.g. [N-s] (for regular plurals)
Idiom (filled)	e.g. *going great guns, give the Devil his due*
Idiom (partially filled)	e.g. *jog* <someone's> *memory, send* <someone> *to the cleaners*
Covariational Conditional	The Xer the Yer (e.g. *the more you think about it, the less you understand*)
Ditransitive (double object)	Subj V Obj1 Obj2 (e.g. *he gave her a fish taco; he baked her a muffin*)
Passive	Subj aux VPpp (PP$_{by}$) (e.g. *the armadillo was hit by a car*)

---

[1] Sag, Wasow, and Bender (2003) prefer to reserve the term construction for combinations of form–meaning pairings, using the term SIGN to refer to individual form–meaning pairings.

As an example of an unusual pattern, consider the Covariational Conditional construction in Table 1.1 above (e.g. *the more you think about it, the less you understand*). The construction is interpreted as involving an independent variable (identified by the first phrase) and a dependent variable (identified by the second phrase). *The* normally occurs with a head noun but in this construction it requires a comparative phrase. The two major phrases resist classification as either noun phrases or clauses. The requirement that two phrases of this type be juxtaposed is another non-predictable aspect of the pattern. Because the pattern is not strictly predictable, a construction must be posited that specifies the particular form and function involved (Culicover and Jackendoff 1999).

Even basic sentence patterns of a language can be understood to involve constructions. That is, the main verb can be understood to combine with an argument structure construction (e.g. transitive, intransitive, ditransitive, etc.). The alternative is to assume that the form and general interpretation of basic sentence patterns of a language are determined by semantic and/or syntactic information specified by the main verb (Grimshaw 1990; Levin and Rappaport Hovav 1995; Pinker 1989). Admittedly, the sentence patterns given in (1) and (2) do appear to be determined by the specifications of *give* and *put* respectively:

(1)   Chris gave Pat a ball.

(2)   Pat put the ball on the table.

Give is a three argument verb and is expected to appear with three complements corresponding to agent, recipient, and theme. *Put*, another three argument verb, requires an agent, a theme, and a location, and appears with the corresponding three complements in (2). However, while (1) and (2) represent the prototypical case, the interpretation and form of sentence patterns of a language are not reliably determined by independent specifications of the main verb. For example, it is implausible to claim that *sneeze* has a three-argument sense, and yet it can appear in (3). The patterns in (4–6) are likewise not naturally attributed to the main verbs:

(3)   "He sneezed his tooth right across town." (Robert Munsch, *Andrew's Loose Tooth*, Scholastic Canada Ltd., 2002)

(4)   "She smiled herself an upgrade." (Douglas Adams, *Hitchhiker's Guide to the Galaxy*, New York: Harmony Books, 1979)

(5)   "We laughed our conversation to an end." (J. Hart, *Sin*, New York: Ivy Books, 1992)

(6) "They could easily co-pay a family to death." (*New York Times,* January 14, 2002)

(7) "You have to consequate your children when they mess up." (Dr. Phil, forwarded by L. Gleitman, January 27, 2005)

Examples need not be particularly novel to make the point. Verbs typically appear with a wide array of complement configurations. Consider the verb *slice* and the various constructions in which it can appear (labeled in parentheses):

(8)   He sliced the bread.   (transitive)

(9)   Pat sliced the carrots into the salad.   (caused motion)

(10) Pat sliced Chris a piece of pie.   (ditransitive)

(11) Emeril sliced and diced his way to stardom. (way construction)

(12) Pat sliced the box open.   (resultative)

In all of these expressions *slice* means to cut with a sharp instrument. It is the argument structure constructions that provide the direct link between surface form and general aspects of the interpretation, such as something acting on something else (8), something causing something else to move (9), someone intending to cause someone to receive something (10), someone moving somewhere despite obstacles (11), someone causing something to change state (12) (Goldberg 1995).

While English has some dramatic instances in which basic argument structure constructions convey contentful meaning, examples exist in other languages as well. For example, Shibatani notes that in Croatian, the dative subject construction can be used to imply an attitudinal stance, unspecified by any particular word or morpheme in the construction (Shibatani 1999):

(13) Pil-o   mi   se   piv-o
     Drink-3SG.PAST I.DAT REF beer-NOM.3SG.NEUT
     Lit. "To me, the beer drank itself": real meaning "I *felt like* drinking beer"

In French, certain verbs such as "to slide" can be used intransitively or transitively, with attendant differences in meaning:

(14) Il glisse.
     He slid.

(15) Il glisse un livre a Marie.
     He slides a book to Marie.   (Willems 1997)

In another French construction, the main clause indirect object is interpreted as the subordinate clause possessor:

(16)   Le fisc   lui   estime   une fortune de 3 millions de francs.
       The IRS to him estimates a   fortune of 3 million   francs
       "The IRS thinks that he has a fortune of 3 million francs." (Koenig 1993)

In Maasai, an External Possessor ("possessor raising") construction allows a second object of the verb to be interpreted as a possessor of the other object:

(17)   ɛ-ya   al-túngání   [en-kitók]   [ol-coní]   (Payne 1997)
       3-take MSG-person.NOM FSG-woman.ACC MSG-skin/ACC
       "The person/man will take the woman's animal skin."

Many languages have constructions in which no verb is expressed at all. These cases are prime examples of argument structure constructions, since their meaning cannot naturally be attributed to a (non-existent) verb. For example, Lambrecht (2004) observes a verbless construction ((*et*) NP *qui* VP) in French is used to convey a focused entire proposition:

(18)   FOC [tout le monde qui part en weekend]
       all the world   who leaves in weekend
       "Everyone is leaving for the weekend."

Russian also has a pattern where the verb can be omitted in certain motion constructions (as well as in copular constructions), particularly when the manner of motion is not relevant, and when a telic goal of motion is expressed as in:

(19)   Kirill   v magazin   (Chidambaram 2004)
       Kirill-NOM to store-ACC
       "Kirill goes/will go to the store."

When a telic goal of motion is not expressed, the required meaning can sometimes be coerced by the construction as in:

(20)   Kirill   iz   magazina   (Chidambaram 2004)
       Kirill-NOM from store-GEN
       "Kirill just got back from the store."

The literal meaning of (20) is simply "K. from store," but because the construction requires an end point, an implicit deictic goal ("here") is inferred, resulting in the interpretation, "K. just got back (arrived here) from the store."

German has an interesting verbless construction which conveys incredulity; it involves the morpheme, *und*, normally used to convey simple conjunction:

(21)   Larry und Arzt?!
       Larry and doctor
       "Larry, a doctor?!"   (Sailer 2002)

It is always possible to posit a null verb in order to account for these verbless constructions, but such a move seems motivated only by the desire to maintain the position that the main verb determines the overall form and meaning of a sentence. The constructionist approach provides an alternative that avoids positing an unseen verb: the phrasal pattern (with or without any morphological indicators) may specify the main relational predicate of the clause.

Other patterns such as passive, topicalization, questions, and relative clauses are learned pairings of form and function—constructions, as well. Each pairs certain formal properties with a certain communicative function. The fact that various formal versions of these constructions recur cross-linguistically stems from their highly useful communicative functions.

Thus, constructions exist in every language. They are essential to an effective account of both unusual or especially complex patterns and they may be invoked to account for the basic, regular patterns of language as well.

An emphasis is placed on subtle aspects of the way we construe the world

Different surface forms are typically associated with slightly different semantic and/or discourse functions. Take, for example, the DITRANSITIVE construction, which involves the form, Subj V Obj1 Obj2. The ditransitive form evokes the notion of transfer or "giving." This is in contrast to possible paraphrases. For example, while (22) can be used to mean that Liza bought a book for a third party because Zach was too busy to buy it himself, (23) can only mean that Liza intended to give Zach the book. Similarly while (24) can be used to entail caused motion to a location (the book is caused to go to storage), the ditransitive pattern requires that the goal argument be an animate being, capable of receiving the transferred item (cf. 25–26). As is clear from considering the paraphrases, the implication of transfer is not an independent fact about the words involved. Rather the implication of transfer comes from the ditransitive construction itself.

(22)   Liza bought a book for Zach.

(23)   Liza bought Zach a book.   (ditransitive construction)

(24)   Liza sent a book to storage.

(25)   Liza sent Stan a book.

(26)   ??Liza sent storage a book.

In addition to semantic generalizations, there also exist generalizations about INFORMATION STRUCTURE properties of the construction, or the way in which a speaker's assumptions about the hearer's state of knowledge and consciousness at the time of speaking is reflected in surface form. In particular, there is a statistically reliable tendency for the recipient argument to have already been mentioned in the discourse (often encoded by a pronoun), which is much more pronounced than in the prepositional paraphrases (see Chapter 7). Facts about the use of entire constructions, including register (e.g. formal or informal) and dialect variation, are stated as part of the construction as well. Constructionist approaches provide a direct way of accounting for these facts, since constructions specify a surface form and a corresponding function.

A *"what you see is what you get" approach to syntactic form is adopted*

Constructionist theories do not derive one construction from another, as is generally done in mainstream generative theory. An actual expression typically involves the combination of at least half a dozen different constructions. For example, the example in (27) involves the list of constructions given in (28)

(27) what did Liza buy Zach?

(28) a. *Liza, buy, Zach, what, do* constructions
      b. Ditransitive construction
      c. Question construction
      d. Subject–Auxiliary inversion construction
      e. VP construction
      f. NP construction

Note that "surface form" need not specify a particular word order, although there are constructions that do specify word order. For example, the form of the ditransitive construction discussed above is characterized in terms of a set of grammatical relations. The overt order of arguments in (27) is determined by a combination of a verb phrase construction with the Question construction, the latter of which allows for the "theme" argument (represented by *What*) to appear sentence-initially. No underlying levels of syntax, nor any phonologically empty elements are posited.

Constructions are combined freely to form actual expressions as long as they are not in conflict. Unresolved conflicts result in judgments of ill-formedness. For example, the specification of the ditransitive construction that requires an animate recipient argument conflicts with the meaning of *storage* in (26) resulting in unacceptability, unless "storage" is construed to mean the people who work in storage.

1.2 Parts II and III

Parts II and III of this monograph focus on EXPLANATION. Chomsky (1965) rightly points out that any valid theory of language must achieve both descriptive and explanatory adequacy. Descriptive adequacy demands that the theory provide a full and accurate description of the language under study. Constructionist approaches excel at being descriptively adequate, since both generalizations and idiosyncratic particulars can be captured.

There has been ample discussion among linguists as to what should "count" as an explanation in linguistics (Croft 2001; Haspelmath 1999; Jackendoff 2002; Newmeyer 2003; Van Valin and LaPolla 1997). The need for lengthy discussions does not, perhaps, reflect well on the state of our field. One would hope that we would share enough of a paradigm to agree on an explanation when we see one. But since we are not yet at that stage, we enter into a brief discussion of the topic here.

Explanations are generally answers to some "how" or "why" questions. The existence of language poses at least two major questions:

1. **How do learners acquire generalizations such that they readily produce a potentially infinite number of novel utterances based on a finite amount of input?**
2. **Why are languages the way they are?**

There are different general types of explanation potentially relevant to language (Haspelmath 1999). For example, consider the following answers to the question, why does my cellphone have a button that is labeled *dial*?

A. **General–formal explanation:** demonstrates that something is an instance of a larger generalization: e.g. because all push-button phones have a button labeled dial.
B. **General–functional explanation:** identifies the purpose or function: e.g. because people use the word out of habit, and because it is short and fits easily on small instruments.
C. **General–historical explanation:** identifies general constraints on historical change that give rise to the phenomenon: all phones used to have rotary dials, and we often retain words that are no longer synchronically motivated, e.g. we also *hang up* our cell phones, *turn* the channel on TVs, and *cut and paste* our *papers* on the computer.

Mainstream generative grammar has traditionally focused on question (1) and has provided generalizing–formal types of explanations (such as A).

Formal generalizations about language are hypothesized to be part of "universal grammar," a genetic endowment of knowledge that is specific to language. It is often assumed that that there are no theoretically interesting reasons for *why* grammars are the way they are beyond formal generalizations. In fact, it is grammar's essentially arbitrary nature, it is argued, that makes it unlearnable, such that critical aspects of it must be hard-wired into our genetic make-up.

Clearly, explanations that generalize (i.e. are independently motivated) are a critical part of explanation for everyone, in any field, since an explanation that refers only to the specific question at hand runs the risk of being ad hoc. General constructs that are independently needed are always preferable. It is for this reason that cognitive and functional linguists prefer explanations that rely on semantic and pragmatic facts, since these sorts of facts are independently required for the sake of interpretation in a way that (underlying) syntactic representations or phonetically null features are not. Moreover, in the same spirit of seeking general explanations, cognitive and functional linguists tend to seek out generalizations that apply beyond language whenever these can be justified; a goal is to posit as little that is specific to language as possible.

Part II: Learning Generalizations

Constructions are understood to be LEARNED on the basis of the input and general cognitive mechanisms. Part II focuses on several interrelated issues related to how and why constructions are learned. In particular, Chapter 3 documents the need for a usage-based model of our linguistic knowledge that allows for input-driven inductive learning. Chapter 4 reports experimental evidence that indicates that constructions can in fact be learned on the basis of the input, and further explores empirical evidence for parallels in the learning of non-linguistic categories. Chapter 5 explores the question of how generalizations are constrained, that is, issues surrounding partial productivity of constructions. Chapter 6 provides motivation for why constructions are learned: exploring the issue of what advantage constructions provide.

Usage-based Models   There is ample evidence from research in non-linguistic categorization that ITEM-SPECIFIC KNOWLEDGE EXISTS ALONGSIDE GENERALIZATIONS. Drawing on parallels between general categorization and linguistic knowledge, Chapter 3 emphasizes the need for both item-specific knowledge and generalizations in language. Patterns are stored if they are sufficiently frequent, even when they are fully regular instances of other constructions and thus predictable (Barlow and Kemmer 2000; Bybee and Hopper 2001; Bybee 1995; Diessel 2001; Goldberg 1999; Langacker 1988; Losiewicz 1992; Thompson and Fox 2004; Tomasello 2003).

For example, there is ample motivation to recognize that we record information about how particular verbs are used in particular argument structure patterns. Evidence comes from several sources: (*a*) issues related to the partial productivity of constructions, (*b*) evidence that children are quite conservative in their productive use of argument structure patterns, and (*c*) evidence that the frequencies with which particular verbs appear in particular argument structure patterns influences speakers' online comprehension.

A usage-based model is needed to account for facts beyond argument structure as well. For example, in our everyday speech, it is often the case that one particular formulation is much more conventional than another, even though both conform to the general grammatical patterns in a language (Pawley and Syder 1983). For example, it's much more idiomatic to say *I like lima beans* than it would be to say *Lima beans please me*. The idiomatic nature of language is made clearly evident by cross-language comparison. For example, in English, a punch in the face can cause a black eye. In German, it's a blue eye: *ein blaues Auge*. An English speaker may boast that she slept like a log or a dog, but a German speaker is more likely to sleep like a woodchuck or marmot (*wie ein Murmeltier schlafen*).[2] An English speaker might complain that someone thinks of themselves as God's gift to the world, whereas in French the complaint would be that the prima donna believed himself sprung from Jupiter's thigh (*se croire sorti de la cuisse de Jupiter*); while an English speaker might bore someone with endless conversation, a French speaker has to avoid holding someone's leg (*tenir la jambe à quelqu'un*). Such idiomatic expressions pervade our everyday speech. Knowing them is part of knowing a language, and clearly their specifics are not determined by universal principles but must be learned on an item-by-item basis (cf. also Jackendoff 2002).

Inheritance hierarchies have long been found useful for representing all types of generalizations. The construction-based framework captures linguistic generalizations within a given language via the same type of inheritance hierarchies that have long been used for representing non-linguistic generalizations (Goldberg 1995, 2003; Hudson 1990; Lakoff 1987; Pollard and Sag 1994). Broad generalizations are captured by constructions that are inherited by many other constructions; subregularities are captured by positing constructions that are at various midpoints of the hierarchical network.

---

[2] Examples from <http://german.about.com/library/weekly/aa030899.htm>.

Exceptional patterns are captured by low-level constructions. For example, the "What's <X> doing <Y>?" construction, which has a fixed form and connotes some sort of unexpectedness, captures a subregularity in the grammar of English. It inherits from several other more general constructions, including the Left Isolation, the Subject–Auxiliary Inversion, the Subject-Predicate and the Verb-Phrase constructions (Kay and Fillmore 1999). Language-specific generalizations across constructions are captured via inheritance networks.

Most construction grammars these days are usage-based, due to the sort of evidence to be reviewed in Chapter 3.

How and why constructions are learned   Crucially, all linguists recognize that a wide range of semi-idiosyncratic constructions exists in every language, constructions that cannot be accounted for by general, universal, or innate principles or constraints. These include the types of examples given in Table 1.2. Generative linguists argue that these constructions exist only on the "periphery" or "residue" of language—that they need not be the focus of linguistic or learning theorists. Constructionists on the other hand have zeroed in on these constructions, arguing that whatever means we use to learn these patterns can easily be extended to account for so-called "core" phenomena. In fact, by definition, the core phenomena are more regular, and tend to occur more frequently within a given language as well. Therefore if anything, they are likely to be easier to learn. Since every linguist agrees that the "peripheral," difficult cases must be learned inductively on the basis of the input, constructionists point out that there is no reason to assume that the more general, regular, frequent cases cannot possibly be.

TABLE 1.2. Productive or semi-productive constructions that are unusual cross-linguistically and must be learned on the basis of the input

Construction Label	Example (reference)
Time *away* construction	*Twistin' the night away* (Jackendoff 1997b)
What's X doing Y?	*What's that fly doing in my soup?!* (Kay and Fillmore 1999)
Nominal Extraposition	*It's amazing the difference!* (Michaelis and Lambrecht 1996b)
Mad Magazine construction	*Him, a doctor?!* (Lambrecht 1990)
N P N construction	*house by house; day after day* (Williams 1994)
Stranded preposition construction	*Who did he give that to?*
Omitted determiners (and vocatives)	*I don't think, Mac/*cabby, that this is the best way to go.* (Zwicky 1974)

In fact, constructionists argue that language *must* be learnable from positive input together with fairly general cognitive abilities since the diversity and complexity witnessed does not yield to nativist accounts (Culicover and Jackendoff 1999; Elman et al. 1996; Tomasello 2003, forthcoming). Research in this area is quickly gaining momentum. A number of constructionists have made good on the promise to explain how particular constructions are learned (Diessel and Tomasello 2001; Israel 2002). It turns out that the input is not nearly as impoverished as is sometimes assumed (Pullum and Scholz 2002; Scholz and Pullum 2002); analogical processes can be seen to be viable, once function as well as form is taken into account (Goldberg 1999; Israel 2002; Tomasello 2003); there is good reason to think that children's early grammar is quite conservative, with generalizations emerging gradually (Lieven, Pine, and Baldwin 1997; Tomasello 2000, 2003); and the ability to record transitional probabilities and statistical generalizations in the input has proven a powerful means by which to learn certain types of generalizations, including word and phrasal boundaries (Saffran, Aslin, and Newport 1996; Saffran 2001a). In Chapter 4, we demonstrate that novel phrasal constructions can indeed be learned, and learned quickly. This chapter emphasizes parallels with the learning of non-linguistic categories, providing experimental results that demonstrate certain facilitory factors. Chapter 5 addresses the flip side of the coin: how generalizations are constrained. It is argued that children are exposed to constant indirect negative evidence that helps them to recover from overgeneralizations.

In suggesting that language is learned as a type of categorization, we undertake the obligation to explain why generalizations exist. We investigate this question from several perspectives. In Chapter 6, we focus on the advantage both in terms of predictive value and in terms of priming that the learning of constructional generalizations provides. In Part III, we address the existence of generalizations across languages and/or across constructions within a single language.

Part III: Explaining Generalizations

Information Structure and Syntax : Information structure, or how information is packaged in a clause so as to convey the relevant information status of various propositions, is a complicated topic. While semantics has come into its own as an explanatory force in linguistics, with linguists of all persuasions paying closer attention to lexical and constructional meaning, information structure has been largely left to specialists. Nonetheless, by building on the previous work in this area that does exist, we will see that attempting to bridge the gap between information structure and syntax allows us to begin to unravel some long-standing puzzles often assumed to only be amenable to formal treatments (Erteschik-Shir 1979; Erteschik-Shir 1998a; Ioup 1975; Kluender 1998; Kluender and Kutas 1993; Van Valin and LaPolla 1997). These include constraints on long-distance dependencies ("Island constraints") and scope phenomena.

Subject–Auxiliary Inversion: A Natural Category :   Mainstream generative grammar has traditionally held a belief in "autonomous syntax"—the idea that formal patterns are, in general, most profitably analyzed without reference to their functions. This early view has recently morphed into the much weaker claim that certain purely syntactic generalizations exist (Newmeyer 1998). In Chapter 8, we critically evaluate this claim with respect to a case that has been cited as a clear example of a purely formal generalization: subject–auxiliary inversion. We observe that the purely formal generalization fails to predict any of the special properties of the family of constructions that require subject–auxiliary inversion. At the same time, recognizing the family of related functions that the relevant constructions serve, enables us strongly to motivate the distribution of the pattern.

Cross-linguistic Generalizations :   A driving question behind much of linguistic research is, what is the typology of possible constructions and what constrains it?

The constructionist approach takes a somewhat different view of what is universal about language than mainstream generative approaches. As Tomasello (2003) observes, what is truly remarkable is the degree to which human languages differ from one another, given that all languages need to express roughly the same types of messages. Constructionist approaches anticipate such fairly wide variability across languages (Croft 2001; Foley and Van Valin 1984; Garry and Rubino 2001).

Nonetheless, there are certain cross-linguistic generalizations that require explanation. For example, constructionist approaches agree that there are recurring semantic prototypes ("conceptual archetypes" in Langacker's terminology) across languages, owing to the fact that humans are overall, more alike than different: we are all born with the same basic conceptual apparatus, with the same basic communicative demands, and we all live in the physical world with forces of gravity, bodies, and night and day (cf. also Lakoff 1987; Webelhuth and Ackerman 1998). Certain semantic/pragmatic functions are so relevant and useful that they can be found in language after language (Croft 2001).

Cross-linguistic generalizations that relate form and function are explained by appeal to general cognitive constraints together with the functions of the constructions involved. Constructionists turn to grammar-external explanations such as universal functional pressures, iconic principles, and processing and learning constraints to explain such empirically observable cross-linguistic generalizations. For example, certain generalizations about how arguments tend to be expressed cross-linguistically can be explained by appeal to iconic and analogical processes (Givón 1991; Givón and Ute Language Program 1980; Haiman 1985; Lambrecht 1994). Constraints on long-distance dependency constructions (traditional "island constraints") appear to yield to processing explanations that take into account the function of the constructions involved (Erteschik-Shir 1998a; Kluender 1998; Kluender and Kutas 1993). Processing accounts have also been suggested to account for word-order options (Hawkins 1994; Yamashita and Chang 2001). Discourse-pragmatic motivations underlie other sorts of generalizations, such as correspondences between the number of semantic arguments and the number of complements expressed.

Even among generative linguists there has been a trend toward the view that many generalizations about language that have traditionally been seen as requiring recourse to innate stipulations that are specific to language can actually be explained by general cognitive mechanisms. For example, the fact that that most languages seem to have noun and verb categories may be explained by the existence of corresponding basic semantic categories (Baker 2004). Hauser, Chomsky, and Fitch go so far as to suggest that the only innate ability specific to language that may be required are the recursive interfaces to phonology and semantics, and they allow that even these may turn out not to be specific to language (Hauser, Chomsky, and Fitch 2002). Indeed, a recursive aspect of semantics is required for our (non-linguistic) theory of mind: the fact that I can imagine what you think about what someone else believes. Recursive structure is also evident in familial relationships (the child of a parent can become a parent herself) and in other non-linguistic domains such as stacking and weaving. Thus the ability to use recursion in language may have been an exaptation from possible precursors in other domains.

Constructionist approaches

There is a growing body of work within the constructionist framework, broadly construed: Barðdal (1999); Bates and Goodman (1997); Bencini and Goldberg (2000); Boas (2000); Booij (2002); Choi (2003); Chung (2001); Croft (2001); Davidse (2000); Davies (2005); Dominey and Inui (submitted); Fillmore, Kay, and O'Connor (1988); Fillmore, Kay, Michaelis, and Sag (in progress); Fried (2002); Gleitman et al. (1996); Goldberg (1992, 1995); Hovav and Levin (1998); Iwata (2000); Jackendoff (2002); Kaschak and Glenberg (2000); Kay (2002a); Kay and Fillmore (1999); Lambrecht, (1994); Michaelis (1994, 2004); Michaelis and Lambrecht (1996a); Mughazy (2002); Pizer (1994); Riehemann (1997); Rowlands (2002); Rudanko (2002); Sag (1997); Schmid and Ungerer (2002); Schmid (2001); Schultze-Berndt (1998); Shibatani (1999); Toivonen (2002); Verhagen (2002); Williams (1994); Zadrozny and Ramer (1995); Zhang (1998); Zwicky (1994).

There are of course fine points of divergence even within these approaches. For example, particular constructionist approaches differ in the types of inheritance that are allowed (default or complete), in the type of semantics that is emphasized, and the degree of emphasis on usage and psychological reality. Several differences are discussed in Chapter 10. Also in Chapter 10, certain less closely related approaches that are occasionally labeled "constructional" in the literature are discussed (Borer 1994, 2001; Hale and Keyser 1998; Marantz 1997). It is argued that while these approaches resemble constructionist approaches insofar as they pair some sort of syntactic representation with some sort of semantic representation, they differ from other constructionist approaches in critical ways. It is also argued that the differences inherent in these approaches lead to serious empirical problems.

What makes a theory that allows constructions to exist a "construction-based theory" is the idea that the network of constructions captures our grammatical knowledge of language *in toto*, i.e. **it's constructions all the way down.**

To summarize, constructionist approaches demand answers to the question of how knowledge of language comes to be in the mind of a learner, and also to the question of *why* languages are the way they are: why the generalizations that exist, exist. These are the questions that are the focus of Parts II and III. But before we turn to these questions, we first must address the issue of what level of generalization requires explanation. This is the focus of Chapter 2.

2

Surface generalizations[1]

> *A mathematician, a physicist, an engineer, and a linguist are trying to decide if all odd numbers are prime. The mathematician says, "one's prime, 3's prime, 5's prime, 7's prime, 9's not prime, so no." The physicist says, "one's prime, 3's prime, 5's prime, 7's prime, 9's not prime, but maybe that's experimental error." The engineer says, "one's prime, 3's prime, 5's prime, 7's prime, 9's prime..."*
>
> *The linguist says, "one's prime, 3's prime, 5's prime, 7's prime. Aha! We have a universal generalization. Nine doesn't seem to be prime, but it MUST be prime at some underlying level of representation!"*
>
> (Joke told by Arnold Zwicky during his Presidential Address at the Linguistic Society of America, 1992)

Since the earliest days of generative grammar, there has existed a strong tendency to consider one construction in relation to a particular rough paraphrase. Initially this was a result of the emphasis on transformations that derived one pattern from another. While today there exist many non-derivational theories for which this motivation no longer exists, the traditional outlook has not completely lost its grip, as can be seen from continuing focus on partial or incomplete generalizations such as the "dative" construction or the "locative" alternation. This chapter argues that it is profitable to look beyond alternations and to consider each surface pattern on its own terms. The arguments in this chapter extend those presented in Goldberg (1995) in addressing the advantages of non-derivational accounts of argument structure (cf. also Michaelis and Ruppenhofer 2001); at the same time, the analysis of particular constructions discussed is consistent with that offered in my earlier work.

It is observed that when considering instances of the *same* surface pattern involving *different* words, similarities should be attributed to the surface

[1] I am grateful to Tsuguro Nakamura, Laura Michaelis, and Hideyuki Sugiura for helpful discussion on this topic and also to Tsuguro and an anonymous reviewer for extensive comments on an earlier draft. This chapter is based on Goldberg (2002).

pattern and differences to the different verbs and arguments involved. A specific proposal by Baker (forthcoming) to derive certain constructions from their rough paraphrases is critiqued below (Section 2.4) in order to demonstrate that what appear to be arguments in favor of derivations are often in fact arguments in favor of attention to surface structure instead.

2.1 What is meant by surface form?

In this section we clarify what is meant by *surface form*. Surface form need not specify a particular word order, nor even particular grammatical categories, although there are constructions that do specify these features. Adopting the notation of Goldberg (1992, 1995) we might characterize the ditransitive construction as in fig. 2.1.

The first line provides the semantics of the construction. The ditransitive involves a predicate with three arguments; these three arguments are labeled "agent," "recipient," and "theme" for convenience but there is no assumption that these thematic role labels are drawn from a universal or limited set. Instead the roles are determined by the meaning of the construction. In this case the main predicate is "CAUSE-RECEIVE" or more informally "give," and the three argument roles correspond to the three major entities involved in the semantics of giving.

As is the case with other constructions, including words and morphemes, constructions typically allow for a range of closely related interpretations. The "CAUSE-RECEIVE" predicate associated with the ditransitive construction is subject to systematic variation depending on which verb class it interacts with. For example, the construction can be used to convey "intention to cause to receive" when used with verbs of creation; "refuse to cause to receive" when used with verbs of refusal, etc. See Bryant (2005); Goldberg (1992, 1995); Kay (2001); Koenig and Davis (2001); Leek (1996); for details and slightly differing analyses.

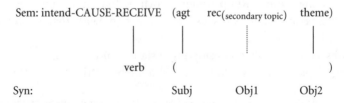

FIGURE 2.1. The ditransitive construction

As indicated in Fig. 2.1 by the lines between the argument roles of the construction and the role array of the verb, the verb and its own arguments are integrated (unified, "fused") with the predicate and arguments of the construction. Solid lines indicate that the argument role of the construction must fuse with an independently existing participant role of the verb. Dashed lines indicate that the argument role of the construction may be contributed by the construction without a corresponding role existing as part of the inherent verbal meaning. That is, a corresponding participant role of the verb may exist, but need not.

Information structure properties of constructions are specified by subscripts. The specification noted is that the recipient argument is a secondary topic. This statistical generalization as well as important syntactic implications of this generalization are discussed in depth in Chapter 7 (Section 7.3).

Finally, the linking of roles to grammatical relations is provided. See Goldberg (1995: ch. 4) for arguments that both generalizations and exceptional mappings can be captured by positing construction-specific linking generalizations when constructions are related within an inheritance hierarchy.[2]

As discussed in Chapter 1, it is important to realize that reference to form in the definition abstracts away from specifics of surface form that can be attributed to other constructions. That is, an actual expression typically involves the combination of many different constructions. For example, the expression in (1) involves the eleven constructions given in (2):

(1)   A dozen roses, Nina sent her mother!

(2)   a. Ditransitive construction
       b. Topicalization construction
       c. VP construction
       d. NP construction
       e. Indefinite determiner construction
       f. Plural construction
       g. *dozen, rose, Nina, send, mother* constructions

---

[2] By appealing to grammatical relations instead of grammatical categories in the syntax of this construction, we do not intend that grammatical categories are irrelevant in general, contra what is assumed in a critique by Newmeyer (forthcoming). In the present case, grammatical relations are found to be more perspicuous because they serve to distinguish the ditransitive from the construction involved in (i):

   (i)   She considered him a fool.
   (ii) She considered him crazy.

Expression (i) is an instance of a construction that has the grammatical relations: Subj V Obj PRED (see Gonzálvez García 2000). Both predicates and second objects can appear as NPs. PRED, however, can also be realized as an AP, as in (ii).

Constructions are combined freely to form actual expressions as long as they can be construed as not being in conflict (invoking the notion of construal here is intended to allow for processes of accommodation or *coercion*; see Kadmon 2001; Michaelis 2004). Thus, the same ditransitive construction is involved in active declarative form as well as in topicalized, clefted, or questioned forms. That is, the recipient argument is an Object whether or not it appears directly after the verb or whether it appears as a distantly instantiated topicalized NP. It is, for example, the (non-echo) question construction that determines the fact that the wh-word appears sentence-initially in English.[3]

Constructional approaches share with mainstream generative grammar the goal of accounting for the creative potential of language (Chomsky 1957, 1965). That is, it is clear that language is not a set of sentences that can be fixed in advance. Allowing constructions to combine freely as long as there are no conflicts, allows for the infinitely creative potential of language. At the same time, constructional approaches generally recognize that grammars don't generate sentences, speakers do. That is, a speaker is free to creatively combine constructions as long as constructions exist in the language that can be combined suitably to categorize the target message, given that there is no conflict among the constructions (cf. Fillmore 1975; Langacker 1987a: ch. 2 for discussion).

2.2 The Surface Generalization Hypothesis

Many theoretical approaches today eschew the need for any kind of trans-formation or derivation (Bresnan 1982, 1994; Fillmore et al. forthcoming; Johnson-Laird 1968; Lakoff 1987; Langacker 1987a, 1991; Pollard and Sag

---

[3] Given the syntactic specifications of the ditransitive construction given in fig. 2.1, a separate but related construction is required to account for passives of ditransitives since such passives do not involve the same linking of grammatical functions to roles. Supporting this idea that there exists a passive ditransitive construction is the fact that the actual form of the passive ditransitive is not strictly predictable. At one time in the history of English, only impersonal passive ditransitives were allowed (Denison 1993). In some languages, both the recipient and patient arguments can passivize, whereas in English only the recipient argument can be passivized (Alsina and Mchombo 1990; Polinsky 1998). In addition, as discussed in Chapter 8, the information structure properties of the passive ditransitive are distinct from that of the active ditransitive. The fact that there is something non-predictable about the passive ditransitive entails that a construction be posited. If it were possible to predict the specifics of passive-ditransitive expressions in some way, an alternative route would be possible. The alternative would be to define the ditransitive construction more abstractly such that it would not specify that there are two objects overtly realized, nor the specifics of the mapping between thematic roles and grammatical functions; instead the only syntactic or linking specification would be that there is an extra object (Kay 1997). In this way, it would be possible to unify the highly abstract "extra object" construction with passive without positing an additional ditransitive-passive construction. See also work by Bryant that aims to provide underspecified characterizations of argument structure constructions such that they unify with passive, active, raising constructions to yield surface forms (Bryant 2005).

1987). A compelling reason to avoid positing derivations in favor of an emphasis on surface form is simply that there are typically powerful generalizations surrounding particular surface forms that are more broad than those captured by derivations or transformations. We refer to these broader generalizations as SURFACE GENERALIZATIONS. The present chapter focuses on the domain of argument structure; the surface formal and semantic/pragmatic generalizations in this domain are captured by ARGUMENT STRUCTURE CONSTRUCTIONS: pairings of form and function that are used to express basic clauses. Several case studies are considered including the "dative" construction and the "locative alternation." It is argued that these traditional divisions underrepresent the generalizations that exist. We address the question of how to account for paraphrase relations, as well as how to account for various differences between instances of the same argument structure construction, in Section 2.8. In this section we review an important historical precedent for the form of argument made here.

Despite being the most influential architect of transformations and later, derivations, Chomsky (1970) put forward one of the most well-known and widely accepted arguments against deriving one subset of data from another. His argument was based on Surface Generalizations. In particular, he demonstrated that NPs based on "derived" nouns (i.e. nouns that have verbal counterparts) have exactly the syntax of NPs based on underived nouns. In particular they both have the same internal and external syntax. Both types occur with the full array of determiners, often pluralize, and take complements marked with *of*. Both types can appear as the subject of passives or can be distantly instantiated by a question word. To avoid an account in which this is mere coincidence, Chomsky reasoned, we need to recognize that both types are base-generated as nouns instead of attempting to derive certain NPs from clausal counterparts (Lees 1960). With Williams (1991), we might call this the "**target syntax argument**": it is preferable to generate A directly instead of deriving it from C if there exists a pattern B that has the same target syntax as A and is clearly not derived from C.

Williams (1991) makes a parallel "target semantics argument." He observes that the meanings of NPs based on underived nouns fall into the same set of categories as the meanings of NPs based on "derived" nouns. For example, extent, temporal duration, and evaluative states can be predicated of both "derived" and underived nouns (1991: 584):

Extent

(3)   a. The destruction of the city was complete. Potentially derived
      b. The carnage was complete.   Underived

Temporal duration

(4)   a. The destruction of the city took four hours. Potentially derived
      b. The war took four hours.   Underived

Evaluative state

(5)   a. The destruction of the city was horrible. Potentially derived
      b. The war was horrible.   Underived
      (not just the fact of the war, but the way the war was)

At the same time, Williams observes, the range of NP meanings is distinct from the range of S meanings, as seen in examples (6)–(8) (1991: 585):[4]

Extent

(6)   *That the city was destroyed was complete.

Temporal duration

(7)   *That the city was destroyed took four hours.

Evaluative state

(8)   That the city was destroyed was horrible.
      (can mean that the fact that the city was destroyed was horrible, but not
      that the way it was destroyed was horrible)

In short, given that the syntax and semantics of derived nouns are like those of underived nouns, and unlike the syntax and semantics of clauses, it is clearly simpler to allow the nouns to be base-generated as nouns as opposed to deriving them from clause structures.

   Beyond target syntax and target semantics arguments are what are referred to below as "input" syntax and semantics arguments. In particular, one should not attempt to derive A from C if there exists a pattern D that has the same syntax and semantics as C and yet cannot serve as input from which to derive A.

---

   [4] In this, Williams echoes Langacker (1987b) insofar as the semantics of Ns are argued to be distinct from that of Ss.

When both target syntax/semantics and input syntax/semantics hold, the relationship between possible input and possible output is symmetric, providing an argument against deriving either type of pattern from the other.

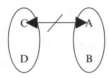

The arguments put forth by Chomsky (1970) (and Williams 1991) have been robust. For more than three decades, the field has resisted the temptation to derive deverbal NPs from clauses. What is less widely acknowledged is that parallel arguments hold in the domain of argument structure. These arguments support the idea that each argument structure pattern is best analyzed on its own terms, without relying on explicit or implicit reference to a possible alternative paraphrase. It is argued that such reliance effectively puts blinders on, and limits a theory's ability to state the full extent of the relevant generalizations.

We might label the hypothesis that the target syntax and target semantics arguments and the input syntax and semantics arguments hold in general for argument structure patterns, the *Surface Generalization Hypothesis*.

Surface Generalization Hypothesis: there are typically broader syntactic and semantic generalizations associated with a surface argument structure form than exist between the same surface form and a distinct form that it is hypothesized to be syntactically or semantically derived from.

Support for the Surface Generalization Hypothesis provides substantial motivation for the assumption that the syntax of argument structure should be represented without recourse to derivations. It also suggests that it is possible to overplay the importance of alternative forms (paraphrases).[5]

---

[5] Bolinger, an early advocate of the Surface Generalization Hypothesis put the problem with ignoring semantic differences between alternative formal patterns this way:

[It is often considered normal] for a language to establish a lunacy ward in its grammar or lexicon where mindless morphs stare vacantly with no purpose other than to be where they are....

2.3 The Ditransitive construction

Many generative theories derive the two ditransitive or double object expressions in (9) and (10) from distinct input expressions on the left, which correspond to their rough paraphrases (Baker 1988; Larson 1988):

(9)   Mina bought a book for Mel.→ Mina bought Mel a book.

(10)   Mina sent a book to Mel.→ Mina sent Mel a book.

Even certain constructionist approaches treat the two examples on the right as instances of two independent constructions (e.g. Jackendoff 1990; Kay 2001). However, both instances of the ditransitive share many properties with each other and differ systematically from their paraphrases (see also Langacker 1991; Oehrle 1975). That is, there are good reasons to group the two "outputs" together as distinct from the "inputs" as follows:

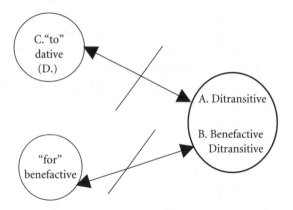

Let us focus on the generalization boldfaced in the diagram above: namely that ditransitives paraphrasable with "to" form a class with those that are paraphrasable with "for." Similarities between the two proposed types of ditransitive expressions (A and B in the diagram above) begin with their shared surface form; in its simple active form, the ditransitive involves an active verb followed by two objects. In both cases questioning the recipient argument is less than fully acceptable (11a,b, in Table 2.1); adverbs may not separate the two object arguments in ditransitives (12a,b); both types of

[C]ontemporary linguistics has carried the fantasy to new heights, and expanded it with a new version of an old vision, that of synonymy: not only are there mindless morphs, but there are mindless differences between one construction and another. (Bolinger 1977)

See also Haiman (1985); Johnson-Laird (1967, 1968); Langacker (1987a); Wierzbicka (1988).

ditransitives prefer the recipient argument to be more given or topical than the theme argument (cf. 13a,b; see Chapter 7 for discussion). Semantically, both so-called *for* ditransitives and so-called *to* ditransitives require that the recipient argument be construed to be animate (14a,b) (Green 1974; Oehrle 1975; Partee 1965/1979).[6] More generally, as noted in Chapter 1, the ditransitive evokes the notion of "giving" in various ways, depending on the verb class involved (15a,b). Each of these parallels are represented in the left-hand column of Table 2.1. The paraphrases are shown to be distinct in each of these ways, in the right-hand column.

Other interpretations for the ditransitive can also be systematically related to the notion of giving, in that they may imply that transfer will occur if certain satisfaction conditions evoked by the main verb occur (16a), that transfer will *not* occur (16b), or that the antonymic relation of giving, that of taking away, occurs (16c).[7]

Ditransitives, whether paraphrasable with "to" or "for," pattern alike and differently from their prepositional paraphrases:

TABLE 2.1. Ditransitives pattern alike (left) and differently than their prepositional paraphrases (right)

Ditransitives : Subj V Obj Obj2 (paraphrasable with "to" or "for")	Paraphrases
(11) a. ??Who did Mina buy a book?	Who did Mina buy a book for?
b. ??Who did Mina send a book?	Who did Mina send a book to?
(12) a. *Mina bought Mel yesterday a book.	Mina bought a book yesterday for Mel.
b. *Mina sent Mel yesterday a book.	Mina sent a book yesterday to Mel.
(13) a. ??Mina bought Mel it.	Mina bought it for Mel.
b. ?? Mina sent Mel it.	Mina sent it to Mel.
(14) a. ??Mina sent that place a box.	Mina sent a box to that place.
b. ??Mina bought that place a box.	Mina bought a box for that place.
(15) a. Mina bought Mel a book. (Mina intends to give Mel the book)	Mina bought a book for Mel. (the book could be intended for Mel's mother, bought by Mina because Mel was too busy to buy it)
b. Mina sent Mel a book. (Mina intends to give Mel the book)	Mina sent a book to storage.

---

[6] See Goldberg (1992, 1995: 146–7) for arguments that the first Object in *The paint job gave the car a higher sales price* is based on a Causal Events as Transfers metaphor. The constraint that the recipient must be animate holds of the source domain of the metaphor.

[7] Goldberg (1995: 150) argues that even instances of such relatively marked examples such as *Cry me a river* can be related to the notion of giving via a metaphorical extension.

(16)   a. Mina guaranteed/offered Mel a book. (If the guarantee or offer is
          satisfied, Mel will receive a book)
       b. Mina refused Mel a book. (Mina caused Mel not to receive a book)
       c. Mina cost Mel his job.   (Mina causes Mel to lose his job)

It has been suggested that the existence of variable meanings undercuts the claim of a unified construction (Nakajima 2002). The criticism stems from the belief that the concepts of, for example, giving, not giving, and taking away cannot naturally be classed together. However, it is clear that both the negation and the antonym of a particular concept are closely associated with that concept. For example, a concept and its antonym typically serve as strong associates for one another in psycholinguistic studies (Meyer and Schvaneveldt 1971): e.g. *hot* primes *cold*, *high* primes *low*, and *giving* primes *taking away*. Negated sentences typically presuppose that the corresponding positive assertion has been asserted or might be believed in the particular context of use (Horn 1989). In this way we can see that giving, not giving, and taking away *are* in fact closely associated concepts.

The existence of a corresponding passive has been thought to differentiate ditransitives into two types; it has been claimed that only those with paraphrases involving *to* can be passivized (Fillmore 1965; Kay 2001). While it may be true that ditransitives that have paraphrases with *to* show a statistical tendency to passivize more easily than those that have paraphrases with *for*, the generalization is far from clear-cut as many have observed (Culicover and Wexler 1973; Erteschik-Shir 1979; Oehrle 1975). For example, the following examples appear to be equally acceptable, or if anything, (17a) is more acceptable than (17b) despite the fact that only (17b) is paraphrasable with *to*:

(17)   a. Mel was cooked a fine dinner by the new chef. (cf. The new chef
          cooked a fine dinner for Mel.)
       b. Mel was tossed a blanket by the babysitter. (cf. The babysitter
          tossed a blanket to Mel.)

Thus we see that ditransitive expressions pattern alike on a number of syntactic and semantic dimensions regardless of their potential paraphrases. Still, perhaps there are empirical facts that would indicate that a derivational relationship is important. A particular proposal is discussed below.

2.4 A Derivational Proposal

Many generative grammar proposals invoke underlying structure to capture paraphrase relations, although there has been a trend toward recognizing surface-level constructional generalizations, even within this general framework (Harley 2002; Marantz 1997). While it is perhaps impossible and certainly beyond the scope of the present chapter to try to critique all possible derivational accounts, it is worth examining at least one in more detail to understand both the possible allure of derivations and the underlying empirical issues that arise. So as to be certain not to argue against a straw man, I present arguments by Baker (1997), a leading proponent of derivational accounts of argument structure.

Baker assumes that all and only sentences with the same truth-conditional semantics must be derived from a common source (the UTAH hypothesis). Thus Baker does not try to defend a derivational account for *all* argument structure alternations. Recognizing the semantic difference between variants of the "load/spray" alternation, for example, he allows that each variant should be base-generated; the two surface forms then reflect two different possible construals of an event (following e.g. Dowty 1991; Goldberg 1995; Pinker 1989; Rappaport and Levin 1985).

As a prime example of an alternation that is claimed to support the derivational approach, Baker offers the ditransitive and its prepositional paraphrase.[8] The assumption is that there is no semantic difference between the ditransitive and its prepositional paraphrases. However, as we have already seen, only in the ditransitive is the requirement that transfer be intended operative (18a). In paraphrases with *for* a larger set of benefactive relationships are possible (Goldberg 1992, 1995; Green 1974; Oehrle 1976), as is evident in (18b):

(18) a. *Bill baked Chris a cake, but never intended for her to have the cake.
      b. Bill baked a cake for Chris, but never intended for her to have the cake—instead he did as a favor for Chris because Chris was too busy to bake it herself.

Thus if we accept that so called *to* ditransitives and *for* ditransitives should be treated under the same general rubric as argued above and assumed by Baker as well, then we can see that the basic assumption of synonymy underlying the derivational proposal is flawed from the outset.

But perhaps there are compelling syntactic motivations for a derivational account. Baker suggests that the recipient ("goal") argument has several special restrictions that distinguish it from other types of objects: it cannot be the subject of a depictive predicate (19a), it cannot be the non-head of a compound (19b), it cannot undergo "wh-movement" (19c), or heavy NP shift

---

[8] Levin and Rappaport Hovav (2003) similarly suggest that the "load/spray" alternation be accounted for by positing two distinct semantic representations, while the ditransitive and prepositional paraphrase, they argue, share the same semantic representation.

(19d), and it must take wide scope with respect to the second NP (19e) (Baker 1997):

(19) a. *She gave Mary$_i$ the towel undressed$_i$. (Williams 1980: 204)
      b. *spy-telling (cf. secret telling) (Baker 1997)
      c. ??Who did she give the towel? (Erteschik-Shir 1979)
      d. *She gave the towel the woman she just met. (Stowell 1981)
      e. The teacher assigned one student every problem: unambiguous scope assignment (Larson 1990: 604)

The derivational account proposes that these restrictions (several of which we will see are only apparent) can be accounted for if one assumes the recipient argument originates within a PP even in the double object construction. In the case of (19a), the logic of the argument is clear; the recipient argument appears to pattern just like the prepositional argument of the paraphrase in disallowing predication by depictive predicates (*hungry, wrapped*):

(20) a. *John gave the meat to Mary$_i$ hungry$_i$. (prepositional paraphrase)
      b. *She gave Mary$_i$ the meat hungry$_i$.   (ditransitive)

(21) a. John gave the meat$_i$ to Mary wrapped$_i$. (prepositional paraphrase)
      b. John gave Mary the meat$_i$ wrapped$_i$.   (ditransitive)

Thus a restriction against depictive predicates applying to recipient arguments would seem to follow from a generalization that depictive predicates only apply to subjects and objects; they cannot be used to predicate properties of prepositional complements (Williams 1980). If the recipient argument is underlyingly a prepositional phrase, then the fact that it patterns just like the prepositional argument of the paraphrase would be expected. However, contra the derivational account, depictive predicates *may* apply to certain ditransitive recipients:

(22) a. They gave her$_i$ communion awfully young$_i$.
      b. The guard gave him$_i$ a pat-down naked$_i$.

The prepositional paraphrases of these expressions differ in acceptability:

(23) a. They gave communion to her awfully young.
      b. ??The guard gave a pat-down to him naked.

Moreover, Pylkkanen (2003) notes that in other languages depictive predicates readily apply to the recipient argument of a ditransitive. Thus the idea that recipients disallow depictive predication is not well supported empirically.

The second observation is that the recipient argument of both the ditransitive and the prepositional paraphrase resists "incorporation" into a synthetic compound:

(24)   *spy-telling, *child-reading (Baker 1997)

The logic of this argument is somewhat less clear. It is true that the generalization does not depend on whether the argument is construed to be a recipient of the ditransitive or a goal argument of the prepositional paraphrase—indeed, it is impossible to tell the difference. There is likely to be a semantic explanation for the resistance of prototypically animate arguments to appear in compounds (Nunberg, Sag, and Wasow 1994). In any case, the restriction against incorporation is not likely to be an effect of the recipient argument being part of a PP, as the derivational account implies, because other arguments regularly expressed as PPs do readily incorporate, including, for example, locations (*river-fishing; sky-diving*).[9] Another reason why the restriction is not likely to be syntactic is that certain counterexamples exist, including *deity-offering*.

Moreover, the logic of the argument for a derivational account is deeply flawed in the case exemplified by the generalizations in (19c,d,e): instead of the recipient argument patterning like the goal prepositional argument in the paraphrase, it patterns *differently* from it. In particular, the prepositional goal argument can readily be questioned (with preposition stranded or not: (25a,b)), whereas the recipient argument of the ditransitive cannot be (25c):

(25)   a. To whom did you give the meat?
       b. Who did you give the meat to?
       c. ??Who did she give the towel?

Similarly, the prepositional dative can be involved in heavy NP shift, whereas the recipient argument of the ditransitive cannot be ((19d), repeated as (26)):

(26)   *She gave the towel the woman she just met. (Stowell 1981)
       (cf. John gave to Mary the meat he just bought at the store.)

As Baker acknowledges, it is not clear on his account what actually accounts then for the ill-formedness of (25c) and (26). Various stipulations are offered and the question is left open (p. 16).

In addressing the fact that the recipient argument of the ditransitive must take wide scope over the theme argument (cf. (19e) repeated as (27)), Baker again observes that the same is *not* true for the prepositional dative:

---

[9] Baker of course recognizes this fact (Baker 1988), but it nonetheless serves to undermine the explanation as to why recipients resist incorporation.

(27)   The teacher assigned one student every problem. (not ambiguous: only wide scope reading of "one student")

(cf. The teacher assigned one problem to every student. (ambiguous))

It is acknowledged that, in fact "Unfortunately, there is no satisfactory analysis available for the scope-freezing effect in double object constructions" (Baker 1997).[10] Still he concludes, "Nevertheless, we can be optimistic that, whatever the final analysis is, it will support the idea that only the dative double object construction has an underlying structure that does not match its surface form" (Baker 1997).

To summarize, let us return to the generalizations observed by Baker (cf. examples (19a–e)). The first two generalizations do not hold: the recipient argument *can* be the subject of a depictive predicate, and the recipient argument can at least occasionally be the non-head of a compound. Other generalizations, namely the resistance of the recipient argument of the ditransitive to appearing in long-distance dependency relations and its preference for a wide-scope interpretation with respect to the theme argument are not properties that motivate a derivational account of the ditransitive, because they serve to distinguish the ditransitive recipient from the recipient/goal argument of the prepositional paraphrase.[11]

---

[10] See Bruening (2001) for a proposal to account for the scope-freezing effect that depends on the syntactic structure of ditransitives. The fact that, as we shall see in Ch. 8, inverse scope is sometimes possible in the ditransitive immediately undermines this account, since the structural proposal would predict that inverse scope is categorically ruled out. In fact Breuning had claimed to have "established that wide scope for the second object is never available in double object . . . constructions, regardless of context or quantifier involved" (2001: 239).

[11] A final argument Baker offers is that while the NP PP variant has an unaccusative counterpart (cf. (i), (ii)), the NP NP does not (cf. (iii),(iv)):

(i)   The ring passed to Mary.
(ii)   The beer opened for Max.
(iii) *Mary passed the ring.
(iv)   *Max opened a beer. (on the reading that Max is a recipient, not an agent)

Once again, this would suggest that the ditransitive and the prepositional variant are distinctly different. Moreover it is clear that Baker's example of *pass* and *open* in (i–ii) are extremely atypical. In general, the agent is very much required in active sentences:

(v)   1.   *The milk gave to Mary.
       2.   *Salad fixed for Mary.
       3.   *The ball threw to Mary.
       4.   *The story told to Mary.
       5.   *The letter sent to Mary.
       6.   *The house built for Mary.

It is true that there do exist certain verbs that can be expressed with <theme goal> arguments, or alternatively with <agent theme goal> arguments, such as *pass* and *open* (also *move*), but there also

Thus Baker's description of the special properties of the ditransitive construction do not provide motivation for a derivational account; instead they beg for an explanation as to what makes the ditransitive construction *distinct* from its prepositional paraphrase. We return to answer this question in Chapter 7, where we will see that the information structure independently associated with the ditransitive construction predicts its behavior with respect to long-distance dependencies and scope assignment. It seems that the only thing that the respective paraphrases share with the ditransitives is the quite rough paraphrase relations themselves. There is no empirical motivation to derive ditransitives from prepositional paraphrases, nor is there motivation to treat ditransitives that admit of distinct paraphrases as more than minimal variants of each other. The robust generalizations are surface generalizations.

2.5 The Caused-Motion construction

Beyond target syntax and target semantics arguments are *input* syntax and semantics arguments: it is preferable to avoid deriving A from C if there exists a pattern D that has the same target syntax and semantics as C and yet cannot serve as input from which to derive A. By widening our focus beyond those expressions that may serve as paraphrases of ditransitives, we see that each paraphrase expression itself is a small part of a much broader generalization. For example, although only (28a) can be paraphrased by a ditransitive, it patterns together with (28b,c,d) both syntactically and semantically; in fact, all of the expressions in (28) can be captured by a single "caused-motion" construction (Goldberg 1995; cf. also Pinker 1989).

(28) a. Mina sent a book to Mel.
      b. Mina sent a book to Chicago.
      c. Mina sent a book toward the front of the room.
      d. Mina sent a book through the metal detector.

Although Baker (forthcoming), as we saw above, argues in favor of a derivational account of ditransitives, he recognizes that examples such as those in

exist certain verbs that appear with <recipient theme> arguments, or alternatively with <agent recipient theme> arguments. These include *get, rent,* and a non-standard use of *learn*:

 (vi)   1. She got the book.
        2. He got her the book.
 (vii) 1. She rented an apartment.
        2. Her mother rented her an apartment.
(viii) 1. She learned how to cook.
        2. She learned me how to cook. (non-standard English)

The facts are clearly variable depending on particular lexical items.

(28) should be treated alike, noting that "it seems artificial to say that the PP in [examples like (28a)] is not a locational path" (Baker forthcoming: 31; cf. also Marantz 1997).

Similar extensions of meaning that we saw above for the ditransitive likewise exist in the case of the caused-motion construction, even though the verb classes involved are distinct:

(29)   a. Mina coaxed Mel into the room.   (if coaxing is successful, Mel moves into the room)

       b. Mina helped Mel into the room.   (Mina helps Mel move into the room)

       c. Mina blocked Mel out of the room. (Mina causes Mel not to move into the room)

These facts motivate treating the caused-motion construction as a general construction, independent of the ditransitive.

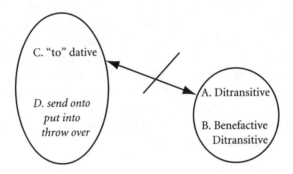

2.6 Load/Spray

Similar arguments can be made for other types of argument structure patterns that are often only considered in terms of alternations (Anderson 1971; Fraser 1971; Hook 1983; Rappaport and Levin 1988). Consider the following examples in (30) and (31):

(30)   Pat loaded the wagon with the hay.

(31)   Pat loaded the hay onto the wagon.

It has been suggested that the *with* variant is derived from the *into* variant (e.g. Rappaport and Levin 1988). Let us consider the "input" syntax and semantics first. The "into" variant can be seen to be an instance of the much broader caused-motion construction already discussed. That is, each of the examples in (32) shares the same surface syntax: each has a DO and prepositional oblique phrase. The semantics are closely related as well; in each case the subject argument serves to cause the motion of the DO argument along the path or to the location specified by the oblique argument:

(32)   a. Pat loaded the hay onto the wagon.
       b. Pat put the hay on the wagon.
       c. Pat shoveled the hay into the wagon.

The (b) and (c) forms of (32) cannot serve as input to any locative alternation, as can be seen in the ill-formedness of the following examples:[12]

(33)   a. *Pat put the wagon with hay.
       b. *Pat shoveled the wagon with the hay.

We thus see that the input syntax and semantics arguments hold for the *into* variant of the so-called locative alternation.

We now turn to the putative "output" syntax.[13] Consider just the following examples that have been independently classified as instances of the "locative" construction by Pinker (1989) and Levin (1993):

---

[12] Recognition of the fact that *load onto* type expressions are instances of the more general caused-motion construction serves to solve a certain paradox in the acquisition literature. It has often been observed that children are more likely to make overgeneralizations such as those in (i) than they are to overgeneralize the pattern with *with* as in (ii):

(i)   She filled the water into the cup. (relatively common)
(ii) She poured the cup with water.   (rare)

The explanation for this has been thought to be mysterious because it has been claimed that far fewer verbs appear in the *into* variant than the *with* variant (Gropen et al. 1991). The overall frequency of the *into* variant was thought to be less than the *with* variant as well. However, once we recognize that the *into* variant is actually part of a much larger generalization, the caused-motion construction, it becomes clear that the frequencies that matter are the frequencies associated with that broader generalization as compared with the causative-plus-instrumental-adjunct pattern. Sethuraman (2002: 146) has calculated just these statistics in the (Bates et al. 1988) corpus of speech between twenty-seven mothers and their twenty-eight-month-old children. The children produced a total of forty-two caused motion tokens compared with two transitive + *with* tokens. Mothers produced 199 caused-motion tokens compared with twenty-five transitive + *with* tokens. If we extrapolate from these patterns is seems that the caused-motion construction is 8–20 times more frequent than the causative + *with* adjunct construction. Figures for the *type* frequencies involved in the causative + *with* variant are not available, but the number could not possibly be higher than the token frequencies (since each unique type requires a new token), and is likely much lower. The type frequency of the caused-motion construction in children's speech is sixteen; in the mothers' speech it is forty. Again the *token* frequencies for the *with* construction are two and twenty-five, respectively. Since type frequency is correlated with productivity (Bybee 1985, 1995), the fact that children more readily overextend the caused-motion construction than the causative + *with* phrase is to be expected.

[13] Arguing that the *with* variant is an instance of a broader generalization is somewhat more controversial than the other cases discussed so far, primarily because *with* has a remarkably wide range of uses, but see Goldberg (2002) for discussion.

(34)   a. Pat loaded the wagon with the hay.
       b. Pat sprayed the wall with paint.
       c. They covered the wall with posters.
       d. Pat adorned the tree with lights.
       e. They tiled their bathroom with blue tiles from Mexico.
       f. They stained the wood with an all-weather protector.
       g. He speckled the canvas with dots.
       h. He wrapped the present with tin foil.

The examples in (34) are arguably all licensed by the combination of two constructions: a causative construction and an independent construction headed by *with*. In this way we account for the well-known fact that the DO in these examples is necessarily interpreted as affected in some way; e.g. the truck must be interpreted to be full or otherwise affected in *Pat loaded the truck (with hay)*. The same is not true for *Pat loaded hay onto the wagon* (Anderson 1971), which only entails that some hay is put on the wagon. That is, the affected status of the DO is rendered completely non-mysterious and requires no ad hoc stipulation (cf. also Rappaport and Levin 1988; Gropen et al. 1991).[14]

Adopting then the idea that the examples in (34 a–h) admit of a causal analysis, notice none of the examples (34 c–h) permit the alternation typically discussed as being relevant to *load* and *spray* as shown in (35c–h) (see also Pinker 1989):

(35)   a. Pat loaded the hay onto the wagon.
       b. Pat sprayed paint onto the wall.
       c. *They covered posters onto the wall.
       d. *Pat adorned lights onto the tree.

---

[14] One would have to be quite an ardent lumper to try to class all of these uses of *with* under a single sense. In (i) is a sampling of its various uses. Again, this is not the claim of the present chapter: we do not deny the existence of constructional homonymy. It is suggested, however, that it is important not to assume massive ambiguity without seeking out broader surface generalizations.

(i)   1. Elena traveled with Maya.
       2. Elena traveled with a hat on.
       3. Aliza traveled with great enthusiasm.
       4. People associate one variant with another.
       5. Be sure to mix the butter with sugar.
       6. The foundation provided the school with funding.
       7. Pat loaded the wagon with hay.
       8. The garden swarmed with bees.
       9. The detective entered the room with a key.
      10. Pat broke the window with a hammer.
      11. Pat watched the bear with a telescope.

    e. *They tiled blue tiles from Mexico onto their bathroom

    f. *They stained an all-weather protector onto the wood.

    g. *He speckled dots onto the canvas.

    h. *He wrapped tin foil onto the present.

Thus in accord with the target syntax argument, it is preferable to generate (35a,b) directly instead of deriving them from (34a,b) due to the fact that there exist (34c–h) that have parallel syntax and semantics and cannot be derived from (35c–h).

Other surface structure generalizations

Applying parallel reasoning, it can be demonstrated using the same input syntax/semantics arguments and target syntax/semantics arguments that the *for* paraphrase of certain ditransitives (e.g. (36a)) patterns together with (36 b,c) syntactically and semantically; each are instances of a transitive construction together with a benefactive adjunct construction. The shared syntax and semantics of these phrases argue for treating them alike (see Goldberg 2002).[15]

(36)   a. Mina sent a book for Mel.

      b. Mina sent a book for the library.

      c. Mina sent a book for her mother's sake.[16]

---

[15] An objection might be raised against the proposal that all *for*-benefactive phrases should be treated as a natural class. It might be argued that because more than one can co-occur, they cannot play the same role in the sentence:

(i)   Mina sent a book for Mel for her mother's sake.

That is, Fillmore (1968) long ago observed that only one semantic role of each type may occur in a single clause. We do not find two distinct agents or patients co-occurring in a single clause:

(ii)   *Bob melted the butter by Paul.

(iii)   *The butter was melted the ice.

But Fillmore's constraint only holds of certain semantic roles, namely those that can be identified as arguments. Adjuncts can freely be added as long as they do not imply a semantic contradiction; in particular they must be construed to have concentric semantic scope such that one more narrowly specifies another. Consider the following sentence with multiple temporal adjuncts:

(iv)   Mina met Bob in the morning yesterday at 11 o'clock.

Notice the hour (11 o'clock) must occur within the part of the day (morning) which is in turn within the day (yesterday). It cannot be claimed that the temporal phrases must be interpreted syntactically as a single complex adjunct because they need not be continuous:

(v)   a. Yesterday Mina met Bob in the morning at 11 o'clock.

     b. At 11 o'clock in the morning Mina met Bob yesterday.

     c. Yesterday Mina met Bob in the morning by the beach at 11 o'clock.

[16] It should be made clear that we are not claiming that *all for* phrases encode benefactives. Clearly there are other uses of the preposition *for* in English which may not be related, for example, those in

Other "alternations" have been analyzed similarly as independent surface generalizations, including the following:

(37)   a. Bees are swarming in the garden.
      b. The garden is swarming with bees. (Fried forthcoming; Jackendoff 1990; Salkoff 1983)

(38)   a. Tom is similar to Bill.
      b. Tom and Bill are similar. (e.g. Gleitman et al. 1996)

(39)   a. She broke it.
      b. It broke. (e.g. Van Valin 1990)

(40)   a. They considered him to be a fool.
      b. They considered him a fool. (e.g. Borkin 1974; Gonzálvez-García 2001)

Target and input syntax and semantics arguments argue against derivations. The formal patterns involved are more profitably viewed as constructions on their own terms. Each of these constructions can be seen to be much more general than is often recognized when only instances that alternate in certain ways are considered.

2.7 The role(s) of the verb

In this section, we address the question of how to account for the overlap in meaning in paraphrases and we examine why the overt interpretation of instances of the same construction may differ, and may allow distinct ranges of paraphrases. One key to these questions lies in the recognition that there is more to the interpretation of a clause than the argument structure construction used to express it. The overall interpretation is arrived at by integrating the argument structure construction with the main verb and various arguments, in light of the pragmatic context in which the clause is uttered.

(i) and (ii). Prepositions are typically highly polysemous and sometimes homonymous (see Brugman 1988; Lakoff 1987; Lindner 1981; Jackendoff 1990).

(i)   The statue stood for three hours.
(ii) He exchanged the socks for a belt.

That is, there do exist instances of *constructional homonymy*: a single surface form having unrelated meanings. In order to identify which argument structure construction is involved in cases of constructional ambiguity, attention must be paid to individual verb classes. In fact, in order to arrive at a full interpretation of any clause, the meaning of the main verb and the individual arguments must be taken into account (see Chapter 6). What is being proposed is simply that if a constituent looks like a benefactive phrase and acts like a benefactive phrase, then there is no reason to be shy about calling it a benefactive phrase.

There is a growing recognition that it is important to recognize a distinction between the frame semantics associated with a verb and the set of phrasal patterns or argument structure constructions that are available for expressing clauses (Gleitman et al. 1996; Goldberg 1992, 1995, forthcoming; Rappaport Hovav and Levin 1998; Iwata 2000; Jackendoff 1997b, 2002; Kay 2001; Pinker 1994). Following Goldberg (1992, 1995) the slots in the argument structure constructions are referred to as "argument roles." That is, phrasal constructions that capture argument structure generalizations have argument roles associated with them; these often correspond roughly to traditional thematic roles such as *agent, patient, instrument, source, theme, location,* etc. At the same time, because they are defined in terms of the semantic requirements of particular constructions, argument roles in this framework are more specific and numerous than traditional thematic roles (see also Jackendoff 1990, 2002).

Argument roles capture surface generalizations over individual verbs' participant roles. That is, each distinct sense of a verb is conventionally associated with rich frame semantic meaning that in part specifies certain *participant roles*: the number and type of slots that are associated with a given sense of a verb. A subset of those roles, namely those roles which are lexically *profiled*, are obligatorily expressed, or, if unexpressed, must receive a definite interpretation.[17] Lexical profiling, following the general spirit of Langacker (1987a, 1991), is designed to indicate which participant roles associated with a verb's meaning are obligatorily accessed, functioning as focal points within the scene, achieving a special degree of prominence. Fillmore (1977) similarly notes that certain participant roles are obligatorily "brought into perspective" achieving a certain degree of "salience." The notion of lexical profiling is intended to be a semantic one: it is a stable aspect of a word's meaning, and can differentiate the meaning difference between lexical items—cf. *buy* versus *sell* (Fillmore 1977) or *rob* versus *steal* (Goldberg 1995). Participant roles may be highly specific and are often unique to a particular verb's meaning; they therefore naturally capture traditional selectional restrictions.

Two general principles can be understood to constrain the ways in which the participant roles of a verb and the argument roles of a construction can be put into correspondence or "fused": the **Semantic Coherence Principle** and

[17] This generalization is true for English. In many other languages profiled arguments are omissable as long as they are given and non-focal in the context. At the same time, lexically profiled roles are expressed by a small set of core grammatical relations, when they are expressed in these languages as well.

the **Correspondence Principle** (see Goldberg 1995 and Goldberg forthcoming for further discussion).

The Semantic Coherence Principle ensures that the participant role of the verb and the argument role of the construction must be semantically compatible. In particular, the more specific participant role of the verb must be construable as an instance of the more general argument role. General categorization processes are responsible for this categorization task and it is always operative. This principle follows from the idea that argument structure constructions are learned by generalizing over the semantics of instances of the pattern used with particular verbs (e.g. Tomasello 1992, 2000; Goldberg 1999; this volume, Chapter 4).

As is the case with lexical items, only certain argument roles are profiled. In the case of simple sentences, only roles expressed in formally prominent positions are considered prominent. Such positions receive a special status in most theories as the set of "terms" which correspond to "core," "nuclear," or "direct" arguments. In English, profiled argument roles are realized as Subj, Obj, or the second object in ditransitives. These positions are afforded a high degree of discourse prominence, being either topical or focal in the discourse (see Keenan 1976, 1984; Comrie 1984; Fillmore 1977; Langacker 1987a for arguments to this effect.). Specifically the Correspondence Principle states that profiled participant roles of the verb must be encoded by profiled argument roles of the construction, with the exception that if a verb has three profiled roles, one can be represented by an unprofiled argument role (and realized as an oblique argument). The Correspondence Principle is a default principle, which is at root iconic.

The intuition behind the Correspondence Principle is that lexical semantics and discourse pragmatics are in general aligned. That is, the participants that are highly relevant to a verb's meaning (the profiled participant roles) are likely to be the ones that are relevant or important to the discourse, since this particular verb was chosen from among other lexical alternatives. In particular, the Correspondence Principle requires that the semantically salient profiled participant roles are encoded by grammatical relations that provide them a sufficient degree of discourse prominence: i.e. by profiled argument roles. As a default principle, the Correspondence Principle can be overridden by particular constructions that specify that a particular argument be deemphasized and expressed by an oblique or not at all. Passive, for example, is a construction that overrides the Correspondence Principle and insures that a normally profiled role (e.g. agent) be optionally expressed in an oblique *by* phrase. See Goldberg (forthcoming) for discussion of other constructions that serve to override the Correspondence Principle.

2.8 Accounting for paraphrase relations

We are now in a position to address the question of how the overlap in meaning between alternants is accounted for. The shared meaning can be attributed directly to the shared verb involved. That is, the verb evokes the same frame semantic scene and the same profiled participant roles. For example, if we assign the participant roles of *load* the labels loader, loaded-theme, and container, we can see that these roles line up with the roles in the caused motion construction and causative + *with* constructions as follows:

(41) Caused motion (e.g. *Pat loaded the hay onto the truck*)

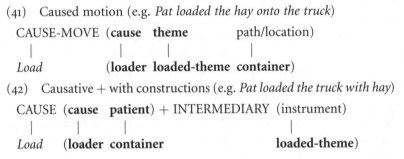

    CAUSE-MOVE (**cause   theme**   path/location)
         | | | |
    Load   (**loader loaded-theme container**)

(42) Causative + with constructions (e.g. *Pat loaded the truck with hay*)

    CAUSE (**cause   patient**) + INTERMEDIARY (instrument)
        | | | |
    Load (**loader container**   loaded-theme**)

All three of *load*'s roles are profiled. This includes the loaded-theme role even though that role is optional. This is because when that role is optional, it receives a definite interpretation as indicated by the strangeness of the following mini-conversation (see Fillmore 1986 for tests to distinguish definite from indefinite omission):

(43) She loaded the truck. #I wonder what she loaded onto it.

Because all three roles are profiled, one of the roles may be expressed as an oblique argument, in accordance with the Correspondence Principle. The Semantic Coherence Principle insures that only semantically compatible roles may be fused. As indicated above, the loaded-theme role of *load* may either be construed to be a type of theme as in (41) or an intermediary as in (42). The container role can either be construed to be a path/location as in (41) or a patient role as in (42). Construing the verb's roles as instances of different argument roles is what results in the different semantic construals of the two constructions.

On this view, there is no need to say that the *with* phrase itself designates a theme relation (cf. e.g. Jackendoff 1990). Instead, the fact that the hay is interpreted to be loaded onto the truck even in the *with* variant is attributed, not to the argument structure construction, but to the specifications of the verb *load*.

2.9 Arguments and Adjuncts

Recognizing that the verb has its own profiled participant roles that are distinct from the argument roles associated with an argument structure construction allows us to recognize four possibilities.

The most common, prototypical case is one in which the profiled participant roles of the verb line up isomorphically with the argument roles of an argument structure construction. This is represented in cell (a) in Table 2.2. Another familiar case is one in which a non-profiled role is expressed by an adjunct construction as represented in cell (d).

In other cases, there is a mismatch between the roles of the verb and the argument structure construction. Sometimes an argument role may not correspond to an independent obligatory participant role of the verb (c). For example, when the ditransitive construction is combined with verbs of creation, the recipient role is associated only with the construction; we do not need to assume that verbs of creation lexically specify a potential recipient. The same is true for certain verbs of motion as well. *Kick*, for example, only has two profiled participant roles; the recipient argument in *She kicked him the ball* is added by the construction.

The fourth logical possibility is that a profiled participant role of the verb is expressed by what is normally considered to be an adjunct phrase. As suggested in the (b) cell of the table, it seems appropriate to identify the *with* phrase that appears with *load* as an instance of this type. Clearly other

TABLE 2.2. Possible routes to argument status

	Role of argument structure construction	Not a role of argument structure construction
Profiled/obligatory participant role of verb	**(a) ARGUMENT of verb and construction** *He* devoured *the artichokes.* *She* gave *him* a letter. *She* put *the package on the table.*	**(b) ARGUMENT contributed by the verb** She loaded the wagon *with hay.*
Not a profiled/ obligatory participant of verb	**(c) ARGUMENT contributed by construction** He baked *her* a cake. She kicked *him* a ball. She sneezed *the foam off the cappuccino.*	**(d) Traditional ADJUNCT** He baked a cake *for her.* She broke the window *with a hammer.* She swam *in the summertime.*

instances of the same construction (including what are usually referred to as instruments) normally function as adjuncts (in being omissible, able to appear sentence-initially or after a clear adjunct such as *yesterday*, etc.). However, we have seen that the loaded-theme participant role of *load* is a profiled role. Because the *with* phrase codes a profiled role but is expressed by a phrase that is normally an adjunct, we might expect the behavior of this argument to fall somewhere in between that of traditional arguments and traditional adjuncts. In (44) we see that this is the case. While placing a clear adjunct before the *with* phrase is not crashingly bad in (44a); it is slightly less felicitous than the corresponding example in (44b).

(44) a. ?Pat loaded the wagon yesterday with hay.
      b. Pat broke the window yesterday with a hammer.

To summarize, we need not be blind to potential differences between uses of a construction with particular verbs. We need to account for verb meaning anyway, so it makes sense to look to verb meaning to determine whether differences in interpretation or in the range of possible paraphrases can be straightforwardly accounted for by it.

2.10 Conclusion

Recognizing surface generalizations surrounding argument structure (i.e. argument structure constructions) is important in that it leads to the recognition of generalizations in language that might otherwise be overlooked. But it is equally important to bear in mind that the meaning of a clause is more than the meaning of the argument structure construction used to express it. Individual verbs as well as particular arguments and context must be factored into the equation. In accounting for similarities among alternative expressions and dissimilarities among instances of the same argument structure construction, careful attention must be given to the verb which is the same in the former and different in the latter.

The arguments in this chapter should not be taken to imply that possible paraphrase relations play *no* role in the learning, processing, or representation of language. The essentially structuralist observation that the semantic interpretation of one linguistic construct tends to be affected by the existence of possible alternatives, receives empirical support from a number of studies (e.g. Lambrecht 1994; Lambrecht and Polinsky 1997; Moore and Ackerman 1999; Spencer 2001; McCawley 1978).

In Chapter 5 it is argued that the statistical use of paraphrases in actual discourse contexts is critical to unlocking Baker's paradox of partial productivity (Brooks and Tomasello 1999; Goldberg 1993, 1995; Pinker 1984; Regier 1996). Paraphrase relations can also be seen to be relevant to online choices made in production (see Chapter 6, Section 6.10).

However, it is less clear that one particular paraphrase should have a privileged status, nor that it is profitable to analyze one phrasal pattern solely by implicit or explicit reference to another. It has been argued here that by carefully examining a fuller range of surface phenomena, broader generalizations, surface generalizations, in the form of argument structure constructions, are revealed.

3

Item-specific knowledge and generalizations

There is always a tension between being a "lumper" and being a "splitter." As a biologist once put it, "splitters see very small, highly differentiated units— their critics say that if they can tell two animals apart, they place them in different genera...and if they cannot tell them apart, they place them in different species....Lumpers, on the other hand, see only large units—their critics say that if a carnivore is neither a dog nor a bear, they call it a cat" (Simpson 1945).

Language contains both large generalizations and idiosyncratic facts, and therefore we unavoidably find those who favor lumping, and those who favor splitting. The constructionist approach to grammar offers a way out of the lumper/splitter dilemma: the approach allows both broad generalizations and more limited patterns to be analyzed and accounted for fully. In particular, constructionist approaches are generally USAGE-BASED: facts about the actual use of linguistic expressions such as frequencies and individual patterns that are fully compositional are recorded alongside more traditional linguistic generalizations. In this chapter we consolidate evidence that such a usage-based model is required to account for the synchronic state of grammar. Before turning to the case of language, let us review some relevant findings in the non-linguistic category literature.

3.1 Exemplar-based knowledge in categorization generally

There is a good deal of evidence in the field of non-linguistic categorization that information about specific exemplars is stored. In a classic dot-recognition study, for example, Posner and Keele (1968) asked subjects to classify random dot patterns of low or high distortion from the average. One group had small distortions from the average; the other group had larger distortions from the same average. Subjects were subsequently tested on dot patterns with more distortion than either training set. The subjects in the high-distortion condition performed better on the task, indicating that they stored more than the simple average (prototype) of the instances on which they were trained.

In related tasks, it has been demonstrated that an instance that is more similar to recently studied instances will be classified more accurately than another which is equally similar to a prototype (Whittlesea 1987). And a recently studied exemplar will tend to be classified more accurately even if less similar to a prototype (Medin and Schaffer 1978).

Other work indicates that people are able to use statistical properties of the features of stored exemplars, including the range of values for each feature and correlations among features (Rips 1989). For example, if you learn of two bird species, one with three times the size of beak of the other, which do you think is more likely to sing? Most people are able to predict that the bird with the smaller beak is more likely to sing, presumably because of correlations between small size and small beak, and small size and ability to sing among bird exemplars. Since these correlations were not likely consciously taught or recognized, it seems that the generalization is made on the fly on the basis of stored exemplars.

Exemplar-based models of categorization have been proposed in order to capture these sorts of empirical facts (Medin and Schaffer 1978). In these models, a category is represented by a collection of instance representations. Classification of new instances is based on their similarity to the stored exemplars. It is fair to say that until very recently such models dominated work on categorization in cognitive psychology.

Exemplars are somewhat abstract

It is important to realize that exemplar-based models of categorization do not do away with abstraction completely. Generally attributes that are more relevant to the task at hand are more likely to be noticed. Any aspect of an exemplar that is not recorded because the learner failed to (unconsciously) notice it, is obviously not stored. This represents a degree of abstraction over the actual input: if a given stimulus, S, has attributes a, b . . . z, but the person witnessing S only records attributes a, b, c, and d, the resulting representation will be more abstract than S, in that it will not specify attributes e–z. Because of this *selective encoding*, what is actually recorded is not a fully specified memory of an encounter, but rather a partial abstraction over what was encountered. In addition, human beings' knowledge erodes over time—the (unconscious) forgetting of attributes (and entire exemplars) also renders our representations more abstract than a collection of actual veridical reproductions of stimuli.

3.2 Generalizations over exemplars

At the same time that much item-specific knowledge is recognized in non-linguistic categorization, there is a growing recognition that exemplars alone do not account for our intricate knowledge of generalizations. That is, exemplar models fail to explain how exactly items cohere as a category. As Ross and Makin put it, "the exemplar view seems to take away the 'categori-ness' of categories" (Ross and Makin 1999: 8). We have certain knowledge about the category *bird* that extends beyond the individual exemplars we have experienced. We know that birds as a class lay eggs, have feathers, and typically fly. We know that some types of dinosaurs may have evolved into birds (without necessarily knowing which particular types of dinosaurs or birds they may have evolved from or into).

Experimental evidence indicates that our knowledge of instances leads to generalizations. For example, Ross, Perkins, and Tenpenny (1990) devised the following category-learning experiment. They initially showed all subjects descriptions of two members of some Club Y:

Member A: likes ice cream
Buys nails

Member B: likes to read Westerns
Buys a swimsuit

Subjects in the C condition were then asked to decide whether a new person was a member of the same club, given the following description:

C: likes sherbet
Buys wood
Buys a towel

Other subjects, in the D condition, were asked to decide whether a different set of features described a member of the club or not.

D: likes to read Cowboy and Indian stories
Buys wood
Buys a towel

Afterwards, subjects in both groups were asked to rank the following features on scale of 1–7 as to their relevance for the category, Members of Club Y:

Plays tennis
Buys a chisel
Has children
Buys sunglasses

Ross, Perkins, and Tenpenny found that subjects who saw C rated "buys a chisel" as more relevant to the category of members than subjects who saw D. Conversely, subjects who saw D rated "buys sunglasses" as more relevant to members than those who saw C. The interpretation of this data is that subjects in the C condition were more reminded of exemplar A, because of the inclusion of the thematic relationship between the first features (liking ice cream and liking sherbet). This in turn led to more attention to the second feature as well, leading subjects to generalize to a superordinate category involving "carpentry" which led to the rating that buying chisels was relevant. In contrast, subjects in condition D were reminded of B, leading them to generalize a "beach" category that in turn led to their ranking of "buys sunglasses" as being more relevant to the category than it was to subjects in condition C.

In recognition of data such as these, there are a growing number of psychological models of categorization that combine exemplar-based knowledge with some type of generalizations. For example, on the *exemplar-based abstraction* view, categorizations are made using exemplars, but the effect is abstraction based on similarity that is additionally stored (Medin and Edelson 1988; Ross, Perkins, and Tenpenny 1990; Spalding and Ross 1994). Abstractions are created locally, on the basis of small numbers of exemplars (even just two). "These abstractions will often be far more specific than [an abstract schema] would be . . . However, if these abstractions are used later in classifying another instance, a still more general abstraction may be made, consisting of the commonalities between the first local abstraction and the new instance" (Ross and Makin 1999).

Another concrete model of categorization that involves both instances and abstractions is Anderson's Rational Model (Anderson 1991). In this model, exemplars are grouped together in clusters. Each cluster has a central tendency that represents that cluster (a mini-prototype). The model determines whether to add a new exemplar to an existing cluster or start a new cluster by comparing a new instance to all existing clusters. Assignment is also affected by the size of the clusters and the likelihood that instances group together. Groups may be of varying size, determined by a variable "coupling" parameter.

In an impressive cross-discipline convergence, certain linguists as well as these cognitive psychologists are embracing combination models that involve both instances and abstraction over those instances (Barlow and Kemmer 2000; Langacker 1987a; Taylor 1995). These theories all acknowledge that while we record a great deal about individual instances of categories, we also discern meaningful relationships among members that make categories cohere together as categories. Let us now turn to the domain of language.

3.3 Item-specific knowledge in adult grammar

Language learning must involve memories of individual examples because the end state of grammar is only partially general (Bybee 1985; Bybee and McClelland 2005; Culicover 1999; Daugherty and Seidenberg 1995; Lakoff 1970; Plunkett and Marchman 1993).

Phonology/Morphology

At the level of phonology, it is clear that very specific aspects of usage events can be and are retained as part of our cognitive representations. For example, there is evidence that particulars of phonetic realizations are retained even if they are predictable by phonological generalizations. For example, what counts as a voiced consonant has been shown to be different in different languages, indicating that speakers retain more specific information than simply [+voiced] (Pierrehumbert 2000). Individual words that are used with higher frequencies tend to be more reduced than other words. For example, Losiewicz (1992) has shown more reduction in the final syllable of *needed* (frequent) than *kneaded* (less frequent). Bybee (2000) observes that *every*, a very high-frequency word, has come to be pronounced as a two-syllable word /evri/, where as low-frequency words like *mammary* or *summery* are pronounced with three syllables. Words of intermediate frequency, such as *camera, family*, and *memory*, allow for variation between pronunciations with two or three syllables. These facts suggest that we index patterns according to their frequencies.

Gahl and Garnsey (2004) demonstrate that phonological reductions (/t,d/ deletions) are more likely in high-probability constructional contexts than in low-probability contexts. In particular, when experimental subjects are asked to produce a sentence in which there is a match between the overt construction used and a verb's statistical bias (as determined by corpora and sentence completion norming studies), they tend to abbreviate the verb form more than when the construction to be produced does not match the bias of the verb involved.

Booij (2002c) has argued that predictable allomorphemic variation is lexically represented, in the case of highly frequent words, since the variation may be retained even when the regular generalization is lost (see also Baayen, Burani, and Schrender 1997 for evidence that highly frequent, regular morphology is lexically represented).

Grammatical category

Idiosyncratic facts about more high-level generalizations such as grammatical categories are retained as well. Consider our knowledge of adjectives. Proto-typical adjectives, such as *red, hot, dry,* and *big,* modify referents and can appear prenominally or predicatively (e.g. after copula verbs such as *seem*), as in (1)–(2). However, neither of these formal properties is necessary. The adjective *mere* can only appear pronominally (3)–(4), while the adjective *aghast* can only appear predicatively (5)–(6):

(1)   a red book

(2)   The book seems red.

(3)   a mere child

(4)   *That child seems mere.

(5)   *an aghast man

(6)   The man seemed aghast.

Even the semantic property of modification does not hold of all adjectives. *Occasional* does not modify or quantify the cigarette in (7), but the act of smoking:

(7)   She smoked an occasional cigarette.

There is also a little construction in English that allows adjectives to appear postnominally, [(all) *things* AP], as in *She loves all things linguistic.* Clearly we must learn the distributional properties of these words and constructions individually. Their distribution does not follow from general facts about adjectives.

English Serial Verb Constructions

To illustrate the partial productivity and idiosyncrasy evident in argument structure patterns within the adult grammar, we briefly consider here a few related, quite understudied constructions. These constructions serve further to illustrate the type of partially idiosyncratic and partially general knowledge that language learners retain.

The first construction, the VVingPP construction, was brought to my attention by Ray Jackendoff (personal communication, 2002). This construction involves a motion verb followed by a verb in progressive form and a directional complement, as in (8):

(8)   The toddler went screaming down the street.

The VVingPP construction clearly has its own peculiar constraints. The directional is an argument of the main verb, not of the second verb. In fact, unlike the paraphrase of motion predicates involving a subordinate clause (illustrated in (9)), the progressive verb in the VVingPP construction may not appear with its own arguments (10):

Subordinate manner clause
(9)   a. Bill went down the street whistling a tune.
      b. Bill took off toward the cops screaming at the thief (all the while).

VVingPP
(10)   a. *Bill went whistling a tune down the street.
       b. *Bill took off screaming at the thief toward the cops.

The main verb in the VVingPP construction is not very productive. Acceptable examples involve intransitive motion verbs with a very general meaning, namely *come, go, run,* and *take off.* With these verbs, the Ving slot is quite open:

(11)   Bill went singing/grinning/waving/laughing down the street.

Other intransitive motion verbs are unacceptable:

(12)   a. *Bill raced whistling down the street.
       b. *Bill walked whistling down the street.

Transitive verbs *take* and *bring* are also acceptable to varying degrees, depending on the choice of Ving:

(13)   Bill took him kicking into the room.

(14)   Bill brought him kicking and screaming into the room.

(15)   ?? Bill took him whistling into the room.

(16)   ?? Bill brought him grinning into the room.

The progressive form of the complement bears its normal semantics such that the activity described must be construed as obtaining over a period of time or as being iterative:

(17)   a. Bill jumped off the bridge. $\neq$
       b. Bill went jumping off the bridge. (VVingPP)

While (17a) is interpreted as a one time, telic action, (17b) is necessarily interpreted as iterative.

The syntax of the active construction appears to be [Subj [VVingPP]]. Notice that [VingPP] is not a constituent in that it cannot appear as a fronted unit:

(18)   Down the hill Bill went screaming.

(19)   ??Screaming down the hill Bill went.

This parse also captures the idea that the PP is an argument of the main verb, since it is a sister to the verb. In addition, the second verb has an adverbial meaning and its distribution mimics to some extent that of adverbs, insofar as it appears without arguments and is sister to the verb as well.[1]

Thus the VVingPP construction appears to be a serial verb construction of English, despite the fact that English does not allow serial verbs in general. The VVingPP construction represents a special form with its own special semantic and syntactic constraints: a conventionalized construction that must be learned from the input the learner receives. The construction is represented below, in Table 3.1.

TABLE 3.1. The VVingPP ("Took-off-Screaming") Construction

Sem:	Move	in a Manner	along a Path
Syntax:	V_ε {go, come, run, take off}	Ving	(Oblique)

In fact a close look at the data reveals a family of related constructions in English. The Took-off-Screaming construction is superficially similar to another conventionalized construction, which we can label the *GoVPing* construction, or more informally, the "Don't go sticking your nose" construction. There are several important reasons to distinguish the two constructions. Unlike the main verbs in the VVingPP construction, *go* in the *GoVPing* construction is not interpreted as a motion verb and therefore does not license a directional. Moreover, the V of the VP expresses its arguments, as indicated by the use of "VP" instead of a simple V. For example, the direct object in (20) is a complement of *read* not *go*:

(20)   You shouldn't go reading the newspaper all day.

Further differentiating the *GoVPing* construction from the VVingPP construction formally is the fact that the *GoVPing* construction only allows the main verb *go* (cf. (21) and (22)), and it prefers that *go* appear in bare form (23):

---

[1] This may be a candidate for the sort of "syntactic mimicry" described by Francis (2005). However, adverbs and not V-ing forms can appear preverbally:

(i)   The barrel quickly rolled down the hill.

(ii)   * Bill screaming went down the hill.

(21) Pat'll go telling Chris what to do, you'll see.

(22) *Pat'll come telling Chris what to do.

(23) ??Pat went telling Chris what to do.

The semantic properties of the two constructions also differ. Unlike the VVingPP construction, the *Go*VPing construction may refer to an instantaneous action:

(24) Don't go spilling your drink!

(25) Don't go jumping off the bridge now!

There is additionally a semantic constraint only associated with the *Go*VPing construction: it implies that there is something negative about performing the action designated by the complement. For example, (21) requires a context in which the speaker disapproves of Pat's telling Chris what to do.

TABLE 3.2. The *Go*VPing, "don't go sticking your nose" Construction

Pragmatics: The action designated by VP is construed negatively by the speaker		
Sem:	Action type	
Syntax:	*go*	[Ving....]$_{VP}$

Finally, while the VVingPP construction is part of Standard English, the *Go*VPing construction is restricted to informal speech.

There is yet another distinct construction in which both verbs are in bare form: the *Go*VP$_{bare}$ construction. In this construction, *go, come,* and *run* are all acceptable (but *take off* is not). Unlike the *Go*VPing construction, the verbs in this construction retain their usual motion interpretations:

(26) Go tell your sister to come here.

(27) Won't you come sit with me?

(28) Would you run get me a pencil?

The motion is interpreted as facilitating the action designated by the VP, where the main assertive event is encoded by the VP. Tensed forms of the first verb (*go*) are unacceptable:

(29) *She came sat/sit with me.

(30) *He goes bring/brings the paper.

The negative implication associated with the *Go*VPing ("don't go sticking your nose") construction is absent from the *Go*VP$_{bare}$ construction:

(31)   She had better go tell her what to do.

(32)   Go do your homework!

This "go tell it to the mountain" construction can be represented as in Table 3.3.

TABLE 3.3. The *Go*VP$_{bare}$, "go tell it to the mountain" Construction

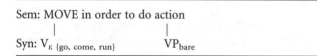

Sem: MOVE in order to do action

Syn: V$_{\varepsilon}$ {go, come, run}   VP$_{bare}$

Thus there are clearly three separate constructions in English. Each must be described on its own terms, with its particular syntactic, semantic, and pragmatic constraints. None is completely general. The idiosyncratic properties of each construction provide an argument that its specifics must be learned on the basis of generalizing over particular examples.

Conventionality and Redundancy

My legal name is Alexander Perchov. But all of my many friends dub me Alex, because that is a more flaccid-to-utter version of my legal name. Mother dubs me Alexi-stop-spleening-me!, because I am always spleening her...because I am always elsewhere with friends, and disseminating so much currency, and performing so many things that can spleen a mother. Father used to dub me Shapka, for the fur hat I would don even in the summer month. He ceased dubbing me that because I ordered him to cease dubbing me that. It sounded boyish to me, and I have always thought of myself as very potent and generative.

Jonathan Safran Foer, *Everything is Illuminated* (Boston: Houghton Mifflin Co., 2002).

The narrator of the passage above is clearly intended to be a non-native speaker. How can we tell? It is because much of the phrasing used and combination of lexical choices are non-conventional, even if fully grammatical.

It is in fact often the case that one particular formulation is much more conventional than another, even though both conform to the general grammatical patterns in a language. Conventions of telling time and reporting height, for example, differ from language to language, forming regular subpatterns that must be learned from the input. Pawley and Syder (1983) point out that this "native-like selection" must ultimately be accounted for as part of a native speaker's knowledge of language (see also Lamb 2002). To do so, however, clearly requires that a certain amount of redundant information must be represented, since the conventional patterns would in any case be generated by the grammar.

Further evidence for some amount of redundancy in language comes from the fact that very typically, a fully general linguistic pattern is instantiated by a few instances that are highly conventional. In such a case, it is clear that both generalizations and instances are stored. For example, conventional instances of the constructions just discussed are given below:

Idiom	don't go sticking your nose in where it doesn't belong
General pattern	*go*VPing
Idiom	go kicking and screaming <path>
General pattern	VVingPP
Idiom	go tell it to the mountain
General pattern	*go*VP$_{bare}$

A few more general examples of this phenomenon are given below, along with a reference to work on the more general pattern:

Idiom:	Boys will be boys.	
General pattern:	NP$_{animatepl}$ will be NP$_{animatepl}$	(Wierzbicka 1988)
Idioms:	The bigger they come, the harder they fall. The more the merrier.	
General pattern:	The Xer the Yer	(Fillmore, Kay, and O'Connor 1988; Culicover and Jackendoff 1999)
Idioms:	What's this fly doing in my soup? What's a nice girl like you doing in a place like this?	
General pattern:	What's X doing Y?	(Kay and Fillmore 1999)
Idiom:	X worked x's way through school.	
General pattern:	subj V poss way PP	(Goldberg 1995; Israel 1996; Jackendoff 1990)
Idiom	Give me a break	
General pattern	Subj V Obj1 Obj2	(Goldberg 1992; Green 1974; Oehrle 1975)

Item specific facts about argument structure

In this section, we review evidence that speakers have exemplar-based knowledge of verb-specific patterns such as that given in (33):

(33)   <actor> *put* < thing > < location >

There exists abundant evidence that children are very conservative in their early argument structure productions. That is, they stick closely to the forms they have heard used with particular verbs (Akhtar and Tomasello 1997; Baker 1979; Bates and MacWhinney 1987; Bowerman 1982; Braine 1976; Brooks and Tomasello 1999; Gropen et al. 1989; Ingram and Thompson 1996; Lieven, Pine, and Baldwin 1997; MacWhinney 1982; Olguin and Tomasello 1993; Pinker 1986; Schlesinger 1982; Tomasello 1992). For example, Olguin and Tomasello (1993) taught twenty-five-month-old children four novel transitive verbs, each in a different syntactic pattern: both participants expressed, agent only, patient only, or neither argument expressed. Children almost always reproduced the same exact pattern they had heard. Of course, in order to restrict their usage to formulations that they have heard or used in the past, they need to record what they have heard.

In a remarkably comprehensive diary study, Tomasello (1992) observed that by far the best predictor of his child's use of a given verb on a particular day was her use of the same verb on the previous few days, not, as might be expected, her use of other verbs on the same day. Tomasello and his colleagues have discussed this verb-centered conservatism under the rubric of *verb islands*, since children readily substitute new nouns into the frames (Akhtar and Tomasello 1997; Clark 1996; Gropen, Epstein, and Schumacher 1997; Tomasello 1992; Tomasello et al. 1997). A simple example of this type of conservatism comes from the diary data of a child, Aliza, collected by the author. Aliza routinely omitted prepositions before the age of approximately twenty-one months. During that time, she produced *come me* and *play me* to mean "come with me" and "play with me," respectively. Beginning at 1;9.9, and subsequently, Aliza reliably produced *come with me*. Nonetheless, she still continued to produce *play me*, without the preposition, for another two months.

There is evidence that adults retain much verb-specific knowledge as well. Verbs are occasionally quite idiosyncratic in the types of argument structure patterns they appear in (Bresnan 1982; Chomsky 1965; Pollard and Sag 1987). For example, the near synonyms *help* and *aid* differ in their distribution:

(34)   a. Pat helped her grandmother walk up the stairs.
        b. *Pat aided her grandmother walk up the stairs.

(35)   a. ??Pat helped her grandmother in walking up the stairs.
       b. Pat aided her grandmother in walking up the stairs.

Even though this sort of example may be rare, a learner cannot possibly know which patterns will turn out to be productive and which will not be on initial encounter. Thus it is clear that all early-learned instances must be stored. Unless we posit some sort of house-cleaning device to erase this early scaffolding, these early-learned forms would continue to be stored.[2]

Psycholinguistic studies have demonstrated that speakers are influenced by the relative frequencies with which they have heard particular verbs used in various argument structure constructions (Ford, Breslan, and Kaplan 1982; Jurafsky forthcoming; MacDonald, Pearlmutter, and Seidenberg 1993). For example, knowledge that *believed* is more likely to appear with a clausal complement than with an object complement influences speakers' online interpretation of potentially ambiguous sentences (Garnsey et al. 1997; Trueswell, Tanenhaus, and Kello 1993). The relative frequencies play a role despite the fact that both possibilities are fully grammatical, as in the examples (36a–b):

(36)   a. Pat believed the speaker might cause a riot.
       b. Pat believed the speaker.

Newmeyer (2003) rightly cautions that frequency information can sometimes be overinterpreted. For example, he argues that the choice of syntactic constructions depends on their differing meanings—that the probabilities of use are a function of their meanings, not some inherent statistical property of the structure. This idea is supported by the fact that statistics are known to vary, sometimes rather dramatically, across different corpora (Roland and Jurafsky forthcoming).

Hare, McRae, and Elman (2004, 2003) explore the idea that semantics drives distribution in some detail. They confirm that subcategorization possibilities are conditioned by a verb's and a construction's senses. For example, the verb *find* must occur with a direct object if it is used to mean "locate," whereas it is biased toward appearing with a sentential complement when it means "realize." However, statistical factors still play a role. *Find* can appear with a direct object, even when it is used to mean "realize;" online reading times indicate that the statistical preference for the sentential complement plays a role, even when the verb's sense is controlled for (see also Argaman 2002; Roland and Jurafsky forthcoming). Findings of this sort

---

[2] Even proponents of "dual route models" of morphology who argue that regular forms are created on the fly by rules while irregular forms are stored, have observed that at least some high-frequency regulars are stored redundantly with their stems (Pinker 1999; Pinker and Jackendoff 2005).

demonstrate that detailed verb-specific knowledge about frequencies of usage influence adult grammar.

We now turn to evidence for the existence of higher-level generalizations, beyond generalizations over particular arguments of a given verb. In Chapter 4 it is argued that argument structure generalizations are *based on* verb-specific patterns.

3.4 Argument Structure Generalizations

To perhaps most linguists, it goes without saying that languages contain generalizations. But if we take item-based knowledge seriously, it raises the question as to whether only individual tokens are stored without any generalization. This possibility has in fact been raised by certain researchers, insofar as they seem to make the claim that the totality of what is stored are specific usage events (Boas 2000; Thompson and Fox 2004; Verhagen 2002). This view deserves pause, in part because, as noted above, a similar suggestion had great currency, and still has its adherents within cognitive psychology in theories known as *exemplar models* of categorization (e.g. Medin and Schaffer 1978).

Still, there is ample evidence that generalizations are essential to language. If generalizations were not necessarily made, we would expect to find languages whose argument structure patterns varied arbitrarily on a verb-by-verb basis. For example, we might expect to find one semantically transitive verb expressed by SVO (Subject Verb Object) word order, another expressed by SOV order, and a third verb expressed by VSO order:

(37)   a. Pat saw Chris.
       b. Pat Chris kissed.
       c. Hate Pat Chris.

But in fact languages are much more regular. Semantically similar verbs show a strong tendency to appear in the same argument structure constructions. *Help* and *aid* cited above are unusual; more typically, verbs that are closely related semantically do appear in the same argument structure constructions (Fisher, Gleitman, and Gleitman 1991; Goldberg 1995; Gross 1975; Levin 1993; Pinker 1989). Newly formed creoles quickly generalize patterns beyond individual verbs (Sandler et al. 2005).

Further evidence that children generalize the patterns they use stems from the fact that they occasionally produce spontaneous overgeneralizations, as in the following examples, from Bowerman (1982) and the author's own diary data:

(38) a. Will you have me a lesson?   Bowerman (1982)
                                                       Christy 4;0
      b. She came it over there.   Bowerman (1982)
                                                       Christy 3;4
      c. I'll hockey over there. (to mean she'll   Aliza 6;7
         move over there in her roller skates, carrying
         a hockey stick)
      d. She unlocked it open.   Zach 3;0
      e. Circle it back up!   Zach 4;8

It is also clear that adults continue spontaneously to generalize argument structures patterns (Aronoff 1976; Clark and Clark 1979; Pinker 1989). The attested examples in (39) provide examples of such adult novel productions:

(39) a. Once you resort to higher-level predicates, you can just lambda your way out of practically anything. (reported by John Moore, May 1995)
      b. He concentrated his hand steady. (reported by Georgia Green; found in Russell Atwood's *East of A*, New York: Ballantine Books, 1999).
      c. They haven't found the time to play him a whole lot of minutes. (Pinker 1989: 154)
      d. Mary presented as an attractive, neatly dressed woman. (Pinker 1989: 155)
      e. I'll just croak my way through, I guess. (reported by Mike Tomasello, May 1996)
      f. Diane hasn't Botoxed and siliconed herself into some kind of weird creature. (reported by Hana Filip, March 2004)

The successful manipulation and comprehension of nonsense verbs in experimental settings also demonstrates that speakers are in fact able to make generalizations (Akhtar and Tomasello 1997; Gropen et al. 1989; Maratsos et al. 1987; Naigles 1990).

KNOWLEDGE OF LANGUAGE IS KNOWLEDGE. Speakers classify the instances they hear into categories. Verb-centered categories are categorized together, ultimately resulting in general, abstract argument structure constructions.

3.5 When do generalizations emerge?

It is sometimes suggested that children are almost totally unaware of argument structure generalizations until the age of three or three-and-a-half (Tomasello 2000, 2003). However, it might be expected that generalizations emerge gradually from early on. In fact, in diary records kept of my children, there exist a number of early overgeneralizations:[3]

(40)   up and down the neigh (requesting that I raise and lower a toy horse) (Aliza 1;8.21)

(41)   come Abbi (requesting that I make toy dog, Abbi, come to Aliza) (Aliza 1;8.2)

(42)   you jump me to the sky (Aliza 2;1.23) (asking me to help her jump on the bed)

(43)   you mad to the pig? (Aliza 2;1.23)

(44)   I reach my hands up (Aliza 2;1.26)

Aliza's first overgeneralizations appeared when she was only twenty months. At that point she used approximately twenty-five verbs, including the transitives *eat, get, give, have, hear, help, hit, hold, make, put, read, ride, take, tickle,* and *wipe*. Thus she had had an opportunity to make some tentative generalizations over the verbs that had already been learned. Her overgeneralizations grew greatly in number and frequency over the next year and a half.

Other early instances of overgeneralizations come from Zach. This data was collected less systematically and there may have been even earlier generalizations. No comprehensive record of his vocabulary was kept (readers with more than one child may understand this lapse):

(45)   It noises. (Zach 2;4) (In answer to "what's that?" about a top when its electronic noise wouldn't turn off)

(46)   Could you reach me up here, Kitty Cat? (Zach 2;4) (playing that one toy cat was talking to another, while raising them to the bookshelf)

(47)   Hold me what I want. (Zach 2;5) (to mean, give me what I want by holding me so that I can reach it: creative extension of the ditransitive construction)

(48)   I becamed to be Spiderman. (Zach 2;7) (cf. I wanted to be Spiderman)

It is conceivable that both children happen to fall on the very early end of the curve of when generalizations emerge as reported by Tomasello (2000). However, there also exists experimental work that suggests that in fact,

---

[3] Note that omission of prepositions cannot account for these novel uses because (40) involves the novel use of particles as verbs, and (41) cannot be paraphrased with any existing preposition: the only candidate, *with* as in *come with Abbi*, could not have been intended because I was bending over Aliza, putting her in her car seat when she asked me to go bring her the toy dog.

argument structure generalizations over verb-centered instances emerge gradually from very early on.

Strong evidence that young children can use more general, abstract argument structures (as well as verb-specific knowledge) is provided by Akhtar (1999). In this study, thirty-six two-, three-, and four-year-olds (mean ages: 2;8, 3;6, and 4;4) were taught meanings for novel verbs that were modeled for the children using non-English word orders as well as canonical English order, for example:

(49)   a. Elmo the car gopping. (SOV)
      b. Dacking Elmo the car. (VSO)
      c. Elmo blicking the car. (SVO: canonical English order)

The children's spontaneous use of these verbs and responses to queries of "what happened?" were recorded. The two- and three-year-olds matched SOV or VSO patterns roughly half the time and changed the order to SVO roughly half the time.[4] The fact that the children produced the non-English orders at all is striking evidence that they are able to learn patterns on a verb-by-verb basis; at the same time, the fact that the children ever produced the unmodeled SVO order that corresponds to the regular English pattern indicates that the children recognized the regular English pattern as a generalization over the particular instances they had heard. The generalization played a greater role in the productions of the four-year-old participants, in that children at this age were overwhelmingly more likely to correct to SVO than to match the modeled order.

Akhtar also ran a control condition in which familiar verbs were modeled in the same non-English orders:

(50)   a. Elmo the car pushing.
      b. Hitting Elmo the car.

In this case, the two- and three-year-olds as well as four-year-olds were significantly more likely to correct to SVO than to use the order that was modeled. This is expected since the argument structure for these particular verbs had already been learned. Thus the children in the experimental condition were not simply mimicking the experimenter's usage blindly, since they did not do so when the verbs involved were already known and their patterns of usage were already familiar.

---

[4] The children were more likely to switch to English order if their utterances were produced with pronouns, e.g. *He dacked it*. This may be because pronouns are so frequent and appear in relatively fixed positions in the input (see Pine, Lieven, and Rowland 1998 for discussion).

Abbott-Smith, Lieven, and Tomasello (2001) replicated Akhtar's study with children that were slightly younger. They found that the youngest children (2;4) corrected non-canonical orders only half as often as the children did at 2;8 in Akhtar's study. Still, even children aged 2;4 corrected the non-canonical orders roughly 25 per cent of the time. The children also used the novel verb that was heard in a grammatical order more often than they used a novel verb that had been heard in an ungrammatical order. This is yet another indication that the generalizations are learned gradually, beginning from very early on (cf. also Ninio 1999, 2005).

By the time children are four years old, it is clear that they readily form generalizations over lists of attested instances (represented at some level of abstraction). Thus, for example, English speakers are aware of a productive transitive construction and readily extend it with appropriate verbs, in addition to being aware of which particular verbs they have heard used in the construction before.

3.6 Representations of constructions capture predictive aspects of the constructions

As was the case with non-linguistic categorization, selective encoding and imperfect memory ensure that our exemplars are somewhat abstract. We do not store an unlimited number of complete utterance representations; rather what we retain are instances at some level of abstraction. That is, we do not passively retain a huge mental corpus, consisting of all the strings we have ever heard, as a computer might do. Instead we constantly parcel out meaning, form abstractions, and generalize over the instances we hear.

For example, in learning constructions whose primary function involves information structure and discourse pragmatics, not semantics and not phonology—constructions such as relative clauses, questions, clefts—learners' representations are likely to abstract quickly over the particular semantics involved. For example, learners' representation of the English relative clause construction may contain almost no information about the *semantic* content that happens to have appeared in actual usage events. Upon hearing, *the man who sat on every hill*, we do not retain the phrase, *sat on every hill* as part of the representation of the relative clause, let alone the phonetic character of the way the word *every* was pronounced (although we do retain this information as part of our representation of the word *every*; recall the discussion in 3.3).

Learners *must* be attempting to assign functions to different parts of the utterances—without this tendency to analyze and decompose strings, we would be unable to assign any meaning to particular words unless the words happened to be used in isolation. This process is not well understood, but it must involve the notion of predictive value. The pronunciation of particular words helps users identify the word (comprehension) and produce the word as others do (production); therefore specific information about pronunciation is stored with particular words. But in other cases, such specific information is undoubtably abstracted away. There is no reason to think that the phonology of determiners is stored with particular verbs that happen to have been heard used with those determiners (the fact that *the* appears in *The man left* is not a fact about the verb *leave*). The co-occurrence of these two features is recognized to be contingent on the particular circumstance. This idea remains to be fleshed out, but it may ultimately help to explain the fact that constraints generally tend to be local (applying to immediate daughters and only less often to granddaughters or more distantly related constituents).

The tendency to seek out predictive correlations is clearly not specific to language. Accounts of our ability to parcel out responsibility in complex events has been discussed under the rubric of Bayesian causal networks (Pearl 1988, 2000). We constantly seek out causal connections within events: the door opens because the handle is turned, not because I happened to be wearing jeans. The cat screams because her tail was pulled, not because it happens to be raining outside. We are expert at identifying predictive correlations (see Chapter 6 for more discussion of this idea).

3.7 Usage-based Models of language

We have seen that in the case of language, as in categorization generally, there is solid evidence that both item-specific knowledge and generalizations coexist. A number of researchers have emphasized the need for both types of knowledge. Langacker (1987a), for example, warns against the "rule *vs.* list fallacy," criticizing the prevailing tendency to view productive generalizations and elaborated lists as being in competition (e.g. Marcus et al. 1995; Pinker 1999). He defines a *usage-based* approach that allows both instances and generalizations to be captured as follows:

Substantial importance is given to the actual use of the linguistic system and a speaker's knowledge of this use; the grammar is held responsible for a speaker's knowledge of the full range of linguistic conventions, regardless of whether these conventions can be subsumed under more general statements. [The usage based model is] a non-reductive approach to linguistic structure that employs fully articulated schematic networks and emphasizes the importance of low-level schemas. (Langacker 1987a: 494)

It is clear that knowledge about language must be learned and stored as such whenever it is not predictable from other facts. Thus evidence that a word or pattern is not strictly predictable provides sufficient evidence that the form must be listed as a construction in what is sometimes called a "constructicon," in allusion to an expanded lexicon (e.g. Jurafsky 1996). At the same time, unpredictability is not a necessary condition for positing a stored construction. There is evidence from psycholinguistic processing that patterns are also stored if they are sufficiently frequent, even when they are fully regular instances of other constructions and thus predictable (Bybee 1995; Bybee and Hopper 2001; Losiewicz 1992; Pinker and Jackendoff 2005). We must recognize that patterns are stored as constructions even when they are fully compositional under these circumstances. Thus the present approach advocates a usage-based model of grammar (Barlow and Kemmer 2000; Bybee and McClelland 2005; Bybee 1995; Goldberg 1999; Langacker 1988). Grammars are usage-based if they record facts about the actual use of linguistic expressions such as frequencies and individual patterns that are fully compositional alongside more traditional linguistic generalizations. Most construction grammars are usage-based, due to the sort of evidence reviewed in this chapter.[5]

Usage-based proposals have been formulated in slightly differing ways by different researchers, but the essential point that both instances and generalizations over instances are stored remains the same. Culicover (1999) suggests two general properties of language learners: they are *conservative* in that they do not generalize significantly beyond the evidence in the input, and they are *attentive* in that they seek out generalizations that are consistent with the evidence presented. Insofar as learners have to record information about the input in order to be conservative with respect to it, Culicover's proposal is essential a version of the usage-based model. Israel (2002) echoes a similar theme. He suggests that language learners seek out both *local* consistency and *global* consistency. Local consistency makes learners aim to be conservative and stick closely with the local instances that they have witnessed. Global consistency makes learners seek out generalizations among instances so that the overall system coheres.

---

[5] Unification Construction Grammar (see Chapter 10), on the other hand, is not uniformly usage-based. That is, according to UCG, constructions are only posited if there is something not strictly predictable about either their form or their function. Fully compositional expressions are not stored even if they are highly frequent unless some aspect of their high frequency such as a register difference is non-predictable. For example, *walked* is not redundantly stored because it is fully predictable from the *walk* lexeme composed with the productive "past tense morphemic" construction.

Some may argue that linguists are not obliged to address the facts outlined in this chapter that argue for a usage-based model of grammar (Newmeyer 2003). However, it must be borne in mind that many of the facts that have been discussed have long been taken to be within the purview of all mainstream linguistic theories. For example, facts about an individual verb's complement taking possibilities or "subcategorization" frames have been assumed to be an essential part of linguistic theorizing since Chomsky (1965). More generally, if our aim is ultimately to characterize grammar in such a way that it is consistent with what we know about the use of language, then, other things being equal, a grammar that accounts for all the facts outlined in this chapter is preferable to one that does not. Moreover, viewing language in terms of a usage-based model allows us the chance to bridge naturally to an empirically grounded theory of how language can be learned. This is the subject of Chapters 4 and 5.

Part II
Learning Generalizations

4

How argument structure constructions are learned[1]

Surely it is premature to give up hope that humans, with our rich cognitive abilities, complex social skills, predilection to imitate, and 100-billion-neuron brains, can learn language from the available input. Children have ample motivation to learn language, hear thousands of utterances every day, and receive constant indirect statistical feedback (see Chapter 5 for discussion of the notion of feedback).

Recent empirical work has demonstrated that even honeybees, with brain volumes of approximately 1 mm³, are capable of quite advanced learning (Collett et al. 1997; Giurfa 1996; Menzel and Giurfa 2001). In one study, honeybees were shown to be able to learn the abstract concepts of "sameness" and "difference" in the following way. Bees were trained to find food in a Y-shaped maze; they individually entered the maze through the bottom of the Y where they encountered a stimulus, A. The entrance-way led to the fork of the Y, where the bee would have to choose a path. At the entrance to one fork was placed matching stimulus A, or a different stimulus B. If the bee matched the stimulus, it was rewarded in that there was food in the fork beyond the matching stimuli but not beyond the non-matching stimuli. Bees were found to learn to match stimulus A to A, B to B at a rate well above chance within four to seven trials. After learning to match the training stimuli, the bee was tested with entirely new stimuli C and D. The bees successfully transferred their new knowledge to the new stimuli with an average of 75 per cent accuracy. In fact they were also able to generalize "different" in that they could be trained to learn "if A is at the entrance then take the fork marked by non-A"; and they then could extend that learning to new stimuli C and D as well (Giurfa et al. 2001).

---

[1] The corpus work described in this chapter was done in collaboration with Devin Casenhiser and Nitya Sethuraman, and the experimental work was done in collaboration with Devin Casenhiser. Please see Goldberg, Casenhiser, and Sethurman (2004, 2005) and Casenhiser and Goldberg (forthcoming) for full results and analysis.

Adding to the impressiveness of these findings is the fact that A and B, and C and D represented distinct modalities. For example in one experiment, A and B were different colors (yellow and blue), whereas the novel testing stimuli C and D were lines of different orientations (horizontal or vertical); in another experiment, A and B were different smells (lemon and mango) and C and D were different colors. That is, in a "difference" experiment, a honeybee could learn that if a yellow patch was at the entryway, then the food would be behind the non-yellow patch; and once that idea was learned, the bee would also know that if there were horizontal lines at the entryway, then the food would be behind the non-horizontal lined (i.e. vertical lined) entrance. This learning goes well beyond simple associative learning in which a specific stimulus triggers a conditioned response. The authors conclude that "bees can, not only learn specific objects and their physical parameters, but also master abstract interrelationships, such as 'sameness' and 'difference'"(Giurfa et al. 2001).

These sorts of advances in our understanding of what even insects are capable of learning could not be envisioned in the 1950s and 1960s when Chomsky asserted that critical aspects of syntax were "unlearnable" by human beings and therefore must be innate; yet the assertion became dogma in our field and led to the continuing, widespread belief in the necessity of a biological endowment that contains knowledge representations that are specific to language: i.e. "universal grammar."

4.1 Learning word segmentation, phrase boundaries, grammatical categories

In the past decade, we have witnessed major discoveries concerning children's ability to extract statistical regularities in the input. Children are able to extract word forms from continuous speech based on transitional probabilities between syllables (Saffran, Aslin, and Newport 1996). For example, the phrase *bananas with milk*, contains four transitional probabilities across syllables (*ba* to *na*; *na* to *nas*; *nas* to *with*; and *with* to *milk*). The probability that *ba* will be followed by *na*, and the probability that *(ba)na* will be followed by *nas* is higher than the probability that *nas* will be followed by *with*. That is, transitional probabilities are generally higher within words than across words. Eight-month-old infants are sensitive to these statistical cues (Saffran, Aslin, and Newport 1996) and treat these newly acquired words as part of their lexical inventory (Saffran 2001b).

These basic learning abilities are neither unique to humans nor specific to language. Cotton-top tamarin monkeys also track transitional probabilities, and show evidence of discovering word boundaries (Hauser, Newport, and Aslin 2001). Moreover, children can discover regularities in the boundaries between sequences of tones (Saffran et al. 1999), and visual patterns (Fiser and Aslin 2002), using the same type of statistical cues.

Statistical cues provide a powerful means by which initial language learning can begin. Children are able to discover syntactic regularities between categories of words as well as the statistical regularities in sound patterns (Marcus et al. 1999). For example, the presence of an article (*the* or *a*) predicts a noun somewhere downstream, and learners can use this type of cue to learn syntactic phrase boundaries (Saffran 2001a). Elman has also demonstrated that grammatical categories can be distinguished on the basis of distribution (Elman 1990). Moreover, children are able to combine word level and syntactic level statistical information: twelve-month-old children can use their newly discovered word boundaries to discover regularities in the syntactic distributions of a novel word-string grammar (Saffran and Wilson 2003). Gerken, Wilson, and Lewis have demonstrated that fifteen-month olds are able to combine multiple cues in order to learn morphophonological paradigmatic constraints (Gerken, Wilson, and Lewis 2005).

It is a lucky thing that children can learn initial aspects of language from statistical features of the input, since **there are no stable formal cues cross-linguistically** to identify word forms, grammatical categories, or relations (Barðdal forthcoming; Croft 2001; Pinker 1984). Are more abstract aspects of language less amenable to learning through exposure? Perhaps. However, the rest of this chapter focuses on children's ability to learn and learn quickly, from the available input, one such aspect of language: linking rules or argument structure constructions.

4.2 Learning argument structure generalizations

Linguists have observed that within a given language, there exist certain formal patterns that correlate strongly with the meanings of the utterances in which they appear. Such correlations between form and meaning have been variously described as linking rules projected from the main verb's specifications (Levin and Rappaport Hovav 1995; Pinker 1989), as lexical templates overlain on specific verbs (Koenig and Davis 2001; Rappaport Hovav and Levin 1998), or as phrasal form and meaning correspondences (*constructions*) that exist independently of particular verbs (Goldberg 1995; Jackendoff 2002).

Of course one way to account for the association of meanings with particular forms is to claim that the association is simply there, biologically determined or innate from the outset (Baker 1988; Chomsky 1982). This claim generally rests on the idea that the input is not rich enough for the relevant generalizations to be learned; this is the well-known "poverty of the stimulus" argument (Chomsky 1980, 1988; Pinker 1994). On this nativist view, learning a grammar can be likened to customizing a software package: everything is there, and the learner simply selects the parameters that are appropriate, given the input (Jackendoff 2002). Many have criticized this approach for its biological implausibility (Bates and Goodman 1998; Deacon 1997; Elman et al. 1996; Sampson 1997). Moreover, there have been virtually no successful proposals for what any specific aspect of the parameters might look like (for discussion of this failure see, e.g. Culicover 1999; Jackendoff 2002; Newmeyer 1998; Webelhuth and Ackerman 1998).

This chapter joins the growing body of literature that detracts from the poverty of the stimulus argument by presenting evidence that the nature and properties of at least certain patterns in language are learnable on the basis of general categorization strategies (see also e.g. Bybee and Slobin 1982; Bybee and Moder 1983; Jackendoff 2002; Lakoff 1987; MacWhinney forthcoming; Pullum and Scholz 2002; Scholz and Pullum 2002; Taylor 1995; Tomasello 2003).

It is argued that the language input children receive provides more than adequate means by which learners can induce the association of meaning with certain argument structure patterns insofar as well-established categorization principles apply straightforwardly to this domain. Throughout this chapter, I adopt constructional terminology, but the ideas presented are not actually exclusive to a constructionist account. Those who favor one of the other terminologies mentioned above need only construe this account as a proposal for how children can learn linking rules or learn the semantics associated with various lexical templates on the basis of the input. What *is* crucial is the uncontroversial notion that there do in fact exist correlations between formal linguistic patterns and meaning. Chapter 5 focuses on the issue of how we avoid overgeneralizations, and Chapter 6 discusses the motivation for learning the generalizations that we learn. The final part of the book (Chapters 7–9) analyzes how to account for further regularities both within and across languages without resorting to claims that the generalizations must be hard-wired or biologically determined.

Table 4.1 provides a partial list of form and meaning correspondences (lexical templates, combination of linking rules, constructions) along with the labels that are used as mnemonics throughout the chapter to refer to them.

Previous work on the acquisition of constructions has focused almost entirely on the question of whether the constructions (or "linking rules") that exist in a given language have been acquired at a certain age. Findings

TABLE 4.1. Examples of correlations between form and meaning

Form/Example	Meaning	Construction Label
1. Subj V Obl$_{path/loc}$ e.g. *The fly buzzed into the room.*	X moves Y$_{path/loc}$	**Intransitive Motion**
2. Subj V Obj Obl$_{path/loc}$ e.g. *Pat sneezed the foam off the cappuccino.*	X causes Y to move Z$_{path/loc}$	**Caused Motion**
3. Subj V Obj Obj2 e.g. *She faxed him a letter.*	X causes Y to receive Z	**Ditransitive**
4. Subj V Obj RP e.g. *She kissed him unconscious.*	X causes Y to become Z$_{state}$	**Resultative**

based on the preferential-looking paradigm have been used to argue that children already have certain linking rules at relatively young ages, the implication being that the linking rules are innate and not learned from the input (Naigles 1990; Fisher 1996; Hirsh-Pasek, Golinkoff, and Naigles 1996). That is, linking rules have been claimed to be "near-universal in their essential aspects and therefore may not be learned at all" (Pinker 1989: 248). These candidates for universal linking rules include a mapping of agent to subject; patient to object; and goal to oblique (prepositional phrase) (Pinker 1989: 74). Naigles, Gleitman, and Gleitman (1993: 136–7) likewise suggest that "there is sufficient cross-linguistic similarity in these linking rules to get the learning procedure started. . . . [T]here is an overwhelming tendency, cross-linguistically, for agents to appear as subjects and themes as direct objects, with other arguments appearing in oblique cases." Baker (1996: 1) likewise notes: "One central task for any theory of grammar is to solve the so-called 'linking problem': the problem of discovering regularities in how participants of an event are expressed in surface grammatical forms." The implication has been that universal aspects of language are innate, proposed specifically to solve the apparent "poverty of the stimulus" problem (Chomsky 1965, 1981, 1988).

On the other side of the debate, the emphasis has been on the conservative nature of children's early learning, with demonstrations focusing on children's failure to generalize beyond the input until learners have been exposed to a vast amount of data at age 3.5 or older (Akhtar and Tomasello 1997; Baker 1979; Bates and MacWhinney 1987; Bowerman 1982; Braine 1976; Brooks and Tomasello 1999; Gropen et al. 1989; Ingram and Thompson 1996; Lieven, Pine, and Baldwin 1997; MacWhinney 1982; Olguin and Tomasello 1993; Schlesinger 1982; Tomasello 1992). The clear implication of this work is that constructions must be learned, since they are acquired so late and in such a piecemeal fashion.

Training studies are required in order to reconcile the issues involved in this debate, since such studies allow the input and the target construction to be manipulated. Yet precious few training studies exist. Moreover, even fewer facilitory or inhibitory factors have been identified. In one training study, Childers and Tomasello (2001) found a single facilitating factor in the acquisition of the English transitive construction: namely the use of pronouns instead of full NP arguments (Akhtar 1999 also found some facilitative effect for pronouns). Abbott-Smith, Lieven, and Tomasello (2004) attempted to look for other facilitory factors in construction learning, including tight semantic homogeneity and shared syntactic distribution in the input, but found null results.

Kaschak and Glenberg (2004) have investigated adults' online processing of the construction exemplified by *This shirt needs washed,* a construction that was novel to their experimental subjects, although it is used by native speakers of western Pennsylvania. They found that speakers were able to read instances of this construction with greater fluency after hearing or reading other instances of the construction. Facilitation was found as well in testing on the same pattern with *wants* after training on *needs,* demonstrating that the facilitation transferred to a related verb. The increased fluency, as measured by shorter reading times, was interpreted to indicate that speakers learned to comprehend the construction; however, the target construction contains familiar words with appropriate inflectional endings and is closely related to familiar expressions such as *This shirt needs to be washed,* with *to be* omitted. A suggestion that subjects were able to comprehend the construction from the outset comes from the fact that they demonstrated increased reading times for semantically inconsistent follow-up sentences even in the initial testing trials. Still the study demonstrates that familiarity with a construction can be acquired quite quickly.

Certain findings indicate that a *failure* to be able to predict aspects of distribution leads learners to generalize the more regular aspects. In order to investigate the processes involved in creolization, Hudson and Newport (1999) taught adult speakers a toy novel syntax, through exposure to sentences that were paired with video clips to provide interpretations. Several different determiners were used in free variation. Adult subjects were then tested on whether they were able to regularize their use of the determiners. The experimenters initially found that subjects failed to regularize and instead produced the various determiners in roughly the proportions they had heard them used. In a follow-up study, Hudson Kam and Newport (MS) have found that adults do regularize (overgeneralizing the use of one determiner) when the input is sufficiently unpredictable. In particular, adults overgeneralized (regularized) a determiner that had appeared 60 per cent of the time, when various other determiners appeared with unpredictable, low frequencies (each of various determiners appearing 2.5 per cent of the time, in free variation). In an artificial grammar-learning task, Gomez (2002) likewise observes that decreasing predictability between adjacent dependencies increased awareness of dependencies between first and third elements (cf. also Monaghan et al. 2005; Valian and Coulson 1988).

To summarize, a few training studies exist, and some have required children to learn a novel word order and/or a novel morpheme, but none has required children to map a novel word order onto a novel meaning: exactly the task that the child faces when naturalistically learning language. The target meaning involved has been simple transitivity in the case of previous novel word-order studies (e.g. Childers and Tomasello 2001), or identifiabilty (in the case of the determiner study by Hudson and Newport 1999), or no meaning at all (in the case of artificial grammar learning by Gomez 2002). Surprisingly little data has been found that has identified particular facilitory or inhibitory factors in learning to map a novel form to a novel meaning, beyond varying overall exposure and levels of predictability.

4.3 Skewed input

In order to examine more closely the input children receive, Goldberg, Casenhiser, and Sethuraman (2004) investigated a corpus of children's early speech. The main language corpus used was the Bates, Bretherton, and Snyder corpus (1988), on the Child Language Data Exchange System (CHILDES) database (MacWhinney 1995). This corpus contains transcripts from the Bates/Bretherton Colorado longitudinal sample of twenty-seven middle-class children–mother dyads, thirteen boys and fourteen girls at age twenty and twenty-eight months. There are transcripts for fifteen minutes, equally divided into three types of mother–infant interaction: free play, reading of the book *Miffy in the Snow*, and snack time.

In analyzing the mothers' speech we found a strong tendency for there to be one verb occurring with very high frequency in comparison to other verbs used in each of the constructions analyzed. That is, the use of a particular construction is typically dominated by the use of that construction with one particular verb. For example, *go* accounts for a full 39 per cent of the uses of the intransitive motion construction in the speech of mothers addressing twenty-eight-month-olds in the Bates et al. (1988) corpus. This high percentage is remarkable since this construction is used with a total of thirty-nine different verbs in the mothers' speech in the corpus. The figures for the three constructions investigated are given below in Table 4.2.[2]

TABLE 4.2. Fifteen mothers' most frequent verb and number of verb types for three constructions in Bates et al. (1988) corpus[3]

Construction	Mothers	Total Number of Verb Types
1. Subj V Obl	39% *go* (136/353)	39 verbs
2. Subj V Obj Obl	38% *put* (99/256)	43 verbs
3. Subj V Obj Obj2	20% *give* (11/54)	13 verbs

The question arises as to why these particular verbs are used more frequently in these constructions by mothers. One factor of course is that these verbs are among the most frequent verbs in the language at large (Carroll, Davies, and Richman 1971). But this does not in itself predict that these verbs should account for such a high proportion of tokens of any single construction, since most frequent verbs appear in multiple constructions. Zipf long ago noted that highly frequent words account for most linguistic tokens (1935). Although he did not claim that there should be a single most highly frequent word for each clause pattern, nor did Zipf's work prepare us for the fact that a single verb accounts for such a large percentage of the tokens, his observation suggests that we may find a similar pattern in constructions other than argument structure constructions.

In fact, Stefanowitsch and Gries (2003) have refined the notion of relative frequencies in order to take into account the overall frequencies of the verbs in the language. Given that one can expect high-frequency verbs to appear with high-frequency constructions, the more refined question asks, how frequent are these particular verbs in these particular constructions over and above chance? Stefanowitsch and Gries advocate applying measures of association (e.g. $\chi 2$ or Fisher exact test) to the following matrix of data:

---

[2] Valeria Quiochi (in prep.) has found a similar pattern for the caused-motion and intransitive motion patterns in Italian. (The ditransitive pattern does not exist in Italian.)

[3] The percentage of uses of *give* in the ditransitive is somewhat less striking than the percentages of *go* and *put* in the intransitive and caused motion constructions, respectively. However, that is likely an effect of the small sample size. Bresnan and Nikitina report that *give* accounts for 226/517, or 44% of the instances of the ditransitive in the parsed Switchboard corpus (Bresnan and Nikitina MS). *Tell*, in our small sample of 54 appeared an equal number of times as *give*. We believe this is an artifact of the story-reading context, since all but one instance of *tell* occurred in the story context, and in 8 out of 10 instances, the theme argument is *story*.

	Argument structure construction (ASC) #1	Other ASCs	Total
*Verb*1	a	b	a+b: frequency of *Verb*1
All other verb tokens	c	d	c+d

If you select all constructions involving *Verb*1 (a+b), how likely is it that there will be (*a*) instances of ASC #1 and (*b*) instance of other ASCs? That is, how biased toward ASC #1 is *Verb*1, given the overall frequencies of *Verb*1 *and ASC#1*? Stefanowitsch and Gries have found that one can never expect a single verb to account for more than 10 per cent of the tokens, even if the verb is very frequent, because there are so many different argument structure constructions: that is, skewing of the magnitude that is found in the data is not expected due to the simple frequencies of the verbs and constructions involved.

The same trends noted in mothers' speech to children are mirrored in children's early speech (Goldberg, Casenhiser, and Sethuraman 2004). This is not surprising since we know from previous studies that children's use of verbs is highly sensitive to their mothers' use of verbs (Choi 1999; De Villiers 1985; Naigles and Hoff-Ginsberg 1998). Moreover the reason certain verbs occur so frequently is constant for both children and mothers as described below.

Accounting for the skewed input

The fact that *go, put,* and *give* are so frequent in the input raises the question as to why that should be so. There seem to be two reasons. First, if we compare, for example, *go* with *amble,* or *put* with *shelve,* it is clear that *go* and *put* are more frequent because they apply to a wider range of arguments and therefore are relevant in a wider range of contexts (Heine 1993; Zipf 1935).

In addition, each of the main uses of these verbs designates a basic pattern of experience; for example, someone causing someone to receive something (*give*), something causing something to move (*put*), or something moving (*go*). These meanings are readily accessible to the child, since they involve concrete actions. Clearly the verb meanings need to be accessible as well as highly frequent in the input in order to be frequently produced in early child language (Slobin 1985).

General Purpose Verbs and Constructional Meaning

As represented in Table 4.3, the meanings of the most frequent verbs used in particular argument structure constructions bear a striking resemblance to

TABLE 4.3. Main verbs and the constructional meanings they correspond to

go	X moves Y	Intransitive Motion
put	X causes Y to move Z	Caused Motion
give	X causes Y to receive Z	Ditransitive
make	X causes Y to become Z	Resultative

the meanings independently posited for those argument structure constructions (Goldberg 1995).

"General purpose" verbs, including *put, go, do,* and *make,* are among the
first and most frequent verbs in many languages (Clark 1978, 1996). Clark cites
data from Bowerman (1973) for Finnish, Grégoire (1937) for French, Sanchés
(1978) for Japanese, and Park (1977) for Korean; Ninio (1999), discussed
below, provides similar data from Hebrew (cf. also Uziel-Karl 1999).

The generality of the meanings of these verbs and their highly frequent and
early appearance in children's speech suggests that they may aid children in
generalizing patterns from the input. Speculations about the close relationship
between certain verbs and argument structure patterns have been made previously by certain researchers both in linguistics and in language acquisition.
Kay (1996) observes that "it is possible to think of the argument structure
patterns as in some sense 'derived from' the semantics of their most neutral
verbs" (cf. also Goldberg 1998). Clark (1996) likewise speculates that certain
early-learned verbs may serve as "templates" for further acquisition on the
basis of their semantic characteristics. She demonstrates that children are
aware of much relevant semantic knowledge pertaining to their early verbs as
evidenced by their discriminating use of various inflectional morphemes.
Ninio (1999) has also suggested that syntactic patterns emerge from generalizing the use of particular verbs. With the possible exception of Ninio, these
researchers do not attempt to flesh out this idea. As Kay (1996) notes, "when we
come to propose this seriously we will have to specify just what sort of
'projection' we are talking about . . . and what the mechanism is according to
which the pattern of the verb is projected to the more general pattern."

Ninio observes that children often begin using a single verb with a direct
object long before a direct object appears with other verbs; moreover, she
notes the overwhelming tendency for these "pathbreaking" verbs to be drawn
from the set of general purpose verbs. In particular, children tend to use verbs
meaning "want," "make/do," "put," "bring," "take out," or "give" before other
verbs are used. In a longitudinal study, Ninio observes that SVO and VO
patterns were initially produced with only one or at most a few verbs for a
prolonged period. More and more verbs came to be used in an exponentially

increasing fashion; that is, there seemed to be more facilitation after ten verbs than after five, and so on. She suggests that this increase stems from the fact that children gradually abstract a more general and purely syntactic pattern on the basis of the early verbs, and that the growing generalization allows them to use new verbs in this syntactic pattern more and more easily.

On both Ninio's account and the present proposal, patterns are learned on the basis of generalizing over particular instances. As vocabulary increases, so does the strength of the generalization, making it progressively more and more easy to assimilate new verbs into the patterns. The two accounts complement each other in that Ninio proposes that general purpose verbs lead the way in the early acquisition of syntax, and the present proposal emphasizes the role of general purpose verbs in the acquisition of the semantics associated with basic syntactic patterns. It seems that early uses of general purpose verbs provide the foundation for both initial syntactic and semantic generalizations, and thus provide a route to the acquisition of form and meaning correspondences: i.e. constructions.

The accounts differ in their explanations as to *why* general purpose verbs should be learned so early. While Ninio notes that general purpose verbs are highly frequent and pragmatically relevant, she argues that the tendency for general purpose verbs to be used early in the VO and SVO patterns stems largely from a high degree of semantic transitivity in these general purpose verbs. However, as Ninio herself notes, many of the early general purpose verbs are not highly semantically transitive according to traditional criteria; i.e. they do not involve an agent acting on, or changing the state of, a patient argument (Hopper and Thompson 1980). For example, the general purpose verbs *want, see, get,* and *have* appear among the very first verbs in Ninio's corpus, and yet they are not highly transitive according to traditional criteria (see Goldberg, Casenhiser, and Sethuraman 2004 for discussion).

The present hypothesis is that the high frequency of particular verbs in particular constructions facilitates children's unconsciously establishing a correlation between the meaning of a particular verb in a constructional pattern and the pattern itself, giving rise to an association between meaning and form.

4.4 Experimental evidence for an effect of skewed input in language learning

Casenhiser and Goldberg (2005) designed an experiment to test learners' ability to learn to pair a novel constructional meaning with a novel form: exactly the task that the child faces when naturalistically learning language.

We created a novel pattern involving known nouns arranged in a non-English word order along with a nonsense verb. At the beginning of each scene, participants heard a simple present-tense sentence describing the scene, and at the end of the scene they heard a past-tense version of the same sentence.

GENERAL FORM:

<NOUN PHRASE$_1$ NOUN PHRASE$_2$ NONSENSE VERB $+ o$ >

EXAMPLE:

The spot the king moopos; The spot the king moopoed

VIDEO CLIP PAIRED WITH EXAMPLE:

a spot appears on the king's nose

The meaning of the phrasal pattern was that of APPEARANCE (a meaning novel for English phrasal patterns): the entity named by the first noun phrase comes to exist in the place named by the second noun phrase. For example, the intended meaning for the sentence *the sailor the pond neebod* was "the sailor sailed onto the pond from out of sight."

Fifty-one children aged 5–7 (mean age 6;4) were randomly and equally assigned to three conditions: the *control* condition, the *balanced frequency* condition, and the *skewed frequency* condition. The number of different novel verbs and the overall number of examples were controlled for: five different novel verbs and sixteen total examples were presented in both training conditions. In the balanced frequency condition, subjects heard the five novel verbs, each with a relatively low token frequency: three novel verbs occurring four times and two novel verbs occurring twice (4-4-4-2-2). In the high token frequency condition, subjects again heard the five novel verbs, but this time one had especially high token frequency of 8, while the other four verbs appeared twice each (8-2-2-2-2). The control condition watched the same film but with the sound turned off; thus any difference among groups can only be attributed to a difference in the linguistic input that subjects were exposed to, as ALL THREE CONDITIONS WATCHED EXACTLY THE SAME VIDEO. Training lasted less than three minutes.

The test was a forced choice comprehension task: subjects saw two film clips presented side-by-side on the screen and heard a sentence describing one of the clips. Sentences included six test trials with the novel phrasal pattern and *new* novel verbs; interspersed were six filler trials with new novel verbs in the familiar transitive pattern. Each test film-clip pair involved the same entity engaged in a similar action, but in only one did the entity appear on the scene within the clip (e.g. in one case, a sailor sails in on a boat from off the screen; in the paired foil clip the sailor sails around in a boat on screen). Half of the foil films involved transitive actions (a clown tossing a ball in the air was matched with a clown falling from out of sight onto the ball), and half involved intransitive actions (a flower growing taller was matched with a flower growing from out of the ground).

Subjects were asked to point to the film clip on the computer screen that corresponded to the description that they heard. Responses were coded for accuracy. The task is reminiscent of the preferential-looking paradigm, the main difference being that our subjects provided an unambiguous behavioral response, pointing to the matching scene instead of simply looking longer at one scene than another. Results are given in Fig. 4.1.

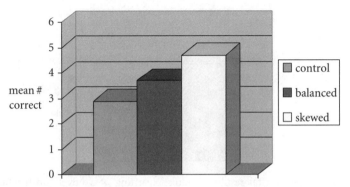

FIGURE 4.1 Experimental results of children's learning of a novel construction with novel verbs (based on Casenhiser and Goldberg 2005)

As expected, subjects in the control (no-sound) condition did no better than chance at choosing the correct scene. The balanced condition showed a statistically significant improvement over the control condition, indicating that they had learned something about the construction's semantics from the training film involving five relatively low token frequency verbs. As predicted by our hypothesis, the skewed frequency condition showed a statistically significant improvement in accuracy over the balanced condition.[4]

The results are striking: after only three minutes of training, children and adults are able to glean the novel abstract meaning that is associated with a

[4] An ANOVA confirmed a significant main effect for group, $F_{(2, 48)} = 11.57$, P < .001. Planned comparisons analyzed with Fisher's PLSD show that both the high-frequency and the balanced groups performed significantly better than the control group (p < .001 and p < .05 respectively). Moreover, the high-frequency group performed significantly better than the balanced group (p < .01).

novel formal pattern involving novel verbs and extend what they have learned to *new* utterances that use *new* novel verbs. Particularly facilitative is input in which one verbal token accounts for the balance of utterances, when the number of verb types is held constant.

The learning involved was implicit insofar as (*a*) no direct instructions were given to the subjects regarding what they were expected to learn during the training, and (*b*) subjects were unable to articulate explicitly the meaning of the construction when asked to paraphrase an instance of the new construction afterwards.

Goldberg, Casenhiser, and Sethuraman (2004) found similar results with adult subjects, as shown in fig. 4.2.

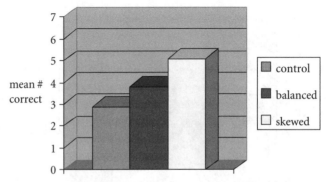

FIGURE 4.2 Experimental results of adults' learning of a novel construction with novel verbs[5]

Thus with less than three minutes of training, both children and adults demonstrated an ability to learn constructional meaning: they were able to extend the semantics of the construction to new novel verbs and new scenes in this forced choice comprehension task. Moreover, the results demonstrate that high token frequency of a single general exemplar does indeed facilitate the acquisition of constructional meaning.

Kidd, Lieven, and Tomasello (2005) have recently found relevant results in an unpublished study. Four-year-old children were asked to repeat sentences which involved complement-taking verbs. Some of the sentences had errors in them (e.g. *I say her give the present to her mom*). They found that 25 per cent of

---

[5] The experiment on adults, performed before the better-controlled experiment described above on children, did not rule out the possibility that watching the scenes helped the children instead of the language. This is because the videos as well as the language differed slightly in the two adult groups that watched the training films. The control condition in the experiment on adults did not hear the language associated with the films *or* watch either film.

the time, children would substitute a different main verb when repeating the sentence. The particular verb *think* accounted for fully 70 per cent of these substitutions (whether or not the sentence was corrected). In a second study, Kidd et al. found that even when none of the input sentences contained *think*, children nonetheless still displayed just as strong a tendency to substitute *think* as the main verb when repeating the sentences (81 per cent of substitutions by four-year-olds; 70 per cent of substitutions by six-year-olds). Since *think* is the most common verb occurring in the [V S] frame (accounting for almost 40 per cent of the tokens in their sample), this provides a further indication that young children's generalizations about constructions appear to be focused around particular verbs that appear frequently in those constructions.

Fast Mapping as evidence of UG?

It is possible that the quick learning of the mapping could be taken as an indication that the particular mapping is a part of universal grammar and is innately available. A mapping between Subj Obj V and <theme location V>, could be added to the set of mapping principles sometimes claimed to be universal. However, it is not clear that languages encode "appearance" in this way. In particular, the mapping violates at least one of the proposed universal linking rules suggested by both Pinker (1989) and Naigles, Gleitman, and Gleitman (1993): namely the generalization that a locative argument should be expressed by an oblique complement. The location argument used in the experiments would require prepositional marking to be considered an oblique in English; yet locations were expressed as simple noun phrases in the experimental stimuli. Moreover, the child's word-order parameter would presumably already be set by age six, and yet children had no trouble learning the SOV order. Therefore the idea that the mapping must be part of UG is without independent support.

4.5 What exactly did they learn? Examining the role of morphology and word order

We considered the possibility that in the experiments described above, subjects attended only to the morphological cue, which was constant: an -*o* suffix on each of the novel verbs. In a follow-up experiment, we removed this morphological ending, so that there was no stable cue to the construction except for word order (Casenhiser and Goldberg 2005).

We also wanted to make certain that children were able to recognize the novel word order in our novel appearance construction. To investigate this, we systematically interspersed in the test films three novel transitive scenes with three novel scenes of appearance. A scene of appearance was available for each test trial; if the children learned that the scenes of appearance were paired with the SOV order, they should choose scenes of appearance when queried by instances involving the SOV order, while choosing transitive scenes when queried by the familiar SVO order. This is just what we found. Results confirmed that children were able successfully to learn the novel construction even without the morphological cue, in that they performed significantly different than the controls, as shown in Fig. 4.3.

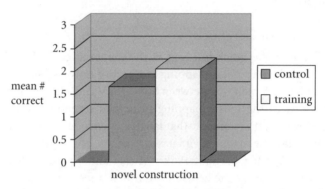

FIGURE 4.3 Average number of trials in which children correctly matched a new instance of the novel construction with a new scene of appearance (out of 3).

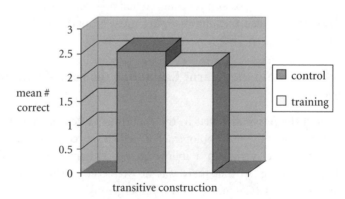

FIGURE 4.4 Average number of transitive stimuli correctly paired with transitive scenes (out of 3)

At the same time, children did not assign a scene of appearance to the transitive stimuli, but instead chose semantically transitive scenes. As expected, children were able to match a transitive stimulus to a transitive scene with or without training, as they were already familiar with the transitive construction: the performance on transitives does not differ significantly across the two groups (Fig. 4.4). See Casenhiser and Goldberg (2005) for specifics.

In the following section we outline why the fact that construction learning is facilitated by high token frequency is in fact expected, given general findings in the non-linguistic categorization literature.

4.6 The role of skewed frequency in non-linguistic categorization

Research in category learning has demonstrated that there is a strong correlation between the frequency with which a token occurs and the likelihood that it will be considered a prototype by the learner (Nosofsky 1988; Rosch and Mervis 1975). Homa, Dunbar, and Nohre (1991) found that token frequency was an important variable at early and intermediate stages of category learning, with increased token frequency facilitating category learning. In learning generalizations about dot patterns, Posner, Goldsmith, and Welton (1967) demonstrated that the rate at which subjects classified patterns correctly was a direct function of the amount of distortion from their respective prototypes: the less variability or distortion, the faster the category was learned.

Elio and Anderson (1984) set up two conditions relevant to the current discussion. In the "centered" condition, subjects were initially trained on more frequently represented, more prototypical instances, with the study sample growing gradually to include more members of the category.[6] In the "representative" condition, subjects were trained on a fully representative sampling from the start. In both conditions, subjects were eventually trained on the full range of instances. Elio and Anderson demonstrated that the order in which subjects received the more prototypical instances played a role in their learning of the category. In particular, they demonstrated that categories were learned more accurately in the "centered" condition; the "representative" condition yielded poorer typicality ratings and accuracy during the test phase on new instances. Elio and Anderson observe, "The superiority of the centered condition over the representative condition suggests that an initial, low-variance sample of the most frequently occurring members may allow the

---

[6] The study involved descriptions of people belonging to one of two clubs, with members' descriptions varying on five four-valued dimensions.

learner to get a 'fix' on what will account for most of the category members" (p. 25). They go on to note that "a low-variance sample, in which there is a maximum amount of similarity among items, is particularly conducive to forming strong category generalizations" (p. 28).[7] Similar results were found by Avrahami et al. (1997) who demonstrated that subjects learned categories better when presented with several ideal positive cases followed by borderline cases than if they were presented with sequences that emphasized category boundaries from the start.[8]

Gentner likewise notes that processes of analogy required for generalization (her "structural alignment") are facilitated when instances being compared are similar to one another. Gentner, Loewenstein, and Hung (2002) performed an experiment that illustrates this idea: they showed children a particular picture of a Martian to be used as a standard for comparison, and two alternative Martian creatures. The standard Martian and one of the alternatives shared one body part, while the distinct Martian didn't. Children were asked, "This one has a *blick*. Which one of these has a *blick*?" The results demonstrated that if the two alternatives were highly similar to the standard, children were better able to pick out the relevant shared body part; when they were only weakly similar, finding the body part was more difficult. In addition, Gentner et al. demonstrated that children who were tested in the high-similarity condition first, were subsequently more successful on the low-similarity items than children who had the same amount of experience with only low-similarity items.

Moreover, categories that are identifiable with a salient type of stable feature are easier to learn than categories in which the feature is instantiated in different ways, even when the variability is relevant to the feature dimension (Markman and Maddox 2003). The analogy to language is that constructions that are instantiated (to a great extent) by a single verb should be initially easier to learn than constructions that are instantiated by many different verbs.

---

[7] Interestingly enough, Elio and Anderson (1984) also found that when subjects were explicitly asked to form hypotheses about what criteria governed category membership, the advantage of learning the centered instances first disappeared. They therefore conclude that the advantage is only evident when the learning is *implicit*. Implicit learning involves knowledge that is not accessible to consciousness, is fairly complex and abstract, an incidental consequence of some task demand, and preserved in cases of amnesia (Seger 1994). Relevantly, language learning is an excellent example of implicit learning, since it is largely learned below the level of consciousness, is very complex and ultimately quite abstract, is a consequence of trying to communicate, and is preserved in cases of amnesia.

[8] Stimuli in this experiment also consisted of non-linguistic stimuli: variable-sized semicircles with variably oriented radial lines.

We performed an experiment with a design parallel to that described for construction learning to test whether the advantage of a single high frequency exemplar would hold in a non-linguistic task as well (Goldberg and Casenhiser forthcoming). We created a random dot pattern (with ten dots) to be used as a prototype as well as four systematic variations from the prototype pattern. Subjects in the skewed frequency group saw twice as many instances of the prototype dot pattern as any of the other dot patterns. Subjects in the balanced group were not given this preferential training with the prototype; instead, they saw a more balanced distribution of the prototype pattern in comparison to the other dot patterns. Subjects were again tested with a forced choice to determine if they were able to distinguish a *new* variation of the prototype from a dot pattern generated randomly. New variations used at test differed from the prototype to the same degree as the variations used in training.

Twenty-four college undergraduates were tested, distributed randomly and equally into the two groups. The results demonstrate that subjects in the skewed frequency group were significantly more accurate at test than those in the balanced frequency group, thus confirming the idea that learning of categories generally is facilitated when a prototype is encountered with high frequency as opposed to experience with the same variety of instances, when the prototype does not account for the balance of items (see Fig. 4.5).

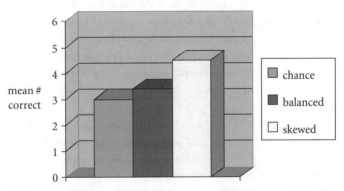

FIGURE 4.5 Mean number of times subjects were able to match correctly the new variation of the random dot pattern (based on Goldberg and Casenhiser, forthcoming).[9]

---

[9] An ANOVA confirmed a significant main effect for group, such that the high frequency training condition performed significantly better than the balanced frequency training condition $F_{(1,27)}=6.78$, $p < .02$. Chi-square test with 6 degrees of freedom was performed to compare subjects' performance to chance. Subjects in the balanced group did not perform significantly above chance $p = .13$. Subjects in the high frequency group did perform significantly above chance $p < .01$.

These results demonstrate that the learning advantage of skewed frequencies is not specific to language.

To summarize, we know that frequency and order of acquisition play key roles in category formation in that training on prototypical instances frequently and/or early facilitates category learning (Bruner, Goodnow, and Austin 1956; Kruschke 1996; Maddox 1995; Nosofsky 1988). This generalization together with the experimental evidence discussed in the previous section suggests that the very frequent and early use of one verb in a pattern facilitates the learning of the semantics of that pattern. The corpus findings demonstrate that exactly this sort of tailor-made input is available to language learners. We suggest, for example, after using many sentences with *put* in the construction in (1), children come to associate the meaning of *put* with the construction even when the verb is not present as in (2):

(1)   She put a finger on that.

(2)   He done boots on. (STE, 28 months; Bates, Bretherton, and Snyder 1988)

The result is that the meaning of roughly "X causes Y to move Z_{loc}" comes to be associated with the Subj V Obj $Obl_{path/loc}$ formal pattern.

The implications of this work are potentially far-reaching, since it is very common for constructions to exhibit statistical "skewing" toward a subset of possible data types. That is, tokens of constructions are typically centered around one or a few specific words, or around a semantic prototype, even when they potentially occur with a much broader range of words or meanings (Brenier and Michaelis 2005; Cameron-Faulkner, Lieven, and Tomasello 2003; Deane 2003; Diessel 2001; Goldberg 1996, 1999; Hunston and Francis 1999; Scheibman 2002; Stefanowitsch and Gries 2003; Thompson and Hopper 2001). In the case of argument structure constructions, we have demonstrated a facilitory effect for a high-frequency verb.[10]

In the case of other constructions, relevant skewing of the input could be around a noun, adjective, or complementizer. For example, Brenier and Michaelis (forthcoming) note that the noun *thing* appears in more than half of the tokens of the double *is* construction (e.g. *The thing is, is that . . .*). Other nouns appear such as *problem, difficulty, question, point, issue,* and *rumor,* but with much less frequency. Thus the general facilitory effect demonstrated in the experiments described above may have a general utility in language learning.

---

[10] See Del'Orletta et al. (forthcoming), Alishahi and Stevenson (forthcoming), and Borovsky and Elman (MS) for computational models that capture this effect.

The advantage of skewed input: an anchoring effect

One way to think of these effects is that they may involve a type of **cognitive anchoring,** where a high-frequency type of example acts as an anchor, i.e. a salient standard of comparison. Numerical anchoring effects have been demonstrated to be quite robust in cognitive psychology. Tversky and Kahneman (1974) demonstrated that people's numerical estimates are influenced by a salient standard of comparison even if that comparison was completely irrelevant to the task at hand. For example, estimations of the percentage of African nations in the UN was influenced by an arbitrary number determined by a manipulated spin of the "wheel of fortune." That is, estimates were significantly higher among the group exposed to a high anchor (guessing 45 per cent if the wheel stopped at 65) than if the group were exposed to a low anchor (guessing 25 per cent if the wheel stopped at 10); i.e. guesses were assimilated towards the anchor. Anchoring effects persist over time (Mussweiler 2001), have an effect even if the anchor values are obviously irrelevant (Strack and Mussweiler 1995), and even when subjects are warned about the distorting effect of anchors (Wilson, Houston, Etling, and Brekke 1996). At the same time, anchoring effects are markedly stronger when the anchor is perceived to be *relevant* to the subsequent task (Wilson, Houston, Etling, and Brekke 1996). The existence of a type of instance that occurs with high token frequency may well provide a highly relevant cognitive anchor, serving to organize memory and reasoning about other related types.

Single high frequency exemplar facilitory, but not necessary

It is important to observe that it is *not necessary* for there to be a single verb with frequency far greater than other verbs for successful learning to take place. The correlation between form and meaning can be learned by noting their association across several distinct verbs, each with relatively low frequency. This is in fact evident from our data insofar as subjects in the balanced condition outperformed those in the control condition: they clearly did learn something from witnessing several verbs in the construction, each with relatively low frequency. This is important because in naturalistic data, there is not always a single verb that has far greater frequency than other verbs, at least if constructions are defined as generally as possible: the transitive construction may be just such a case (Sethuraman and Goodman 2004).

I need to emphasize that I am *not* claiming that general purpose verbs are necessarily the very first verbs uttered. Neither the cross-sectional corpus data nor the experimental data address this question. Moreover, longitudinal studies have yielded differing answers (see Ninio 1999 for a suggestion that such verbs are likely to be the very first or second verbs uttered; but see Campbell and Tomasello 2001 for evidence that they are not always the very first verbs).[11]

Reconciling results with the observation that high token frequency is inversely related to productivity

Bybee (1995) has argued that morphological tokens with especially high frequency do *not* lead to generalizations because they are routinized to such an extent that their internal structure is unanalyzed and therefore unavailable for analogical extension. Bybee's argument is based on irregular morphological items such as *went* and *am* which clearly do not lend themselves to generalizations. It is quite possible that such morphological forms are used without internal analysis. However, it is clear that the constructions under discussion represent a different case. They must be analyzed because they contain argument positions that must be filled. The caused-motion pattern with *put,* for example, has slots that are filled by different arguments from one use to the next. The same is true with our constructed stimuli. Psycholinguistic experiment has revealed that even frequent VP idioms such as *kick the bucket* are analyzed in online sentence comprehension (Peterson et al. 2001). In fact, VP idioms have to be analyzed since their internal structure is minimally variable: the verb may be variably marked for tense or agreement (*kick the bucket; kicked the bucket; kicks the bucket*).

The experiments discussed above had a type frequency of five, not one, and so were unlikely to be treated as fixed idioms. However, we have since run an experiment that includes a training condition in which the only novel verb is *moop.* In this case, subjects do in fact show evidence of less robust generalization (Goldberg and Casenhiser in prep.). Thus a combination of type and token frequencies are relevant.

4.7 Reconciling evidence for fast mapping of phrasal forms and meanings with conservative learning

The finding that the mapping between a new form and meaning pair can be generalized so quickly, with so little input, appears to run counter to the large body of evidence that indicates that children are very conservative learners.

---

[11] See Tomasello and Stahl (2004) for arguments that extreme care must be taken to avoid confusing high frequency with early acquisition when intermittent sampling techniques are used. Ninio's (1999) data combined parental reports with intermittent sampling, so the data should be reliable (unless high frequency affects the veridicality of maternal reports). See Goldberg, Casenhiser, and Sethuraman (2004) for discussion of Ninio's Pathbreaking Verb analysis.

That is, as discussed in Chapter 3, many studies have demonstrated that the initial production of argument structure patterns is very conservative in that children stick closely to the forms they have heard used with particular verbs (Akhtar 1999; Baker 1979; Bates and MacWhinney 1987; Bowerman 1982; Braine 1976; Brooks and Tomasello 1999; Gropen et al. 1989; Ingram and Thompson, 1996; Lieven, Pine, and Baldwin 1997; MacWhinney 1982; Olguin and Tomasello 1993; Schlesinger 1982; Tomasello 1992, 2000, 2003).

It is possible that the difference between conservative learning found in other tasks and the fast mapping discussed here is age-related. Clearly work on younger children is needed to demonstrate that the categorization strategies at play in the experiments discussed above are operative at younger ages, when children actually begin to acquire language.

However, the reason for the conservative learning has been claimed to be that children—and *adults*—operate with a usage-based model of language (Tomasello 2003). The difference between children and adults has been thought to involve a difference in the amount of experience with the ambient language. Therefore we would not necessarily expect to find quicker generalizations in older children than in younger children if they are both exposed to the same amount of input on a novel construction.

Therefore, it seems more likely that the difference is task-dependent. Studies that have documented conservative learning have used a variety of methods including (*a*) spontaneous production, (*b*) elicited production, and (*c*) act-out tasks. These tasks require *recall* of at least aspects of the pairing of form and meaning. Clearly this is true in the case of production, since in order to produce an utterance, the child must be able to recall its form correctly and use it appropriately. In act-out tasks, children are encouraged to act out scenes that they hear verbal descriptions of; this also requires that the child recall the relevant meaning associated with the given form. The task outlined here, on the other hand, only requires that children *recognize* the relevant meaning from among two given alternatives. This is more akin to the preferential-looking paradigm that has been argued in fact to demonstrate early generalizations (Gleitman 1994; Naigles and Bavin 2001), although somewhat controversially (Tomasello 2000, 2003). It may be that learners are able to make tentative generalizations on the basis of very little input; only if those generalizations are reinforced, however, do they become a stable source of productive language creation (see Section 3.7 for evidence of early tentative generalizations).

It seems that children are both conservative and quick generalizers. Indeed, if in fact language is usage-based, as argued in Chapter 3, then we should expect to find evidence of both item-based learning and the quick grasping for generalizations. Children must "make sense of" their language so that they are able productively to use it in new situations. Therefore they are likely constantly to seek out generalizations. The advantages to learning constructions are discussed in Chapter 6. But before we turn our attention there, we first address the issue of how generalizations are constrained. This is the subject of the following chapter.

4.8 Summary

To summarize, it appears that the input is structured in such a way as to make the generalization of argument structure constructions straightforward. One particular verb accounts for the lion's share of tokens of each argument frame considered in an extensive corpus study on the Bates et al. (1988) corpus, in both mothers' and twenty-eight-month-old children's speech. The dominance of a single verb in the construction facilitates the association of the meaning of the verb in the construction with the construction itself, allowing learners to get a "fix" on the construction's meaning. Research on construction learning and on the categorization of random dot patterns presented here supports this idea. In this way, grammatical constructions may arise developmentally as generalizations over lexical items in particular patterns. As Elman has suggested, "Knowledge of constructions is a straightforward extension, by generalization, of knowledge of groups of words that behave similarly" (Elman forthcoming: 13).

The present proposal for how the semantics associated with constructions is learnable from the input directly undermines the "paucity of the stimulus" argument as it is aimed at the particular issue of linking generalizations. Before we decide that language-specific properties must be innate, it is worth investigating how they might be learned, given general cognitive processes such as categorization, together with a closer look at the input children receive.

Still, it might be argued that while linking generalizations may be learnable, they are not learned, insofar as they exhibit some striking regularities across languages. We address this argument in Chapters 7 and 9, where it is argued that the cross-linguistic generalizations that exist are readily attributed to general cognitive, pragmatic, and processing constraints and do not require recourse to any genetic, domain-specific linguistic knowledge.

5

How generalizations are constrained

A boulder is a ROCK? ... TWO names?! <incredulous> ... Is "boulder" a LAST name?

(Zach 3;3)

The previous chapter argued that categorization of attested instances leads learners to generalize grammatical constructions beyond their original contexts. In this chapter, we address the question of how the learner knows whether a pattern can be extended for use with new verbs for the sake of production, that is, the question of productivity. We need to explain how generalizations are constrained: How do children avoid or recover from overgeneralizing their constructions? Children are not strictly conservative, producing only what they have heard, and yet they are not reliably corrected when they produce overgeneralizations or ungrammatical utterances of other kinds. As many have noted, the most obvious possible solutions are not viable, including a reliance on overt corrections or corrective repetitions (Bowerman 1996; Brooks and Tomasello 1999; Pinker 1989). How then can children retreat or avoid overgeneralizations?

There has been much discussion in the literature about productivity and I do not attempt to review it all here (Baker 1979; Bowerman 1988; Brooks and Tomasello 1999; Goldberg 1995; Pinker 1989). At least four factors have been proposed as relevant to predicting a pattern's productivity: (*a*) the number of times an item occurs—its token frequency or degree of *entrenchment*; (*b*) *statistical pre-emption*: the repeated witnessing of the word in a competing pattern (Brooks and Tomasello 1999; Goldberg 1993, 1995; Marcotte 2005; Pinker 1981); (*c*) the absolute number of distinct items that occur in a given pattern or a pattern's *type frequency* (Bybee 1985; Goldberg 1995; MacWhinney 1978; Plunkett and Marchman 1991, 1993); and (*d*) the variability of the items that occur in a given pattern: a pattern's *degree of openness* (Bowerman and Choi 2001; Bybee 1995; Janda 1990; Pinker 1989).

In order for *any* of these factors to work in constraining generalizations, some memory of how particular words are used in particular constructions is essential. That is, the only way to account for partial productivity is to recognize item-specific knowledge (cf. discussion in Chapter 3).

5.1 Statistical Pre-emption

Several theorists have argued that the process of *entrenchment* or hearing a pattern with sufficient frequency plays a key role in constraining overgeneralizations (Braine and Brooks 1995; Brooks and Tomasello 1999). For example, Braine and Brooks propose a "unique argument-structure preference" such that once an argument structure pattern has been learned for a particular verb, that argument structure pattern tends to block the creative use of the verb in any other argument structure pattern, unless a second pattern is also witnessed in the input. Brooks et al. (1999) demonstrated that children in an experimental setting were more likely to overgeneralize verbs that were used infrequently (e.g. to use *vanish* transitively), and less likely to overgeneralize frequently occurring verbs (e.g. to use *disappear* transitively). The difference was attributed to the difference in frequency. This sort of explanation, however, does not address the fact that verbs that frequently appear in one argument structure pattern can in fact be used creatively in new argument structure patterns, without any trace of ill-formedness as in:

(1) She sneezed the foam off the cappuccino.
(2) She danced her way to fame and fortune.
(3) The truck screeched down the street.

Upon closer inspection, effects that might be ascribed to entrenchment are better attributed to a statistical process of pre-emption, critically involving the role of semantic or pragmatic contrast.

That is, one way that overgeneralizations can be minimized is based on the idea that more specific knowledge always pre-empts general knowledge in production, *as long as either would satisfy the functional demands of the context equally well*. That is, more specific items are preferentially produced over items that are licensed but are represented more abstractly, as long as the items share the same semantic and pragmatic constraints. The idea that more specific information should override more general information when the two are functionally equivalent is one with much precedent (cf. e.g. the Elsewhere Condition of Kiparsky 1973, who attributes the generalization to Panini).

In the case of morphological pre-emption (or blocking), this idea is already familiar. While the agentive nominalizing suffix, *–er*, for example, is partially productive (one who is prone to squabbles can be called a *squabbler*), it does not apply to words for which there already exists an agentive nominal counterpart. For example, while someone can *ref* a game, he is not a *reffer*, because *referee* pre-empts the creation of the new term *reffer*. Similarly, *went* pre-empts *goed*, *children* pre-empts *childs*, etc. The pre-emption process is straightforward in these cases because the actual form serves the identical semantic/pragmatic purpose as the pre-empted form. This idea implies that there is no complete synonymy—while two words may refer to the same thing (*auto* and *car*), they will generally differ in terms of register (as *auto* and *car* do), construal (as *thrifty* and *stingy* do), or in terms of dialect (as *soda* and *pop* do) (Clark 1987).

DiSciullo and Williams (1987) discuss a case of pre-emption in which the existence of a morphological form pre-empts the use of a phrasal pattern. In particular, the ready availability of a lexical comparative pre-empts the formation of a comparative phrase: e.g. *better* renders the adjective phrase *more good* ill-formed. This is expected on a constructionist view, since the morphological form [adj-er] and the phrasal pattern [more adj] are both stored constructions, and they have nearly identical meaning and pragmatics. At the same time, if the instance of the morphological comparative is not stored as an entrenched lexical item, there should be some leeway in choosing the phrasal form, even when the phonology of the adjective would allow it to appear with the morphological comparative. That is, the process of pre-emption requires that an alternative form be more readily available than the pre-empted form. As expected, in fact, a cake can be *moister* or *more moist* than another cake, *fresher* or *more fresh*, *duller* or *more dull*. *Moister*, *fresher*, *duller*, being relatively infrequent, appear to be created on the fly from the [adj-er] lexical construction and not stored as independent words that would block the creative formation of *more moist*, *more fresh*, or *more dull*.[1]

The role of pre-emption between two phrasal forms requires explanation, since expressions formed from distinct phrasal constructions are virtually never semantically and pragmatically identical. Any two phrasal constructions will differ either semantically or pragmatically (or both). As we discussed in Chapter 2, the ditransitive construction in (4) is distinct semantically and pragmatically from the prepositional paraphrase. Thus knowledge that the

---

[1] The role of frequency is sometimes overlooked in discussions of these constructions because the [adj-er] form requires single syllable adjectives and such shorter forms tend to be highly frequent. Therefore, the comparative forms are also often sufficiently frequent to pre-empt the phrasal forms.

prepositional paraphrase is licensed as in (5) (based on positive evidence) should not in any simple way pre-empt the use of the ditransitive (Bowerman 1996) in(4), which is ill formed:

(4) *She explained me the story.
(5) She explained the story to me.

In fact, a large number of verbs do freely appear in both constructions. Goldberg (1995), following up on a suggestion made by Pinker (1984: 400), argued that a statistical form of pre-emption could play an important role in learning to avoid expressions such as (4), once a speaker's expectations are taken into account in the following way. In a situation in which construction A might have been expected to be uttered, the learner can infer that construction A is not after all appropriate if, consistently, construction B is heard instead.

The type of counterfactual reasoning required may seem overly complex. However, it has been demonstrated in another domain that young infants are entirely capable of a very similar sort of logic. Gergely, Bekkering, and Kiraly (2002) divided fourteen-month-old babies into two conditions. In one condition the babies watched an experimenter turn on a light in front of him by using his head instead of his hands. In the second condition, the experimenter also turned on the light with his head, but was simultaneously holding a blanket close to his chest with both hands, feigning chills. They found that when the demonstrator's hands were free, 69 per cent of the babies mimicked his head action to turn on the light (a good example of humans' predilection to imitate). But only 21 per cent of the infants did so when the adult's hands were occupied. In the latter case, the infants' reasoning appeared to be: "if the experimenter were able to use her hands she would have (but they were busy holding the blanket)." In the condition which saw the experimenter use the head action despite having her hands free, the child appeared to reason, "if the experimenter meant to use her hands she would have; since she didn't, perhaps she used her head for some reason." Similarly, the reasoning required for pre-emptive processes to work is "if the person meant to use the other formulation she would have; therefore, since she didn't, perhaps she used the alternate formulation for a reason."

The fact that statistically based pre-emption involving related, but non-synonymous constructions, plays a role in avoiding overgeneralizations has in fact been demonstrated empirically. Brooks and Tomasello (1999) found that children aged six or seven were less than half as likely to productively produce a novel verb in a transitive frame when the verb had been modeled in both an intransitive and periphrastic causative construction, than when it was only modeled in the simple intransitive. For example, if the child had heard both *The ball is tamming*, and *He's making the ball tam*, then they were less likely to respond to "what's the boy doing"? with *He's tamming the ball*, than they were if only the simple intransitive had been witnessed. It seems that hearing the novel verb used in the periphrastic causative provided a readily available alternative to the causative construction, statistically pre-empting the use of the latter. That is, hearing a periphrastic causative in a context in which the transitive causative would have been at least equally appropriate led children to avoid generating a transitive causative in a similar contextual situation.

The Brooks et al. (1999) finding that high-frequency verbs are less likely to be overgeneralized than low-frequency verbs is consistent with the idea that it is pre-emption that prevents overgeneralization, not the frequency of the verb per se. That is, the pre-emptive context in which *disappear* might have been expected to occur transitively but instead is witnessed intransitively (in a periphrastic causative construction) occurs more frequently than the same pre-emptive context for *vanish*.

It might seem that the conditions for applying statistical pre-emption are not common enough to constrain generalizations. However, defending the same type of pre-emptive process, Marcotte (2005) observes that instances of such indirect negative evidence are readily available to the child:

children's ability to detect shared meanings between their own utterances and adult ones is an unspoken but crucial precondition to obtaining even positive evidence. Both positive and negative evidence are the outcome of a process of comparison between the child's parse of an adult utterance in its context, and a child-generated representation expressing the same meaning in that context. Matches yield positive evidence, mismatches yield negative evidence.

In a computer modeling study designed to analyze how spatial terms can be learned on the basis of positive evidence, Regier (1996) found that learning was dramatically improved if each positive use of a spatial term was taken as a statistical indication by the system that all of the other possible spatial terms were inappropriate. The inference is necessarily only statistical: the model would have been ill-advised to assume that every use of *above* indicated that *over* had not been a possible alternative, since the two are often both equally applicable. Still, by treating each use of *above* as a tentative indication of "not *over*" and "not *across*" and "not *under*," etc., the model was able to learn to map words successfully onto an impressive variety of spatial configurations. Alishahi and Stevenson (forthcoming) have successfully applied statistical pre-emption in a computational model of argument structure learning; the system recovers from overgeneralizations such as *She falled the cup*, by consistently hearing *fall* used intransitively even when an actor argument was part of the message to be conveyed (as in *She made the cup fall*).

As is discussed more in Chapter 7, there is a clash in information-structure properties that results in a preference for (7) over (6). In learning to avoid examples like (6), the child may be aided by statistical preemption in the input:

(6) ??Who did she give a book?

(7) Who did she give a book to?   (preferred, despite prescriptive injunction against stranded prepositions)

That is, when a learner might expect to hear a form like that in (6), she is statistically overwhelmingly more likely to hear a form such as (7). (In online data, actual occurrences of questioned prepositional goals outnumber questioned ditransitive recipients by roughly forty to one; see Chapter 7 for discussion). This statistical pre-emption may lead the child to disprefer questions such as that in (6) in favor of ones such as (7).

The pre-emptive process, unlike the notion of simple high token frequency, predicts that an expression like (8) would *not* be pre-empted by the overwhelmingly more frequent use of *sneeze* as a simple intransitive (as in (9)) because the expressions do not mean at all the same things.

(8) She sneezed the foam off the cappuccino.

(9) She sneezed.

At the same time, frequency does play some role in the process of statistical pre-emption exactly because the pre-emption is statistical. Only upon repeated exposures to one construction in lieu of another related construction can the learner infer that the second construction is not conventional. As noted above, this requires that a given pattern occur with sufficient frequency.

5.2 Type frequency/Degree of Openness of a pattern

The process of statistical pre-emption is a powerful way in which indirect negative evidence can be gathered by learners. At the same time, it cannot account fully for children's lack of overgeneralizations. Constructions may be either too low frequency or too semantically or pragmatically specialized for another construction effectively to pre-empt their appearance (cf. discussion in Goldberg 1995: ch. 5). Moreover, upon first encountering a novel verb, speakers presumably know something about the contexts in which it can appear and the contexts in which it cannot, without there being a possibility of a pre-emptive context (since it is a new word).

Several authors have proposed that *type frequency* correlates with productivity (Bybee 1985, 1995; Clausner and Croft 1997; Goldberg 1995). Constructions that have appeared with many different types are more likely to appear with new types than constructions that have only appeared with few types. For example, argument structure constructions that have been witnessed with many different verbs are more likely to be extended to appear with additional verbs. To some extent, this observation has to be correct: A PATTERN IS CONSIDERED EXTENDABLE BY LEARNERS ONLY IF THEY HAVE WITNESSED THE PATTERN BEING EXTENDED.

At the same time, it is clear that learners do not generate new instances on the basis of type frequency alone. In fact, a training study by Childers and Tomasello (2001) sought to find a role for increased type frequency in the productive use of the transitive construction, but failed to find an effect. The degree of semantic relatedness of the new instances to instances that have been witnessed is likely to play at least as important a role as the simple type frequency. Constructions that have been heard used with a wide *variety* of types are more likely to be extended broadly than constructions that have been heard used with a semantically circumscribed set of types. That is, learners are fairly cautious in producing utterances based on generalizing beyond the input; they can only be expected confidently to use a new verb in a familiar pattern when that new verb is relevantly close in meaning to verbs they have already heard used in the pattern.

In writing about how non-linguistic inductions are made, Osherson and colleagues (Osherson et al. 1990) propose a relevant notion of COVERAGE. They demonstrate that speakers are more confident about generalizing a property to a new instance to the degree that the new instance fits within the category determined by entities known to exhibit the property. For example, speakers are more confident of the soundness of the conclusion in (A), that rabbits have some property X,[2] than they are of the same conclusion in (B):

(A) assumption 1: Lions have property X.
     assumption 2: Giraffes have property X.
     - - - - - - - - -
     Conclusion: Rabbits have property X.

(B) assumption 1: Lions have property X.
     assumption 2: Tigers have property X
     - - - - - - - - -
     Conclusion: Rabbits have property X.

[2] The property X in the above syllogisms is typically filled in by a "blank" predicate, i.e. a predicate of which subjects have no knowledge.

Intuitively this is because the assumptions in (B), that lions and tigers have some property X, tells us something only about large felines, and says nothing at all about rabbits, whereas the assumptions in (A) lead us to suspect that the generalization may hold of all mammals, in which case there is more reason to believe the property holds also of rabbits as an instance of the category mammal. Osherson et al. characterize coverage as the degee to which the premise categories are similar to members of the lowest-level category that includes both the premise and the conclusion categories. In the case of language, the analogy is clear: The greater the degree to which previously attested instances fill a semantic space that includes the potential target instance, the more confident speakers will be in using the target instance.

5.3 Applying pre-emption and openness to particular examples

Let us consider again the novel utterances in (1)–(3) repeated below:

  (10) She sneezed the foam off the cappuccino.
  (11) She danced her way to fame and fortune.
  (12) The truck screeched down the street.

The reason *sneeze* can readily appear in the caused-motion construction as in (10) is because *sneeze* can be construed to have a meaning relevantly like other verbs that readily appear in that construction, as a verb that effects a causal force. Other verbs that appear in the construction indicate that the causal force may involve air (*blow*), and need not be volitional (*knock*). Since *sneeze* has not been pre-empted in this use—given that this meaning has only rarely if ever been expressed—(10) is fully acceptable. Example (11) of the *way* construction is fully acceptable since a large variety of verbs have been attested in that particular construction. *Dance* is relevantly like any of a number of these attested verbs including in particular various verbs of performance (e.g. *sing*). The intended meaning in (11) is also not pre-empted by another construction, since the *way* construction is both relatively infrequent and has a very specialized meaning, roughly "to (metaphorically) travel despite difficulty or obstacles" (Goldberg 1995). That is, since it can only very rarely be expected with any degree of confidence, its non-occurrence in a given context cannot be taken as evidence that it is infelicitous. Finally, (12) is an acceptable use of *screech* because other verbs of sound emission are attested in the intransitive motion construction with a similar meaning (e.g. *rumble*, used to mean "to move causing a rumbling sound") and since again, it is not likely that the meaning "to move causing a screeching sound" could have been systematically pre-empted by another construction.

Thus a combination of both conservative extension based on semantic proximity to a cluster of attested instances, together with statistical preemption can go along way toward an avoidance of overgeneralizations in the domain of argument structure.

5.4 Combining multiple cues

Recent work in automated learning algorithms has made possibly relevant discoveries. It has been shown that any collection of rules of thumb ("weak hypotheses") that are imperfect but correct more often that chance can be combined to yield a highly accurate predictive system through a "boosting" algorithm (Freund and Schapire 1999; Meir and Rätsch 2003; Schapire 1990). Boosting has been applied to both traditional symbolic and to connectionist network systems. The algorithm works roughly as follows. It takes a representative subset of data to use as training and formulates the first weak hypothesis (h1), where $h1(x_i)$ is the function that classifies each x_i in the training set according to h1. The training items x_i, for $i = 1$ to n, are then weighted more heavily if their classification was incorrect according to h1, less heavily if their classification was correct. The relevance of this sort of procedure to language learning clearly requires some sort of indirect negative evidence, such as the statistical preemption just discussed. This procedure provides a distribution for all the x's.

The value of a weak hypothesis is measured by its error rate, taking into account the distribution. That is, it is equal to the probability that x is misclassified by h, where x is chosen randomly on the basis of the distribution of weights of x's.

A second weak hypothesis (h2) is formulated on the basis of the revised data set (the data set is distinct from the original data set insofar as the distribution assigned to x's is distinct, with the system treating those examples with the strongest weights as the most important to get correct). Again the system iterates, slightly increasing the weight of all incorrectly classified examples and decreasing the weight of all correctly classified examples. These weak hypotheses are then combined via an algorithm "ADABoost" to yield $H(x)$, where $H(x)$ is the weighted sum of all weak hypotheses, where the weight of each hypothesis is determined by its degree of value as described above. Boosting has been shown to yield an algorithm with an arbitrarily small error rate on the basis of such a collection of rules of thumb that are simply above chance.

This sort of algorithm appears to be well suited for determining the conditions in which one construction is chosen over an alternative, when several factors are involved. For example, it is well known that the choice of the ditransitive construction over its prepositional paraphrase is conditioned by the semantic class of the verb, the phonology of the verb (Germanic sounding versus Latinate sounding), semantic characteristics of the recipient argument, and the length, complexity, and focus structure of the two non-subject arguments. Each of these factors can be identified as a heuristic—the boosting algorithm would provide a relevant tool to identify interactions and weights among the factors in order to predict the preferred form for new instances.

5.5 Conclusion

A pattern can be extended to a target form only if learners have witnessed the pattern being extended to related target forms, and if the target form has not systematically been pre-empted by a different paraphrase. Statistical pre-emption provides indirect negative evidence to learners—allowing them to learn to avoid overgeneralizations.

In choosing between allowable alternatives that are conditioned by multiple factors, speakers must combine multiple cues. Successes in machine-learning algorithms that involve iterative refinements of combinations of cues provide promising avenues to explore.

In some ways the task of learning would seem to be made easier if speakers never generalized beyond what they had positive evidence for. For example, it would seem to simplify the task if languages used each particular verb in its own particular frame, without generalizing across verbs or using verbs in novel ways. However, in the following chapter we investigate the benefits of generalizing beyond the input to the level of argument structure constructions.

6

Why generalizations are learned

People do not rely on simple observation or feature learning in order to learn new concepts. They pay attention to the features that their prior knowledge says are the important ones.

(Murphy 2002: 63)

As many psychologists have emphasized, human categorization is generally driven by some functional pressure, typically the need to predict or infer certain properties on the basis of perceived characteristics (Anderson 1991; Holland et al. 1989; Kersten and Billman 1997; Leake and Ram 1995; Murphy 2002; Ross and Makin 1999; Wisniewski 1995). That is, cognitive systems do not generalize randomly or completely. Holland et al. (1989), in their monograph on induction, emphasize that generalizations are constrained in that "the inferences drawn by a cognitive system will tend to be . . . relevant to the system's goals" (p. 5). In the case of language, the language learner's goal is to understand and to be understood: to comprehend and produce language. There is ample functional pressure to predict meaning on the basis of given lexical items and grammatical characteristics (comprehension); conversely, there is pressure to predict the choice of lexical items and grammatical characteristics given the message to be conveyed (production). Since the sentences the child is learning to understand and produce form an open-ended set, it is not sufficient simply to memorize the sentences that have been heard. The child must necessarily generalize those patterns at least to some extent in order to understand and produce new utterances.

In the first part of this chapter, it is argued that the predictive value of constructions encourages speakers to learn them. A second motivation for representing generalized constructions is suggested in Section 6.10, namely that constructions are primed in production.

6.1 Background: the predictive value of verbs in argument structure patterns

There is a long history in the field of linguistics of considering the main verb to be the key word in a clause (Chomsky 1965; Grimshaw 1990; Lakoff 1970; Levin and Rappaport Hovav 1995; Pinker 1989). This has also been true in the field of language acquisition (e.g. Tomasello 1992, 2000). A critical factor in the primacy of verbs in argument structure patterns stems from their relevant predictive value. If we compare verbs with other words (e.g. nouns), verbs are much better predictors of overall sentence meaning, where by "overall sentence meaning" we basically intend "who did what to whom," a level of generalization that is uncontroversially required for adequate sentence comprehension.

Experimental evidence for the idea that verbs play a key role in semantic interpretation is provided by Healy and Miller (1970). Healy and Miller compared the relative contribution of verbs and subject arguments to overall sentence meaning. These two candidates, verb and subject, were presumably chosen because they appear to be the best candidates for representing overall sentence meaning. The subject argument is often referred to as the "topic" argument in a sentence or what the sentence is "about" (Kuno 1972; Lambrecht 1994; Reinhart 1982). At the same time, the verb provides a great deal of information about who did what to whom. Healy and Miller constructed twenty-five sentences by crossing five subject arguments (*the salesman, the writer, the critic, the student, the publisher*), five verbs (*sold, wrote, criticized, studied, published*), and one patient (*the book*). Participants were asked to sort the sentences into five piles according to similarity in meaning. Results showed that participants reliably sorted sentences together that had the same verb much more often than sentences that had the same subject argument. That is, for example, all five sentences with the verb *criticized* were categorized together much more often than five sentences with the subject *the critic*. Given these results, Healy and Miller concluded that the verb is the main determinant of sentence meaning.

Another source of evidence for the idea that the verb is a good predictor of sentence meaning comes from work on analogy. It has been richly documented that relational aspects of meaning are fruitful sources of analogy and similarity judgments (Gentner 1982). Markman and Gentner (1993), for example, found that in making non-linguistic judgments, similarity is judged to be greater when two representations share the same relations between the entities in each representation. That is, the entities are aligned based on the structure that relates them, rather than on the basis of independent characteristics of the entities. The relevance to language is straightforward. In comparing two sentences, the main relational predicates, the verbs, are more likely to be used than the independent characteristics of the arguments (cf. also Tomasello 2000). Why should this be so? The purpose of analogies is generally one of drawing inferences and making predictions: what can be predicted on the basis of one situation about another situation (Gentner and Medina 1998). Thus it is the value of verbs as good cues to sentence meaning that results in the child's early learning of verb-centered argument structure patterns ("verb islands").

This chapter focuses on the question of why learners generalize beyond the verb to the more abstract level of argument structure constructions.

6.2 The value of constructions as predictors of sentence meaning

In the first part this chapter (Sections 6.2–6.9) we demonstrate that generalizing beyond a particular verb to a more abstract pattern is useful in predicting overall sentence meaning, more useful in fact than knowledge of individual verbs. Bates and MacWhinney (1987) have stressed the importance of weighting different cues, dependent on how reliable and available each cue is. Goldberg, Casenhiser, and Sethuraman (2005) hypothesize that the predictive value encourages speakers to generalize beyond knowledge of specific verbs to ultimately learn the semantic side of linking generalizations, or constructional meaning.

Precedent for this idea comes from work in the non-linguistic categorization literature. Kruschke (1996) and Dennis and Kruschke (1998) discuss how learners shift attention away from less reliable (i.e. less distinctive) cues toward more reliable cues, when learning overlapping instances that belong to distinct categories. For example, if two diseases share one symptom but have their own distinctive symptom, subjects will attend more to the distinctive symptoms than the shared one.[1]

---

[1] Kruschke discusses how this tendency is so strong that it can account for the neglect of base-rate information (the *inverse base-rate effect* discovered by Medin and Edelson (1988)). In Medin and Edelson's study, subjects were taught to classify diseases on the basis of symptoms. Subjects were trained to discriminate disease C (for common) and R (for rare), with C being presented three times as often as R. In the training, every instance of C had two symptoms, I and PC, and every instance of R had two symptoms, I and PR. Since I appeared with both diseases, it was an imperfect predictor; PC was a perfect predictor of the common disease, PR was a perfect predictor of the rare disease. When tested with the ambiguous symptom I, subjects acted in accord with the disease's overall frequency and chose the common disease, C. But when presented with conflicting symptoms PC and PR, people

Consider the construction types below in Table 6.1:

TABLE 6.1. Construction types, defined formally

Label	Form
VOL:	(Subj) V Obj Obl$_{path/loc}$
VOO:	(Subj) V Obj Obj2

It is clear that constructions are sometimes better predictors of overall meaning than many verbs. For example, when *get* appears in the VOL pattern, it conveys caused motion, but when it appears in the VOO pattern, it conveys transfer:

(1)   a. Pat got the ball over the fence.
          get + VOL pattern → "caused motion"
       b. Pat got Bob a cake.
          get + VOO pattern → "transfer"

As quantified below, *get* in isolation has low cue validity as a predictor of sentence meaning. Since most verbs appear in more than one construction with corresponding differences in interpretation, speakers would do well to learn to attend to the constructions. As an indication of the fact that the construction is at least as good a predictor of overall sentence meaning as the verb, we consider the actual predictive value of verbs versus formal patterns in a corpus of speech to young children.

Clearly if we compare the contribution of verb and construction to subtle aspects of meaning involving manner or means, the verb would be more predictive than the construction. This is necessarily true since constructions rarely encode specific meanings: compare "X causes Y to receive Z," the meaning of the ditransitive construction with the meaning of the verbs *hand* or *mail*. At the same time, both verbs and constructions have the potential to convey the overall event-level interpretation, roughly "who did what to whom." Since the event-level interpretation (who did what to whom) is clearly a *necessary* component of interpretation, we chose to compare the relative contribution of constructions and verbs at this level. Clearly, in order to arrive at a *full* interpretation of a sentence, the specifics contributed by only the verb (and its arguments) are required as well.

---

tended to choose the rare disease, contrary to what would be expected if base rates were taken into account in a simple way. Krushke (1996) suggests that subjects learn that the shared symptom I tends to be misleading for the less frequent disease, inferring that PR is a correspondingly better cue.

6.3 Corpus evidence of the construction as a reliable predictor of overall sentence meaning

Goldberg, Casenhiser, and Sethuraman (2005) examined the Bates corpus (Bates et al. 1988) on the Child Language Data Exchange System (CHILDES) database (MacWhinney 1995), as described in Chapter 4.

Results for the VOL pattern

We first examined whether the formal pattern VOL predicted the semantic caused-motion meaning. "Cue validity" is the conditional probability that an object is in a particular category, given that it has a particular feature or cue (Murphy 1982). Two coders classified mothers' utterances as either entailing caused motion or not; those that we judged not to entail caused motion were separated and further analyzed as discussed below. Agreement between the two independent coders was 99 per cent for classifying utterances as instances of the VOL pattern. Agreement for classifying VOL utterances as entailing literal caused motion, metaphorical caused motion, caused location, or not was 97 per cent. Disagreements were resolved through discussion.

P(A|B) is the probability of A, given B. As detailed below, the cue validity of VOL as a predictor of "caused-motion" meaning, or P("caused motion" | VOL), is somewhere between .63 and .83, depending on how inclusive we take the notion of caused motion to be, and how inclusively we define the VOL formal pattern. We found that 63 per cent (159/256) of the mothers' instances of the construction clearly entail literal caused motion. The following examples are representative:

(2)   a. get some more in it
       b. bring 'em back over here
       c. stuff that all in your mouth
       d. put 'em in the box

Another twenty instances involve the verbs *keep, have, get,* or *leave* as in the following type of examples:

(3)   a. keeping these people in the garage
       b. leave it right there

The utterances in (3) entail that the subject argument acts to keep or allow the theme argument to stay in a particular location. The subject argument is agentive and the locative phrase is predicated of the direct object argument just as in instances that entail prototypical caused motion. Many researchers have related these instances to cases of caused motion independently (e.g. Goldberg 1995; Matsumoto 1992; Talmy 1976). If we include these cases in the final tally, 70 per cent of VOL utterances imply caused motion or caused location. Another 2 per cent (5) of instances involve the verb *want* as in:

(4)   Oh, you want them in a cup?

These instances convey possible future caused motion. If we include these in the tally, the percentage of instances that are related to caused motion increases to 72 per cent. Another 5 per cent (13) of instances involve the verbs *read* or *say*, which could be argued to encode metaphorical caused motion (Ackerman and Webelhuth 1998; Goldberg 1995; Pinker 1989; Reddy 1979). Including these cases would raise the total number of VOL utterances whose meanings are related to caused motion to 77 per cent.

Of the remaining VOL utterances, 25, or 10 per cent involved locative adjuncts. If we exclude these, the total number of utterances included as VOL utterances would be reduced from 256 to 231. The total percentage of VOL utterances that involved caused motion would be 85 per cent.

The remaining 34 tokens include examples such as the following, which do not convey caused motion:

(5)   a. What is your foot doing on the table? (The WXDY construction: 16 instances)
      b. What did Ivy do to her arm? (1 instance)
      c. find the bird in the snow (utterances with find: 2 instances)
      d. get Papa at the airport (move-from interpretation: 1 instance)
      e. stand it up (verb particle interpretations: 14 instances)

To summarize, the cue validity of the VOL pattern as a predictor of caused-motion meaning is provided in Table 6.2 below and in the pie chart of Figure 6.1. on the following page.

We then investigated the extent to which individual verbs predicted caused-motion meaning. Table 6.3 shows our calculations of the cue validities of individual verbs that appear at least five times in mothers' speech in the Bates et al. (1988) corpus.[2] For reliability, a second coder independently classified a

TABLE 6.2. Cue validity of VOL construction as a predictor of caused motion

	Strict encoding of caused-motion meaning	Inclusive encoding
VOL	.63	.85

[2] Verbs appearing in the VOL pattern less than 5 times each accounted for 56 instances. These verbs were: *eat, pick, set, throw, want, clean, close, cook, dump, find, give, hold, keep, leave, let, make, move, park, pour, push, send, stack, stick, stuff, try, wake, walk, wear, wipe.*

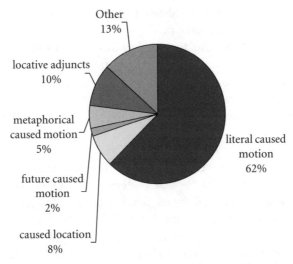

FIGURE 6.1 Proportion of utterances that were related to caused motion (all but those indicated by "other" or "locative adjuncts")

sample of 34 per cent (404/1195) of the total number of utterances, including all of the tokens in the corpus, for the verbs *put, get, take, read, see, stand,* and *turn*. The two coders agreed on whether the verb determined the overall sentence meaning reliably 89 per cent (360/404) of the time. The other

TABLE 6.3. Cue validity of verbs as predictors of whatever meaning they predominantly have in the VOL pattern

Verb	A. Number of instances of stable verb meaning	B. Total number of times verb appears in corpus	C. Cue validity (A/B)	D. Number of times in VOL pattern	E. Weighted cue validity (C × D/200) High (low)
put	113	114	1	99	.50
do	147	601	.24	26	.03
have	15	115	.13	16	.01
get	18	108	.17	14	.01
take	9	44	.20	14	.01
read	14	24	.58	7	.02
see	30	86	.35	7	.01
stand	8	8	1	7	.04
say	6	65	.09	6	.00
bring	10	10	1	6	.03
turn	10	20	.5	6	.02
Total		1195		200	**.68**

utterances were also classified independently by two coders, with disagreements resolved through discussion.

Column A of Table 6.3 lists the number of utterances in which the verb's meaning as it is determined to appear most frequently in the VOL pattern, appears overall in the corpus (including appearances in the VOL pattern). Column B lists the total number of times the verb appears in the corpus. Simple cue validity was calculated by dividing column A by column B; this is recorded in Column C.

In order to determine the cue validity of verbs as they appear in the VOL pattern, it is necessary to weight the cue validities of each verb according to how often the verb occurs in the VOL pattern. We therefore multiply the cue validity obtained in Column C by the number of times the verb occurs in the VOL pattern (recorded in Column D) and divide by the number of VOL tokens in the corpus (200). Summing over the weighted cue validities in Column D provides us with the overall cue validity of .68 for verbs in the VOL pattern in our corpus. If we compare the .63—.85 cue validity for the VOL pattern as a predictor of caused-motion meaning, we can see the construction is roughly as valid a cue.

To see that the weighted average of cue validities is more revealing than the simple average, it is illustrative to consider the following hypothetical situation. Imagine that there were one verb that accounted for 90 per cent of the tokens of a particular construction and had a cue validity of 1. In this particular case, the predictive value of verbs in the construction would clearly be quite high. Yet if there happened to be ten other verbs appearing in the construction, each accounting for 1 per cent of the tokens, and each having low cue validity (in the limiting case close to 0), the average cue validity would only be approximately 0.09. This is not the number we are after, since it does not reveal the fact that the most likely verb to appear is highly predictive. The weighted average in this circumstance would be roughly 0.9, accurately reflecting the predictive nature of verbs in this hypothetical construction. Thus it is the weighted average of cue validities that more accurately reflects the predictive value of verbs.[3]

It is clear from Table 6.3 that there is a wide variability of cue validities across verbs. While a few verbs have perfect or near perfect cue validities (*put, bring, stand*) in our corpus, other verbs' cue validities were low (*do, get, have, let,* and *take*). For the latter verbs, relying on the construction in conjunction with the verb is essential to determining sentence meaning. This fact in itself is

---

[3] The simple average of cue validities would be .5 instead of .68, which would only strengthen our claim that the cue validity of constructions is at least as high as that of verbs.

sufficient to conclude that attention to the semantic contribution of constructions is required for determining overall sentence meaning.

6.4 Results of an analysis of the VOO pattern

Comparable results exist for the VOO pattern. We first examined whether the formal pattern predicted the meaning of "transfer." There were a total of 54 VOO utterances in our database. After initial discussion of criteria to be used, agreement was 100 per cent for classifying mothers' VOO utterances as entailing transfer: literally, metaphorically, or not (n=54). If we include instances that involve metaphorical transfer (specifically those involving the verbs *read* and *tell*), 51 of those 54 (94 per cent) convey transfer. If we exclude instances of *read* and *tell*, 34/54 (61 per cent) code transfer. These figures are given in Table 6.4, with the breakdown given in Figure 6.2.

Goldberg, Casenhiser, and Sethuraman (2005) also investigated the extent to which the verbs predicted overall sentence meaning. Agreement among the two coders was 97 per cent for classifying mothers' uses of verbs as predictive of overall sentence meaning (who did what to whom) (n=307).

We determined for each utterance whether the predominant meaning (who did what to whom) conveyed by the verb's use in the VOO pattern held in each of the remaining utterances involving the same verb. For example, we decided that *tell* involved a speaker, a listener, and some kind of content

TABLE 6.4. Cue validity of the VOO pattern as a predictor of the meaning of transfer

VOO	Strict encoding of transfer	Inclusive encoding of transfer
	.61	.94

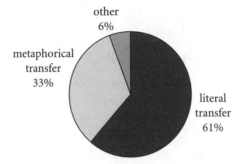

FIGURE 6.2 Proportion of utterances involved literal or metaphorical transfer

conveyed in all uses of the VOO pattern and also in every other use in our corpus; therefore *tell* has a perfect cue validity of 1. On the other hand *read* involved a reader, a listener, and some kind of content in its three appearances in the VOO pattern and in eleven other utterances (phrased using "someone read something to someone"); in the remaining ten utterances in our corpus, *read* did not involve a listener. Therefore the cue validity of *read* was determined to be: $(3+11)/24=.58$.

Table 6.5 shows our calculations of the cue validities of each of the thirteen verbs that appeared in the VOO pattern in our corpus. As in Table 6.4, Column A lists the number of utterances in which the verb's meaning as it is determined to appear most frequently in the VOO pattern, appears overall in the corpus (including appearances in the VOO pattern). Column B lists the total number of times the verb appears in the corpus. Simple cue validity is recorded in Column C and was calculated by dividing column A by column B. To determine cue validity across verbs, it is necessary to weight this number according to how often the verb occurs in the VOO pattern. We therefore multiply the cue validity obtained in Column C by the number of times the verb occurs in the VOO pattern (recorded in Column D) and divide by the number of VOO tokens in the corpus (54). Summing over the weighted cue validities in Column D provides us with the overall cue validity of .61 for verbs in the VOL pattern in our corpus.

TABLE 6.5. Cue validities of verbs in the VOO pattern as predictors of whatever meaning they predominantly have in the VOO pattern

Verb	A. Number of times verb has stable meaning	B. Number of instances in corpus:	C. Cue validity (A/B)	D. Number of times in VOO pattern	Weighted cue validity (C × D/54)
Give	14	14	1	11	.20
Tell	37	37	1	11	.20
Get	7	108	.06	7	.01
Build	6	24	.25	5	.02
Make	3	56	.05	4	.00
Read	14	24	.58	3	.03
Show	6	6	1	3	.06
Bring	2	10	.2	2	.01
Feed	2	2	1	2	.04
Pour	2	4	.5	2	.02
Buy	1	9	.11	1	.00
Fix	1	7	.14	1	.00
Call	4	6	.67	2	.02
TOTAL		307		54	**.61**

The weighted average cue validity for verbs is .61. We again see that the overall cue validity of constructions is at least as high as the cue validity of verbs. If we are generous in deciding what utterances involve transfer, the cue validity of the construction is markedly higher than the cue validity for verbs.

Once again there is a wide variability of cue validities across verbs. While a few verbs had perfect cue validities (*feed, give, show, tell*) in our corpus, other verbs' cue validities were quite low (*fix, get, make*). Again, regardless of the overall cue validity of verbs, this fact in itself indicates that attention to the construction's contribution is key to determining who did what to whom.

What about verbs in other constructions? It may be that verbs are more predictive for some constructions than others. For example, in the simple intransitive construction, the verb supplies almost all of the lexical content. There is a large difference in sentence meaning between *The vase broke* and *She shouted*. Still, even in these cases, the verbs involved are far from perfect predictors of overall sentence meaning. *Break* can appear both transitively and intransitively—to know whether an agent is known or relevant, one needs to know which construction was used. *Shouted*, too, can be used as a verb of communication (e.g. *She shouted the directions*) or simply a verb of sound emission (e.g. *She shouted for joy*).

The fact that the cue validities calculated (.68 for verbs in the VOL and .61 for verbs in the VOO) are close is intriguing. It is possible that there is a generalization about the overall cue validity of verbs: they may be predictive of sentence meaning roughly two-thirds of the time in English. Calculations on other constructions and other corpora are needed to confirm this figure.

6.5 Experimental evidence for constructions as predictors of sentence meaning

Bencini and Goldberg (2000) conducted an experiment inspired by the Healy and Miller (1970) sorting experiment described in Section 6.1, which had been titled, "The Verb as the Main Determinant of Sentence Meaning." In this earlier experiment, stimuli were created by crossing subject arguments with verbs, since it was assumed that the two best candidates for determining what the sentence was about were the verb and the subject argument. We aimed to compare the semantic contribution of the construction with that of the morphological form of the verb. The stimuli were sixteen sentences created by crossing four verbs with four different constructions.

Undergraduate students were asked to sort these sixteen sentences, provided in random order, into four piles based on "overall sentence meaning." They were instructed that there was no right or wrong answer, that the experiment was only intended to determine how people sorted sentences according to sentence meaning. Subjects could sort equally well by verb: e.g. all instances of *throw* (1a-d) being put into the same pile, regardless of construction; or subjects could sort by construction: all instances of e.g. the VOO (ditransitive construction) (1a, 2a, 3a, and 4a) being put into the same pile.

It would of course be possible to design stimuli with a great deal of overlapping propositional content such that we could a priori predict either a verb or constructional sort. For example, the sentences *Pat shot the duck* and *Pat shot the duck dead* would very likely be grouped together on the basis of overall meaning despite the fact that the argument structure patterns are distinct. Conversely, *Pat shot the elephant* and *Patricia stabbed a pachyderm* would likely be grouped together despite the fact that no exact words were shared. The stimuli were designed to minimize such contentful overlap contributed by anything other than the lexical verb. No other lexical items in the stimuli were identical or near synonyms.

The use of the sorting paradigm is a particularly stringent test to demonstrate the role of constructions. Medin, Wattenmaker, and Hampson (1987) have shown that there is a strong, domain-independent bias towards sorting on the basis of a single dimension, even with categories that are designed to resist such one-dimensional sorts in favor of a sort based on a family resemblance

TABLE 6.6. Stimuli for sorting experiment

1a. Pat threw the hammer.	(VO) Transitive
b. Chris threw Linda the pencil.	(VOO) Ditransitive
c. Pat threw the key onto the roof.	(VOL) Caused Motion
d. Lyn threw the box apart.	(VOR) Resultative
2a. Michelle got the book.	(VO) Transitive
b. Beth got Liz an invitation.	(VOO) Ditransitive
c. Laura got the ball into the net.	(VOL) Caused Motion
d. Dana got the mattress inflated.	(VOR) Resultative
3a. Barbara sliced the bread.	(VO) Transitive
b. Jennifer sliced Terry an apple.	(VOO) Ditransitive
c. Meg sliced the ham onto the plate.	(VOL) Caused Motion
d. Nancy sliced the tire open.	(VOR) Resultative
4a. Audrey took the watch.	(VO) Transitive
b. Paula took Sue a message.	(VOO) Ditransitive
c. Kim took the rose into the house.	(VOL) Caused Motion
d. Rachel took the wall down.	(VOR) Resultative

structure (Rosch and Mervis 1975). One-dimensional sorting has been found even with large numbers of dimensions (Smith 1981), ternary values on each dimension (Anh and Medin 1992), holistic stimuli, and stimuli for which an obvious multidimensional descriptor was available (Regehr and Brooks 1995). The stimuli presented subjects with an opportunity to sort according to a single dimension: the verb. Constructional sorts required subjects to note an abstract relational similarity involving the recognition that several grammatical functions co-occur. Thus we would expect verb sorts to have an inherent advantage over constructional sorts.

Six subjects produced entirely construction sorts, seven subjects produced entirely verb sorts, and four subjects provided mixed sorts. In order to include the mixed sorts in the analysis, results were analyzed according to how many changes would be required from the subject's sort to either a sort entirely by verb (VS) or a sort entirely by construction (CS). The average number of changes required for the sort to be entirely by the verb was 5.5; the average number of changes required for the sort to be entirely by construction was 5.7. The difference between these scores does not approach significance. That is, subjects were just as likely to sort by construction as they were to sort according to the single dimension of the morphological form of the verb. If verbs provided equally good cues to overall sentence meaning, there would be no motivation to overcome the well-documented preference for one-dimensional sorts: subjects would have no motivation to sort by construction instead of by verb. Bencini and Goldberg hypothesize that constructional sorts were able to overcome the one-dimensional sorting bias to this extent because constructions may be better predictors of overall sentence meaning than the morphological form of the verb.

This experiment was performed with adults, but the implications for language learning are clear. Insofar as constructions are at least as good predictors of overall sentence meaning as any other word in the sentence, learners would do well to learn to identify construction types, since their goal is to understand sentences.

Kaschak and Glenberg (2000) demonstrate that subjects rely on constructional meaning when they encounter nouns used as verbs in novel ways (e.g. *to crutch*). In particular they show that different constructions differentially influence the interpretations of the novel verbs. For example, *She crutched him the ball* (ditransitive) is interpreted to mean that she used the crutch to transfer the ball to him, perhaps using it as one would a hockey stick. On the other hand, *She crutched him* (transitive) might be interpreted to mean that she hit him over the head with the crutch. Kaschak and Glenberg suggest that the constructional pattern specifies a general scene and that the "affordances" of particular objects are used to specify the scene in detail. It cannot be the semantics of the verb alone that is used in comprehension because the word form is not stored as a verb but as a noun. Ahrens (1994) conducted an experiment with a novel verb form. She asked 100 native English speakers to decide what *moop* meant in the sentence *She mooped him something*. Sixty percent of subjects responded by saying that *moop* meant "give," despite the fact that several verbs exist that have higher overall frequency than *give* and could be used in that frame, including *take* and *tell*. Similarly, Kako (2005) finds that subjects' semantic interpretations of constructions and their semantic interpretations of verbs that fit those constructions are highly correlated, concluding as well that syntactic frames are "semantically potent linguistic entities."

A question arises as to why constructions should be at least as good predictors of overall sentence meaning as verbs. The answer I believe stems from the fact that in context, knowing the number and type of arguments tells us a great deal about the scene being conveyed. To the extent that verbs encode rich semantic frames that can be related to a number of different basic scenes (Goldberg 1995), the complement configuration or construction will be as good a predictor of sentence meaning as the semantically richer, but more flexible verb.

6.7 Increased reliance on constructions in second-language acquisition

Liang (2002) replicated the sorting task of Bencini and Goldberg (2000) with Chinese learners of English of varying proficiencies. Learners categorized as advanced passed the Chinese national test for non-English majors, a test that is generally recognized in China as indicating advanced English ability. Learners categorized as at the intermediate level had passed the national entrance examination to college, which indicates an intermediate level of proficiency with English. Beginning English learners had only two years of English instruction. Liang found that subjects produced relatively more construction-based sorts as their English improved. Her data is provided in Fig. 6.3 on the following page.

For early learners (n=46), the average deviation from an entirely verb-based sort was 5.8; the deviation from an entirely construction-based sort was 6.2. For intermediate learners (n= 31), the average deviation from a verb sort was 6.2; from a construction sort, 5.3. For advanced learners (n=33), the average deviation from a verb sort was 8.2, from a constructional sort 4.9.

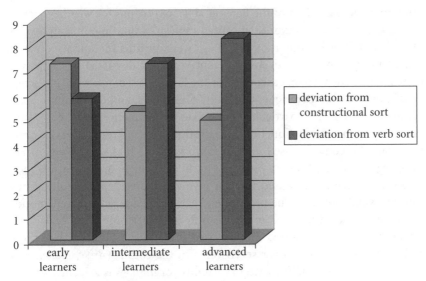

FIGURE 6.3 Results from Liang (2002)

These results indicate that the ability to use language proficiently is correlated with the recognition of constructional generalizations.[4]

6.8 Category Validity

We have discussed cue validity, the probability that an item belongs to a category, given that it has a particular feature: P(cat | feature), and we have found that when the category is taken to be overall sentence meaning, constructions have roughly equivalent cue validity compared with verbs. There is also a second relevant factor. CATEGORY VALIDITY is the probability that an item has a feature, given that the item belongs in the category: P(feature | cat). Thus category validity measures how common or available a feature is among members of a category. The relevant category is, again, sentence meaning.

The category validity of particular verbs as a feature of the semantic category caused motion was determined by hand-coding each utterance in a

[4] Gries and Wulff (2004) also replicated the sorting study, this time with advanced German learners of English, finding similar results to those found for advanced learners by Liang: the average deviation from a verb sort was 8.9, and from a constructional sort was 5.4, a significantly stronger reliance on constructions. These studies raise an interesting issue as to why it might be that learners of a second language appear to rely more heavily on constructions than do native English speakers, at least in this sorting paradigm.

randomly selected subset of the Bates et al. (1998) corpus for whether each of the mothers' utterances expressed caused motion or not. In our sample of all of the utterances of four mothers, there were 47 utterances that conveyed caused motion involving twelve different verbs. As discussed in Chapter 4, there is often one verb that accounts for the lion's share of tokens of particular constructions (Goldberg 1999; Goldberg, Casenhiser, and Sethuraman 2004; Sethuraman 2002); in particular, *put* accounts for many the tokens of the caused-motion construction, but since the transitive and resultative constructions can also convey caused motion (with verbs such as *send, bring, carry*), the category validity for even *put* is not particularly high; in our corpus, 29/47 expressions conveying caused motion involved the verb *put*, resulting in a category validity of .62. The probability that a sentence with caused-motion meaning contained the verb *bring* was only .02, since only 2 per cent of the utterances expressing caused motion used *bring* (1/47). Similarly low probability was found for another seven verbs in the corpus (*drive, make, open, ride, stack, leave, wear*). The category validity for *dump* was .04, *stick* was .06, and *turn* was .11.

The average category validity of all verbs that may convey caused motion is equal to $1/n$, where $n =$ the number of verbs that express caused motion, or in our sample, $1/12 = .08$. Clearly as the sample size increases, the average category validity for verbs is lowered. The actual average category for verbs approaches 0, since more than a hundred different verbs can be used to convey caused motion ($n > 100$; average cue validity $= 1/100^+ < .01$). Another relevant number is the MAXIMUM CATEGORY VALIDITY, since the maximum category validity provides an estimate of the category validity associated with the "best guess" of a relevant verb. In our sample, *put* had the highest category validity of .62; the other eleven verbs conveying caused motion had markedly lower category validities.

The category validity of a construction as a feature of the semantic category caused motion is the probability that the particular construction will be involved, given the interpretation of caused motion. There were only three constructions used to convey caused motion (the VOL, the resultative, and the transitive construction). If we make the very conservative assumption that these three constructions are independent, we find an average category validity of .33 for constructions. The average category validity for constructions may also go down as the sample size increases; but since there are less than a handful of constructions that can be used to convey caused motion, the average category would not dip below .20. The VOL pattern has the maximum category validity for "caused motion" meaning of .83 (39/47 utterances that expressed caused motion involved the VOL pattern). *Put* is only grammatical in the VOL pattern (*She put on the table; *She put the book*): P (*put* | "caused motion") = P (*put* & VOL | "caused motion"). Since hundreds of verbs in addition to *put* can appear in the VOL pattern with caused-motion interpretation, P (*put* & VOL | "caused motion") is necessarily less than P (VOL | "caused motion"). Therefore, P (*put* | "caused motion") < P (VOL | "caused motion"). That is, the VOL pattern must have a higher category validity than *put*; it is more *available* as a cue to caused-motion meaning. The comparison between verbs and constructions is given in Tables 6.6 and 6.7. Table 6.6 provides the AVERAGE CATEGORY VALIDITY for the VOL pattern and verbs that may be used to convey caused motion. Table 6.7 provides the MAXIMUM category validity of the VOL pattern and verbs for caused motion meaning.

On both measures, the average category validity and the maximum category validity, the construction has a higher score than the verb. All things being equal, if two cues have roughly equal validity, the higher category validity of one cue will naturally result in a greater reliance on that cue in categorization tasks (Bates and MacWhinney 1987; Estes 1986; Hintzman 1986; Nosofsky 1988). Thus constructions are better cues to sentence meaning than verbs insofar as they are as reliable (with equivalent cue validity) and more available (having higher category validity).

TABLE 6.6. Average category validity for the VOL pattern and verbs as features of the category of caused motion meaning in a sample of 47 utterances (to illustrate) and more generally, based on rational assumptions

	In sample of 47 utterances	Asymptotic category validity
n	(n = 12)	(n > 100)
$\sum_{i=1}$ P (**verb**$_i$ | "caused motion")/n	=.08	<.01
where verb$_i$ is a verb that may encode caused motion		
n	(n=3)	(since n < 5)
$\sum_{i=1}$ P (**construction**$_i$ | "caused motion")/n	=.33	>.20
where construction$_i$ is a construction that may encode caused motion		

TABLE 6.7. Maximum category validity for the construction and verbs as features of the category of caused motion meaning in a sample of 47 utterances (to illustrate) and more generally, based on rational assumptions

	In sample of 47 utterances	In general:
Verb: P (*put* | "caused motion")	=.62	P (*put* | "caused motion") = P (*put* & VOL | "caused motion")
Construction: P (VOL | "caused motion")	=.83	P (*put* & VOL | "caused motion") < P (VOL | "caused motion") Therefore, P (*put* | "caused motion") < P (VOL | "caused motion")

6.9 Languages in which verbs are more predictive

The verbs in many languages are more restrictive than they are in English, only appearing in constructions that match their meanings. Verbs in Latinate languages, Turkish, and Hindi, for example, do not appear in anything like the range of constructions that they do in English even though they have quite parallel meanings (see, e.g., Narasimhan 1998). Therefore it would seem that the verbs in e.g. Turkish have much higher cue validity than they do in English. And yet it seems unlikely that they fail to form argument structure constructions in such languages. Dan Slobin (personal communication, Feb. 14, 2004) has found in unpublished experimental work that speakers of Turkish readily interpret novel verbs presented in familiar constructions, indicating that they are at least able to construct information about an abstract argument structure construction for the purpose of comprehension. The fact that the category validity for constructions is generally higher than that for verbs—insofar as there are more verbs that can be used to convey a particular event frame than there are constructions—may be responsible in part for yielding constructional generalizations.

In addition, there is a second factor that may well play a role in encouraging speakers to form argument structure constructions, even when the cue validity of the verbs in the language is consistently high. This factor involves the phenomenon of CONSTRUCTIONAL PRIMING.

6.10 Structural Priming and its relation to constructions

A second type of motivation for learning constructions, outlined in this section, is that constructions are primed in production. That is, saying or hearing instances of one grammatical pattern primes speakers to produce other instances of the same. Kathryn Bock and colleagues (Bock and Loebell 1990; Bock, Loebell, and Morey 1992; Bock 1986; Loebell and Bock 2003) have shown in a number of experimental studies that passives prime passives, ditransitives prime ditransitives, and datives prime datives (cf. also Bock and Griffin 2000; Loebell and Bock 2003; Branigan et al. 1995; Chang et al. 2000; Friederici, Schriefers, and Lindenberger, 1998; Hare and Goldberg 1999; Nicol 1996; Potter and Lombardi 1998; Saffran and Martin 1997; Savage et al. 2003; Scheepers 2003; Smith and Wheeldon 2001; Tomasello 2003; Yamashita, Chang, and Hirose 2003).

This sort of priming provides a useful tool to investigate the mental representation of linguistic expressions (Branigan et al. 1995; Bencini 2002). The naturalness of the priming paradigm is supported by the fact that a tendency towards structural repetition occurs in natural unmonitored speech or text (Kempen 1977; Tannen 1987; Weiner and Labov 1983; Levelt and Kelter 1982). This suggests that structural priming is not simply a laboratory-induced phenomenon.

Priming has been argued to represent implicit learning in that its effect is unconscious and long-lasting (Bock and Griffin 2000; Chang et al. 2000). Thus the existence of structural priming may be an important factor underlying the fact that there are generalizations in languages. The same or similar patterns are easier to learn and produce. At the same time, priming of course is not particular to language—repetition of the same motor programs also leads to priming effects.

Bock's original claim was that syntactic tree structures, not constructions with associated meanings, were involved in priming (Bock and Loebell 1990; Bock, Loebell, and Morey 1992; Bock 1986; Loebell and Bock 2003). In recent work, the question of whether constructional priming exists has been investigated. That is, can abstract pairings of form with meaning be primed? Chang, Bock, and Goldberg (2003) conducted a simple experiment in which syntactic structure was controlled for, while two different constructions were used as primes. Sample prime target sentences are given below:

Sample Primes:
(6) a. She loaded the wagon with hay. ("load with")
     b. She loaded hay onto the wagon. ("load onto")

Sample Targets:
(7) a. He embroidered the shirt with flowers.
     b. He embroidered flowers onto the shirt.

Subjects were asked to recall a sentence as it was presented after a short distractor task. Such rapid serial visual presentation (RSVP) tasks have been shown to yield priming effects (Potter and Lombardi 1998). If semantics matters in priming, then we should see "load with" structures priming other "load with" structures more than "load onto" structures. In fact this is exactly what was found.

Also, as predicted by constructional priming, subjects produced more load-with types of sentences after load-with type primes than after load-onto primes as shown in fig. 6.4; and more load-onto sentences after load-onto primes than after load-with primes as shown in fig. 6.5.

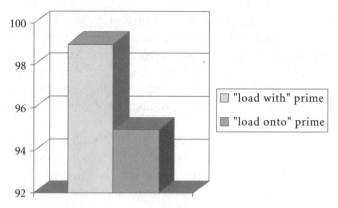

FIGURE 6.4 Percentage of "load with" responses to "load with" target (n=80)

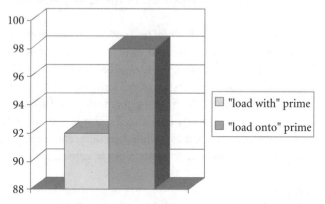

FIGURE 6.5 Percentage of "load onto" responses to "load onto" target (n=80)

The constructional priming found cannot be wholly attributed to an overlap in prepositions, since the "load onto" sentences used a variety of prepositions including *over, onto, into, around, on.* Moreover, Griffin and Weinstein-Tull (2003) have shown that object-raising sentences prime object-raising sentences more than object-control sentences, despite a lack of any shared morphology. This also suggests constructional priming; the results are unexpected if only formal cues were taken into account, since the two constructions arguably have the same form.

Given these results, it is worth returning to the original motivation for earlier claims that syntactic constituent structure, not constructions (form–meaning pairings) are primed. Bock and Loebell (1990) made perhaps the strongest case for this claim with a series of experiments. In one experiment, they showed that both datives and locatives primed dative descriptions of (unrelated) pictures equally well. Example primes are given below:

Primes:
(8) a. The wealthy widow gave her Mercedes to the church. (dative)
  b. The wealthy widow drove her Mercedes to the church. (locative)

The constructional interpretation of this result stems from a claim discussed in Chapter 2, namely that so called "dative" and "locative" expressions are actually both instances of the same caused-motion construction (cf. also Goldberg 1995).

(9) Caused-motion construction:

CAUSE-MOVE   (cause   theme   path)
  | | | |
  V   Subj   Obj   Obl

(10) Examples:
    a. She drove the box to Missouri.
    b. She drove the box to Mary.
    c. She threw the box to Mary.
    d. She gave the box to Mary.

Therefore, the findings are that caused-motion expressions prime caused-motion expressions, a result that is expected by a constructionist account of priming. In fact, Bock and Loebell also acknowledge that locative and dative expressions are semantically similar. They therefore performed a second experiment in which they investigated whether intransitive locative expressions such as found in Table 6.8 (example b) primed passives: a

TABLE 6.8. Stimuli types used in Bock and Loebell (1990)

Primes Type	Example
a. Passives:	*The construction worker was hit by the bulldozer.*
b. Intransitive Locatives:	*The construction worker was digging by the bulldozer.*
c. Actives (control):	*The construction worker drove the bulldozer.*

construction with the same syntax as locatives but with clearly distinct meaning.

Bock and Loebell (1990) found that in fact intransitive locatives did prime passives. This is the strongest evidence for purely syntactic, non-constructional priming. Yet all of the intransitive locative primes used as stimuli included the preposition *by* and the auxiliary *be*. A question naturally arises, was it the shared morphemes, and not the shared syntactic structure, that produced the priming (Hare and Goldberg 1999)? In order to address this question, Bencini, Bock, and Goldberg (in preparation) attempted to replicate the Bock and Loebell findings while adding a fourth condition in which intransitive locatives without shared morphology were used as primes (prime type d in Table 6.9).

TABLE 6.9. Stimuli types used in Bencini, Bock, and Goldberg (in prep.)

Primes Type	Example
a. Passive	*The construction worker was hit by the bulldozer.*
b. Locatives w/shared morphology	*The construction worker was digging by the bulldozer.*
c. Actives (control)	*The construction worker drove the bulldozer.*
d. **Locatives w/o shared morphology**	***The construction worker might dig near the bulldozer.***

Bock and Loebell was replicated, demonstrating that locatives with the shared morphology prime passives and as also expected, passives prime passives. At the same time, a significant difference between the passive condition and the locative condition without shared morphology was also found, and the locatives without shared morphology condition did *not* prime passives significantly more than the control group. This finding is intriguing because it may indicate that shared syntactic structure is not sufficient to induce priming.[5]

Hare and Goldberg (1999) designed a different test of the idea that pure syntactic tree structure and not some sort of form–meaning pairing was involved in priming. Recall that it has been well established that ditransitives prime ditransitives, and also that instances of the caused-motion construction prime other instances of the caused-motion construction. We attempted to

---

[5] At the same time, the data are a bit ambiguous, because there is a stepward trend such that passives and by-locatives prime passives (significantly), and in addition, numerically more passives were produced after non-by locatives than after controls; however the latter difference was non-significant despite the running of 130 subjects.

determine whether a third sort of prime, "provide with" primes, would differentially prime either caused-motion expressions ("datives") or ditransitive descriptions of scenes of transfer. Examples of the "provide with" sort of primes are given in Table 6.10.

TABLE 6.10. Key priming condition in Hare and Goldberg (1999)

Prime type	Examples
"provide with" condition	*The government provided the troops with arms.*
	His editor credited Bob with the hot story.
	The father entrusted his daughter with the keys.

"Provide with" sentences arguably have the same syntactic form as caused-motion expressions: NP [V NP PP], and yet the order of rough semantic roles involved parallels the ditransitive: Agent Recipient Theme. Results demonstrated that "provide with" expressions prime ditransitive descriptions of (unrelated) pictures as much as ditransitives do. There was no evidence at all of priming of caused-motion expressions, despite the shared syntactic form (Hare and Goldberg 1999). Thus when order of semantic roles is contrasted with constituent structure, the order of semantic roles shows priming, with no apparent interaction with constituent structure.[6]

What do the structural priming facts mean? First of all, constructions can be primed, which means that the level of generalization involved in argument structure constructions is a useful one to acquire. It is further possible that priming of structure may not be independent of meaning. Thus the priming mechanism may encourage speakers to categorize on the basis of form *and* meaning.

6.11 Conclusion

We have offered two factors that likely encourage speakers to form the argument structure generalizations they do. Children initially generalize at

---

[6] One interpretation of the Hare and Goldberg findings is that it was order of animate participants that effected priming, not the order of semantic roles. This possibility is exists because animacy has been shown to induce priming, even when the overall construction is held constant (Bock, Loebell, and Morey 1992). In fact, it remains to be shown that ditransitive vs. dative priming is not induced by differing order of animate participants as well. But, Yamashita, Chang, and Hirose (2003) have shown that dative sentences with the order AGENT-*wa* RECIPIENT-*ni* PATIENT-*o* (*wa-ni-o*) prime other *wa-ni-o* ordered productions, even though the animacy of recipients and patients were controlled for. These results suggest that structural priming can be sensitive to the order of syntactic functions or thematic roles.

the level of specific verbs plus argument slots (Tomasello's "verb islands") because the verb in an argument frame is the best single word predictor of overall sentence meaning. We argue further that children generalize beyond specific verbs to form more abstract argument structure constructions because the argument frame or construction has roughly equivalent cue validity as a predictor of overall sentence meaning to the morphological form of the verb, and has much greater category validity. That is, the construction is at least as reliable and much more available. Moreover, given the fact that many verbs have quite low cue validity in isolation, attention to the contribution of the construction is essential.

Motivating constructional generalizations in a different way is the simple fact that hearing or producing a particular construction makes it easier to produce the same construction. Instead of learning a myriad of unrelated constructions, speakers do well to learn a smaller inventory of patterns in order to facilitate online production.

Part III
Explaining Generalizations

7

Island constraints and scope

This chapter explores the relevance of information structure and processing demands in an explanation of constraints on movement ("island constraints") and constraints on relative scope assignment. We build on previous accounts in order to give a motivated account of a wide range of facts, emphasizing an analysis of the ditransitive that predicts many of the special properties that were observed in Chapter 2.

At the outset, certain terminology is introduced that will be critical to the discussion that follows. Gundel (1985: 35) makes a useful distinction between two types of given/new distinctions: referential givenness/newness and relational givenness/newness. Each is discussed below in turn.

Referential givenness/newness is a relationship between a linguistic expression and a non-linguistic entity. It is correlated with degrees of cognitive activation or identifiability (Ariel 1990; Chafe 1987, 1994; Lambrecht 1994; Prince 1981). There are strong correlations between NP marking and given or new status as follows:

- **Given arguments** are typically expressed by weakly accented pronouns or not at all. They can be established by linguistic or extra-linguistic context. They are considered to be cognitively "active" in the mind of the addressee.
- **Accessible arguments** are normally expressed by definite full NPs. They are considered to be semi-active in the mind of the addressee.
- **New arguments** are normally expressed by indefinite NPs. They are considered to be inactive in the mind of the addressee at the time of utterance.

Relational givenness/newness refers to the assumed informational contribution made by a particular utterance to the knowledge state of the addressee: the INFORMATION STRUCTURE of a sentence (Allen 1999; Halliday 1967; Lambrecht 1994). The choice of particular constructions often determines the information structure of a sentence, including its topic and potential focus domain. Differences in the packaging of information are perhaps the most important reason why languages have alternative ways to say the "same" thing.

A sentence **topic** is a "matter of [already established] current interest which a statement is about and with respect to which a proposition is to be interpreted as relevant" (Lambrecht 1994). The topic serves to contextualize other elements in the clause (Chafe 1994; Kuno 1972; Langacker 1987a; Strawson 1964).

In languages that have uncontroversial subjects, the **subject argument is the default topic** in the clause (Chafe 1987; Lambrecht 1994; Langacker 1987a; MacWhinney 1977).

The **potential** focus domain of a sentence is that part of a sentence that is interpretable as being asserted.

Test for being within the focal domain: propositions expressed within the potential focus domain can be understood to be negated by sentential negation.

The focus domain is thus "one kind of emphasis, that whereby the speaker marks out a part (which may be the whole) of a message block as that which he wishes to be interpreted as informative" (Halliday 1967). Similarly Lambrecht (1994) defines the focus relation as relating "the pragmatically non-recoverable to the recoverable component of a proposition [thereby creating] a new state of information in the mind of the addressee."

The primary topic and the focus domain together do not exhaustively identify the information units of a sentence. We will refer to elements of a sentence that are neither the primary topic nor part of the focus-domain as BACK-GROUNDED elements (corresponding roughly to the TAIL of Vallduví 1993).

BACKGROUNDED elements: constituents that do correspond neither to the primary topic nor to part of the potential focus domain.

Elements that are a part of presupposed clauses are backgrounded. For example, consider the restrictive relative clause in (1):

(1)   I read the book that Maya loaned me.

We can see that the proposition conveyed by the relative clause is not part of the focus domain because it is not negated by sentential negation. As a presupposition, it is implied by both the positive and the negative form of the sentence:

(2)   I read the book that Maya loaned me. → Maya loaned me the book.

(3)   I didn't read the book that Maya loaned me. → Maya loaned me the
                                                          book.

Of course, aspects of presuppositions can be negated with "metalinguistic" negation, signaled by heavy lexical stress on the negated constituent (*I didn't read the book that Maya gave me because she didn't GIVE me any book!*). But then metalinguistic negation can negate anything at all, including intonation, lexical choice, or accent. Modulo the possibility for metalinguistic negation, the presupposed parts of a sentence are taken for granted, and are not understood to be part of what is asserted by the sentence. Contrastive focus, like metalinguistic negation, is also an orthogonal dimension: it is marked by stress on a constituent in any position—even on a topic or on a backgrounded element. Contrastive focus is often indicated by a fall–rise pitch accent. It will not be central to concerns discussed in this chapter.

The three relevant categories of relational information structure are exemplified in Table 7.1.

TABLE 7.1. General categories of relational information structure

	Example (relevant constituent underlined)
primary topic	She hit a pole.
within the potential FOCUS DOMAIN	George met her.
backgrounded elements	The man who she told him about called.

7.1 "Island" Constraints

John Robert Ross, in his stunning dissertation, noticed that it was not possible to create unbounded dependencies involving just any aspect of a sentence (Ross 1967). In particular, certain syntactic constructions are "islands" to unbounded dependency relations or "extraction." These include complex noun phrases, complex subjects, complements of manner-of-speaking verbs, and adjunct clauses as illustrated in Table 7.2.

The judgments in the case of the complex NPs and subject islands are more robust, and less dependent on context, than in either of the latter two instances, each of which is marginally acceptable (despite the fact that all of these types are classified as "strong" islands in the generative literature).[1] Exploring these subtle differences in judgments requires us to look in a more detailed way at the discourse functions of each of the constructions involved, and is beyond the scope of the present chapter.

---

[1] Baltin (1982) has suggested that manner-of-speaking complements are adjuncts, not arguments, in that they are generally omissable. Under that interpretation, this case would be an instance of the generalization about adjuncts.

TABLE 7.2. Classic examples of "island" constraints

*Who did she see the report that was about? (cf. She saw the report that was about x)	**Complex NPs** (both noun complements and relative clauses)
*Who did that she knew bother him? (cf. That she knew x bothered him)	**Subjects**
??What did she whisper that he left? (cf. She whispered that he left x)	**Complements of manner-of-speaking verbs**
??What did she leave the movie 'cause they were eating?[2] (cf. She left the movie because they were eating x)	**Presupposed adjuncts**

In a constructional approach, "movement" phenomena are understood to involve the combination of some construction with an unbounded dependency construction (e.g. a question, relative clause, topicalization). The constructions that are combined each have particular information-structure properties, and those properties must be consistent in order to avoid a pragmatic clash. Most if not all of the traditional constraints on "movement"—i.e. the impossibility of combining a construction involving a long-distance dependency with another construction—derive from clashes of information-structure properties of the constructions involved. In Section 7.10, we will address the role of processing in judgments of ill-formedness.

Direct replies are sensitive to islands

Largely ignored are other types of discourse-level phenomena that are sensitive to islands. For example, Morgan (1975) long ago observed that DIRECT REPLIES TO QUESTIONS are sensitive to islands. Let us assume that the answer to (4) is that Laura was dating someone new. None of the replies in (5)–(8) is an appropriate answer to the question posed in (4), since the proposition that would answer the question (namely, that Laura was dating someone new) is expressed within an island. The answer cannot felicitously be expressed in a relative clause (5), in a sentential subject (6), nor in the sentential complement of a manner-of-speaking verb (7), nor by a presupposed adverb (8):

(4)   Why was Laura so happy?

Relative clauses are islands to appropriate answers

(5)   #The woman who thought she was dating someone new lives next door. (cf. The woman who lives next door thought she was dating someone new.)

---

[2] 'Cause is used here instead of *because* to encourage the presupposed interpreation of the adjnct.

Sentential subjects are islands to appropriate answers

(6) #That she's dating someone new is likely.
(cf. It's likely that she's dating someone new.)

Complements of manner-of-speaking verbs are islands to appropriate answers

(7) #John shouted that she was dating someone new.
(cf. John said she was dating someone new.)

Presupposed adverbials are islands to appropriate answers:

(8) #John was hysterical 'cause she was dating someone new.
(cf. John left Manhattan in order that she could date someone new.)

Through Gricean implicatures of relevance, contexts can be found in which the sentences marked as infelicitous above, or closely related ones, are much improved, interpreted as *indirect* responses to the question in (4). But as direct responses to the question posed, each of the responses above is markedly odd.[3] Since this island phenomenon exists across sentences, indeed, across interlocutors, it strongly raises the possibility that constraints on islands are fundamentally related to discourse; the phenomenon is not easily described in purely syntactic terms.

Exclamative ah! *is sensitive to islands*   Another source of island effects that cries out for a discourse-level explanation is James' (1972) observation that certain discourse particles such as EXCLAMATIVE *ah!* cannot be used to remark on propositions within islands. For example, the following formulations in (9) cannot be used to convey an exclamation about the fact that Laura was dating someone new, since that fact is conveyed within a complex NP, an island. The examples in (10)–(12) demonstrate that other islands are similarly outside the scope of the exclamation.

Relative clauses are islands to scope of *ah!*

(9) Ah! the woman who thought Laura was dating someone new lives next door! (exclamative cannot refer to the proposition that she was dating someone new)
cf. Ah! the woman who lives next door thought she was dating someone new!

---

[3] It is possible directly to answer the question in (4) with a sentence such as *I heard a rumor that she was dating someone new*, where the answer appears to be within a RC. But such expressions are equally well interpreted such that the entire NP, *a rumor that she was dating someone new*, is the answer, and of course the entire NP can be extracted (*What did you hear?*).

Sentential Subjects are islands to scope of *ah!*

(10)   Ah! That she is dating someone new is likely! (exclamative cannot refer to the proposition that she was dating someone new)
cf. Ah! it is likely that she was dating someone new!

Complements of manner-of-speaking verbs are islands to scope of *ah!*

(11)   Ah! John shouted that she was dating someone new! (exclamative cannot refer to the proposition that she was dating someone new)
cf. Ah! John said she was dating someone new!

Complements of presupposed adjuncts are islands to the scope of *ah!*

(12)   Ah! John was hysterical 'cause she was dating someone new. (exclamative cannot refer to the proposition that she was dating someone new)
cf. Ah! John left Manhattan in order that she could date someone new.

The facts about indirect questions and *ah* exclamatives cannot naturally be accounted for by purely syntactic accounts (Cole et al. 1977). Both phenomena cry out for an explanation in terms of discourse properties of the constructions involved.

7.2 Backgrounded constructions are islands

Several researchers have suggested that the extraction site must be a *potential focus domain* (Erteschik-Shir 1979, 1998a; Takami 1989; Van Valin 1998; Van Valin and LaPolla 1997). That is, the constituent in which the gap exists (i.e. the constituent containing the canonical position for the fronted element) must be within the part of the utterance that is asserted. It cannot be presupposed. In accord with this observation, notice that none of the constructions in Fig. 7.1 is part of the focus domain—they are all pragmatically

Complex NPs
1. She didn't saw the report that was about him. → The report was about him.

Sentential subjects
2. That she knew it didn't bother him → She knew it.

Complements of manner-of-speaking verbs
3. She didn't whisper that he left. → He left.

Presupposed adverbials
4. She didn't leave the movie after they ate it. → They ate it.

FIGURE 7.1 Islands that involve presupposed information

PRESUPPOSED. That is, their propositional content is implied by both the positive and negative form of the sentence.

Elements within these presupposed clauses are not part of the potential focus domain. In accord with this idea, Erteschik-Shir (1979), Takami (1989), and Van Valin (1998; Van Valin and LaPolla 1997) each propose some type of a **negation test**, as independent verification that constructions such as those identified in Figure 7.1 are not part of the potential focus domain; cf. the test for being part of the potential focus domain above. When an assertion is negated, only elements within the potential focus domain are contradicted.

The idea that the extraction site must be within the potential focus domain can be used to explain why these particular constructions are islands to unbounded dependency relations. But a constraint that extraction can only occur from potential focus domains does not explain how it is that the SUBJECT argument (the whole subject constituent), which is also not part of the focus domain, is readily available for unbounded dependencies. In fact on Keenan and Comrie's (1977) accessibility hierarchy, subjects are the *most* likely candidates for potential extraction:

(13)   subject > direct object > oblique object > object of comparison

If a language permits a relative clause to be formed on a noun phrase associated with a grammatical function low in the hierarchy, it will permit relativization on NPs representing all grammatical functions above it. Work in Centering Theory, a computational linguistics tool, has found that the same hierarchy predicts the likelihood of subsequent mention (Grosz, Joshi, and Weinstein 1983, 1995).

It is possible to account for both facts, that unbounded dependencies are normally available to clausal subjects or to elements within the focus domain with the following generalization:

(14)   Backgrounded constructions are islands (BCI)

Given the definition of backgrounded elements provided at the outset of this chapter, this claim entails that only the primary topic in a clause, or elements within the potential focus domain are candidates for unbounded dependencies. Notice that elements *within* clausal subjects are backgrounded in that they are not themselves the primary topic, nor are they part of the focus domain.

The restriction on backgrounded constructions is clearly motivated by the function of the constructions involved. Elements involved in unbounded dependencies are positioned in discourse-prominent slots. *It is pragmatically anomalous to treat an element as at once backgrounded and discourse-prominent.* A critical role for processing comes into play as well, as discussed in Section 7.10.

The definition of backgroundedness implicitly acknowledges that the notions of topic and focus are not opposites: both allow for constituents to be interpreted as having a certain degree of discourse prominence (see, e.g., Arnold (MS) for experimental and corpus evidence demonstrating the close relationship between topic and focus). One sentence's focus is often the next sentence's topic. That is, once new material is introduced into the discourse, it is available to persist as a continuing topic during subsequent discourse: i.e. it may have high *topic persistence.* Centering Theory captures the relationship between topic and focus very naturally (Grosz, Joshi, and Weinstein 1983, 1995). In the theory, discourse referents in the speaker's focus of attention are called *centers.* All arguments in each utterance are forward-looking centers, which become potential antecedents for referential terms in a subsequent utterance. A special member of the forward-looking centers is also a backward-looking center, corresponding roughly to "topic," in that it indicates what the utterance is "about" and serves to link the utterance to the preceding utterance.

The fact that topic and focus are not opposites goes some way toward explaining the pervasive confusion about the terms. Both topic and focus are sometimes described as the "locus of attention." There is likely a sense in which that is exactly accurate: both the primary topic and focus are centers of cognitive attention (Deane 1991). These stand in contrast to elements that are neither the primary topic nor within the focal domain of a sentence: *backgrounded* elements.

The formulation that "extracted" elements cannot be backgrounded predicts that certain aspects of sentences heretofore unclassified as traditional "islands" should in fact resist unbounded dependency relations. This is true, for example, of parentheticals, which are not part of the focus domain as evidenced by the fact that they are not understood to be negated by sentential negation, and neither are they the primary topic:

(15)   I just read—stop me if I have already told you about this—a great new book.

(16)   I didn't just read—stop me if I have already told you about this—that great new book.

(17)   *Who$_i$ did I just read—stop me if I have already told [i] about this—a great new book.

The generalization that extracted elements cannot be backgrounded accounts for a wide range of facts. Since backgrounded propositions are not part of what is asserted, they do not provide felicitous answers to questions; this explains the fact that answers are sensitive to island phenomena. Since the exclamative marker *ah*! has scope only over what is part of the focal domain, it follows that it, too, cannot refer to backgrounded propositions, since they are by definition not part of the focus domain. Many other facts about the resistance of certain constructions to unbounded dependencies are accounted for as well. The facts surrounding the ditransitive construction are discussed below.

7.3 The ditransitive recipient argument resists unbounded dependencies

A statistical generalization about the information structure of ditransitives can be used to account for how the ditransitive construction interacts with unbounded dependency constructions. In particular, recall from Chapter 2 that the recipient argument of the ditransitive resists unbounded dependency relations (Erteschik-Shir 1979; Oehrle 1975):

(18)   ??Who did Chris give the book?

(19)   ??The boy who Mary had already given the key let himself in.

These judgments are somewhat subtle. Therefore, a Google search was performed to attempt to quantify the dispreference. Results showed that when a recipient was questioned (e.g. *who did she give...*), prepositional paraphrases (e.g. *who did she give the money **to**?*) outnumbered ditransitives by forty to one. In particular, only three questioned recipients of a ditransitive were returned out of the first 120 examples, accounting for only 2.5 per cent of the examples considered.[4] This skewing of the data towards questioning the recipient of the prepositional paraphrase and not the ditransitive recipient, exists despite the prescriptive injunction against stranding prepositions. Moreover, *give* is lexically biased to appear in the ditransitive over the prepositional paraphrase when there is no long-distance dependency

---

[4] The three attested instances of questioned recipients of ditransitives found are provided below. Two of these involved particularly long theme phrases, strongly motivating the use of the ditransitive (Wasow 2002).

(i)   When Julia left the Valley, who did she give control of her interest in Falcon Crest?
(ii)   In Paul's report to James and to the elders, who did he give credit for the work among the Gentiles?
(iii)   Jack: Yes, but who did she give the eye? ☺

Example (iii) involves an idiomatic phrase *to give someone the eye*, "to look seductively at someone." The expression with *to* (*she gave an eye to him*) only has a literal interpretation.

relation.[5] Therefore it is fair to say that there is a systematic and strong dispreference for questioning the recipient argument of the ditransitive construction. In order to account for the judgments in (18) and (19), we take a brief detour, outlining the discourse properties of the recipient argument of the ditransitive.

The ditransitive recipient as secondary topic

While the subject argument is generally agreed to be the default primary topic in a clause, the recipient argument of the ditransitive construction has been described as a secondary clausal topic (Dryer 1986; Givón 1979, 1984; Langacker 1987a; Van Hoek 1995; see also Nikolaeva 1991 for a general discussion of secondary topic status). Since it is not the primary topic, and as we shall see, it is generally not within the potential focus domain, it qualifies as being backgrounded.

In both corpus and experimental studies, it has been demonstrated that argument status as new or given plays a role in conditioning whether the ditransitive construction is chosen over the dative paraphrase (Arnold et al. 2000; Bresnan and Nikitina ms; Dryer 1986; Givón 1979, 1984; Wasow 2002). In contrast to the ditransitive recipient argument, the theme argument of the ditransitive strongly tends to be new information, rarely being already given in the discourse context. The proposed generalizations with example sentences are provided below:

(20)   Ditransitive: Subj   V   Obj1   Obj2
                      agent   recipient   theme
                      topic   secondary topic   new/accessible

(21)   She gave him a book.

(22)   ??She gave a man them.

The paraphrase with *to* is not constrained in this way, as indicated below:

(23)   "Dative": Subj   V   Obj   PP
                  agent   theme goal
                  topic

(24)   She gave a book to him.

(25)   She gave it to a man.

---

[5] Wasow (2002) cites the lexical preference for ditransitives over prepositional paraphrases when *give* is used to be roughly four to one.

What is the evidence for the claim that the recipient argument of the ditransitive is a secondary topic? Corpus studies have demonstrated that the recipient argument is typically pronominal and if it is not expressed pronominally, it tends to be expressed with a definite NP description. That is, the recipient argument of the ditransitive construction rarely introduces a new argument into the discourse. These strong trends have been observed by Thompson (1990) with a database of 162 tokens, and by Collins (1995) who analyzes a corpus of spoken and written language containing 108 instances of the ditransitive construction and 57 prepositional paraphrases. In both studies, the ditransitive recipient is overwhelmingly already given in the discourse.[6] Because these corpus studies were relatively small, and because statistics are known to differ somewhat across different corpora, I replicated these earlier studies on two distinct databases as described in the Appendix to this chapter. The first database consisted of spoken child-directed language from the Suppes corpus in the CHILDES database (MacWhinney 1995).[7] The second database involved primarily written texts gathered from the web using the Linguists' Search Engine on Alta Vista. In fact, the ditransitive recipient argument is highly likely to be pronominal as compared with either the goal argument of the prepositional paraphrase or the theme argument of the ditransitive. In neither corpus were there significant instances of new recipient arguments. See also Ruppenhofer (2004) for additional corpus analysis of the ditransitive.

Referential givenness is not identical to topicality, but the two are correlated in the following way. Continuing topics are given in that they have to have been mentioned in order to be continuing as topics, and even newly established topics tend to be accessible or anchored in the discourse as opposed to brand new, insofar as they typically appear with a definite determiner or are explicitly related to a given entity by means of a possessive determiner or relative clause (Francis, Gregory, and Michaelis 1999; Lambrecht 1994).

The ditransitive recipient has other hallmarks of topicality as well: it is animate and its existence is presupposed (Polinsky 1998). Animate referents are more likely to be topical than inanimate referents (e.g. Bock, Loebell, and Morey 1992), and topical referents are generally presupposed to exist (Strawson 1964). The fact that both topics and ditransitive recipient arguments tend

---

[6] In data from an experiment reported in Wasow (2002), with the relative weight of recipient and theme controlled for, we see a strong preference for the recipient argument to be given as opposed to accessible. The discourse context the experimenters created was not amenable to instances of new recipients.

[7] I am grateful to Mike Tomasello for making these data available to me.

to be given, animate, and presupposed to exist is explained if we assume that the recipient argument is a secondary topic.

Moreover, designating the recipient argument of ditransitives as a secondary topic predicts that it should not be part of the focus domain. This prediction holds; notice that it is not understood to be negated by simple negation (Erteschik-Shir 1979):

(26)   She gave her a ball.
        #No, him.

Only if there is lexical stress (contrastive focus) on the recipient argument can a given ditransitive recipient be construed to be part of the focus domain:

(27)   She gave HER a ball. (recipient is contrastive focus)
        No, him.

This is in contrast to the prepositional goal argument which *can* be interpreted as part of the focus domain without contrastive stress.[8]

(28)   She gave a ball to her.
        No, (to) him.

Since the recipient argument is not the primary topic and is not within the focal domain, it qualifies as being a backgrounded element. An independent indication of the backgrounded nature of the recipient argument comes from the fact that a full 26 per cent (50/190) of examples involving *give* on a search using the Linguists' Search Engine (Alta Vista) were non-idiomatic examples such as the following in which the recipient or goal argument was unexpressed:

(29)   But he *gave the glad tidings* that despite all the negative propaganda, Islam was spreading rapidly in America.
(30)   Furthermore we *give exact algorithms* for interval graphs ... and graphs of bounded asteroidal number.

Backgrounded elements are often candidates for omission (see Chapter 9). Thus it is safe to conclude that the recipient argument is generally backgrounded (as a secondary topic) in the clause.

---

[8] Parallel judgments hold for the following version of the negation test:

(i)   She didn't give him a ball. It was a bat.
(ii)   She didn't give him a ball. #It was her/Mary.

Again, with contrastive stress, it is possible to interpret the scope of negation to include the recipient:

(iii)   She didn't give HIM a ball. It was Mary (she gave it to).

Statistical generalization, not hard and fast constraint

Despite the strong statistical trend for the recipient argument of the ditransitive construction to be non-new and not part of the focus domain, it is important to acknowledge that introspective grammaticality judgments are less robust. Constructed examples such as the one below are acceptable:

(31)   The US committee hoped to give an American the award.

In this example, the recipient argument, *an American*, is new and may receive either a specific or a non-specific interpretation: either the committee wanted to give a specific American the award or they wanted to give some American or other the award. In the same vein, while the focus domain tends not to include the recipient argument, when the recipient argument is new, it can be part of the potential focus domain, as it is within the scope of simple negation:

(32)   The US committee hoped to give an American the award.
        No, a Canadian.

To account for this fact, it may be necessary to introduce degrees of backgroundedness. If backgrounded arguments correspond to a lack of cognitive attention, it would make sense that backgroundedness might be a gradient term. We return to this idea below.

The analysis of the ditransitive in (20) finds additional support in that it directly predicts both the fact that the recipient argument resists unbounded dependencies and the scope facts concerning the ditransitive, as we shall see in Section 7.12. These are two aspects of the construction that have been emphasized but not adequately explained by formal accounts (recall the discussion in Section 2.4).

As defined above, elements that do not correspond to the primary topic and are not within the focus domain are backgrounded and therefore are not candidates for extraction. Because the status as backgrounded in the ditransitive is actually a statistical generalization, not a categorical constraint, the fact that unbounded dependencies involving the recipient argument are occasionally found is also expected. In addition, this information structure account of the ditransitive facts serves to unlock an often overlooked puzzle: **passive recipients can be questioned and relativized.** The active ditransitive recipient resists unbounded dependencies because it strongly tends to be backgrounded: although topical, it is not the primary topic, and it is not within the focus domain. Nonetheless, the recipient argument can be freely questioned or relativized if it is already the subject of a passive:

(33)   Who was given the book?   passive
        (cf. ??Who did John give the book?)   active

(34)   The man who was given a book left early.   passive
        (cf. ??The man who she gave a book left early.)   active

That is, if the recipient argument is a subject (via passivization), then it is free to be involved in unbounded dependency relations that are otherwise only marginal. This makes sense since passivized recipients are the primary topics in a clause, and primary topics are readily involved in unbounded dependencies.

Empirical evidence exists to support the idea that the recipient argument is not backgrounded when it is in subject position. It turns out that the information structure generalizations about the recipient argument differ in the active and passive. The passive-ditransitive recipient patterns like other passive subjects, not like recipients in the active voice. In particular, the subject-recipient argument of the passive ditransitive is markedly less likely to be already given, i.e. marked with a pronominal, than the recipient argument of active ditransitives. Of the first ninety-two passive ditransitives found by the Linguists' Search Engine, the subject-recipient argument was marked as indefinite 10 per cent of the time, a definite lexical NP 70 per cent of the time, and a pronominal only 20 per cent of the time. Similar percentages were found for passive sentences generally (12 per cent, 67 per cent, and 21 per cent, respectively of the first 100 passive sentences returned). On the other hand, the recipient argument of an active ditransitive was only marked as indefinite 1.5 per cent of the time, and definite 32.5 per cent of the time. It was marked with a pronominal a full 66 per cent of the time. These comparisons are shown in Fig. 7.2.

Given this empirical finding, the fact that the recipient argument is available for unbounded dependency constructions when it is passivized is expected on an account that predicts that unbounded dependency restrictions stem from information structure properties of the constructions involved.[9]

The statistical generalization that the recipient strongly tends to be given in the discourse and not part of the focus domain is used to explain the scope relations of the ditransitive as well in Section 7.12.

---

[9] The percentages of lexical NP subjects are known to vary greatly across different types of corpora (Francis, Gregory, and Michaelis 1999). However, since I used the same corpus to search for all of the arguments under discussion, it is fair to compare the *relative* percentages.

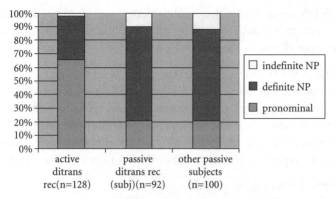

FIGURE 7.2 **Comparison of recipient argument in active ditransitives and in passive ditransitives, and passive subjects generally, in data collected from Alta Vista using the Linguists' Search Engine.** Active ditransitive recipients are different from passive ditransitive recipients ($\chi^2(2, N = 211) = 67.0$, p $<$ .001). Passive ditransitive recipients and other passive subjects are not different from each other ($\chi^2(2, N = 192) = .26$, p $=$ .88).

7.4 Subordinate Clauses

Are subordinate clauses backgrounded? It might seem that negating the main clause would not negate the subordinate clause, so that subordinate clauses should uniformly be backgrounded. In fact as will be discussed below, many subordinate clauses are backgrounded. However, in other cases, sentential negation can be used to imply a negation of the proposition expressed by the subordinate clause. For example,

(35) She doesn't think they sent the letter.

(36) He didn't say they went to the market.

(37) They don't believe she left early.

The complement clauses in (35)–(37) are within the potential focus domain of the main clause negation. That is, (35) for example, will be true if she thinks they didn't send the letter (or if she didn't think anything at all). On the other hand, negating other main verbs much less readily conveys the implication that the complement clause is within the scope of negation. We have already seen that complements of manner-of-speaking verbs are generally islands. As predicted, the complement of manner-of-speaking verbs is generally not within the potential focus domain (without special context):

(38)   I didn't grumble that they sent the letter.   (manner-of-speaking verb)
(asserts that I didn't grumble; there is typically no implication about
whether they sent the letter)

This is because the main focus of the clause is on the manner of speaking,
since otherwise a simpler verb such as *say* could have been used. The subordinate clauses in (35)–(37) are not necessarily construed to be backgrounded,
whereas the subordinate clause in (38) strongly tends to be. In accord with this
idea is the fact that it is acceptable to question elements within subordinate
clauses of the types in (35)–(37) but not those in (38), as illustrated below:

(39)   What did you think that they sent?

(40)   What did you say that they sent?

(41)   What did you believe that they sent?

(42)   ??What did you grumble that they sent?
(manner-of-speaking complement)

At the same time, if it is clear in the context that the manner of speaking is
already topical, the complement clause can be construed to convey the focus
domain of the sentence. In this case, long-distance dependencies from within
the manner-of-speaking complement are improved.

7.5 Reason clauses

Reason clauses may be backgrounded or not, depending on context, position,
intonation, and choice of connector. The reason clause may be part of what is
asserted, particularly if the main sentence accent falls within the reason clause.
This interpretation is clear in (43):

(43)   She didn't travel to Memphis because she wanted to see ELVIS. (can be
used to imply that while she did travel to Memphis, it was not to see Elvis)

Under this interpretation, unbounded dependencies from within the *be-*
cause clause are acceptable.

(44)   ?Who did she travel to Memphis because she wanted to see?

As a type of adjunct, reason clauses are considered to be "strong" islands
within mainstream generative grammar (Cinque 1990). This predicts that
examples such as (44) should be unacceptable, and yet they are not (cf. also
Kluender 1998). Reason clauses involving *in order to* are even more problem-
atic for the notion that all adjuncts are "strong" islands. *In order to* reason

clauses differ from those expressed by *because* phrases in that the scope of negation tends to include the *in order to* verb phrase even without special intonation (45):

(45)   She didn't travel to Memphis in order to see Elvis (can be used to imply that the traveling was done but not in order to meet Elvis)

That is, *in order to* clauses are not presupposed and are not backgrounded, even though they are adjuncts (in that they are omissible and apply to a wide range of expressions). In accord with the BCI, questioning elements from within *in order to* clauses is fully acceptable:

(46)   Who did she travel to Memphis in order to see?

Similarly the following attested cases, all from Santorini (2005), involve unbounded dependencies from within adverbial clauses that are not presupposed (the dependent filler is boldfaced, the adjunct phrase underlined):

(47)   Why did this admirable man turn to **the very tyranny** he sacrificed so much to overthrow? (J. Blatt and S. Jacobs (2002), "Things fall apart", *The Nation* 274, no. 13: 30)

(48)   Enron ... ingratiated itself with **those very politicians** it gloried in mocking in its ads. (T. Frank (2002), "Shocked, shocked! Enronian myths exposed", *The Nation* 274, no. 13: 17)

(49)   ... Bush declared in **a victory speech** that he was forced to wait 36 days to deliver. (Kathy Kieler, "We can unite," *USA Today*, December 12, 2000, p. 1A)

(50)   **a scenario** that government agencies are spending billions of dollars preparing for (*The World*, NPR, February 10, 1999)

Thus it is clear that adjuncts are not islands across the board; only backgrounded (presupposed) adjuncts are islands.

7.6 Non-restrictive relative clauses

The BCI account predicts straightforwardly that definite restrictive relative clauses and noun complements should be unavailable for long-distance dependencies, because both are backgrounded. *Non*-restrictive relative clauses might seem to pose a problem insofar as they often convey new information. Yet, the negation test still clearly demonstrates that they are backgrounded: they act as informational asides, not unlike the parentheticals mentioned above.

(51)   I saw John, who I told you about last week.

(52)   I didn't see John, who I told you about last week. → I told you about John last week.

(53)   *Who did John, who I told _ about last week leave early?

Thus the BCI correctly predicts that restrictive as well as non-restrictive relative clauses should be islands.

7.7 Presentational relative clauses

Not all relative clauses are equally backgrounded. "Presentational" relative clauses can serve to convey the main assertion in a clause. In Danish, and to some extent, in English as well, these relative clauses are, as predicted by the BCI, available for unbounded dependencies:[10]

(54)   Hvad for en slags is er der mange born der kan li?   Danish (Erteschik-Shir 2002)
       What kind of ice cream are there many children who like?

(55)   We have a visitor who there's no one who's willing to host. (Chung and McCloskey 1983)

(56)   John is the sort of guy that I don't know a lot of people who think well of. (Culicover 1999: 230)

(57)   That's the article that we need to find someone who understands. (Kluender 1998)

Notice that in these cases, the content of the relative clause is negated by sentential negation. For example:

(58)   There are not many children who like this kind of ice cream. → many children don't like this kind of ice cream.

(59)   That's not the article that we need to find someone who understands. → we don't need to find someone who understands that article.

These "exceptional" cases of presentational relative clauses that allow long distance dependencies are also expected on the BCI account.

7.8 Factive complements

Complements of factive verbs presuppose the truth of their complements by definition, as in (60):

---

[10] Relative clauses in French can be used presentationally, serving to convey the main assertion in the clause (Lambrecht 2004), and yet they are unavailable for unbounded extraction for reasons that remain mysterious.

(60) It bothered Sue that the mayor smoked cigars. → The mayor smoked cigars.

The BCI account predicts, then, that the complements of factive verbs should be islands, and in fact, long-distance dependencies from within the complement of a factive verb are not fully acceptable (Kiparsky 1971; Ross 1967):

(61) ??What did it bother Sue that the mayor smoked? (factive complement)

Factive complements are sometimes discussed as "weak" islands insofar as complements are more readily available for unbounded dependencies than are adjuncts:

(62) *Why did it bother Sue that the mayor smoked cigars_?
(the sentence is acceptable if the question is understood to ask why Sue was bothered, but it is unacceptable under the interpretation that the reason for the mayor smoking is being queried)

The negation test would seem to indicate that factive complements should be quite robust islands, whereas in fact it is clear that unbounded dependencies from within these complements are less than crashingly bad. This fact may be taken as undermining the account, or it might instead suggest that the negation test is not a perfect indicator of backgrounded status. Intuitively the proposition expressed by the complement clause of factive verbs is more central to the discourse than that expressed in relative clauses. I leave this question aside until a better gauge of backgrounded status is found.

There are other unsolved mysteries that exist on an account that relies purely on backgrounded status. These include indefinite full relative clauses and wh-complements, as discussed below.

7.9 Tricky cases

Indefinite Relative clauses

In the case of relative clauses with *indefinite* heads, the content of the relative clause appears to be within the focus domain, at least according to the negation test. That is, the content of relative clauses that are headed by indefinite NPs is not presupposed (Hooper and Thompson 1973):

(63) She didn't meet a boy who resembled her father... the boy resembled her mother.

Thus the BCI predicts that indefinitely headed relative clauses should not be islands, insofar as they are within the focus domain and are therefore not backgrounded. In fact, we see the predicted contrast between definite and indefinite head nouns in the case of "reduced" relative clauses:[11]

(64)   Who did she see a report about?

(65)   ??Who did she see the report about?

(see Deane 1991 for discussion and analysis of such cases).

However, contrary to the prediction of the BCI, full relative clauses on indefinitely headed arguments *are* islands:

(66)   *Who did she see a report that was about?

An explanation of this fact remains elusive; in order to investigate the contrast between (64) and (66) it is clearly necessary to gain a better understanding of the distinct discourse properties of reduced versus full relative clauses. It seems, however, the contrast is in the right direction—intuitively, full relative clauses are more backgrounded than reduced relative clauses. Again, this suggest that the negation test may not be a refined enough measure of background status. Also it is clear that if anything, definitely headed RCs are more island-like than indefinitely headed RCs. Postal (1998), for example, argues that indefinitely headed RCs are "selective" islands, whereas definitely headed RCs are "absolute" on the basis of the following types of differences in judgments:

(67)   a. *It was the distance to the chasm that Frank liked the man who
            was able to determine.
        b. ?It was the distance to the chasm that Frank knew someone who
            was able to determine.

Clearly more work is needed to understand fully the restrictions on long-distance dependencies out of indefinitely headed relative clauses, but at least the preference for such dependencies when compared with those out of definitely headed relative clauses is in the predicted direction.

Wh-complements

Wh-complements are part of the potential focus domain, as is evidenced by the fact that they may be negated by sentential negation without special intonation:

---

[11] On the basis of their surface structure, these cases are probably better understood to be noun complements instead of relative clauses. Their classification makes no difference to the issues discussed here—as part of complex noun phrases, traditional linguistic theory predicts that they should be islands.

(68)   She wasn't wondering whether she would meet William, she was
       wondering whether she would meet Bob.

This then predicts that wh-complements should *not* be islands, although they
are generally taken to disallow unbounded dependencies. In fact, judgments
about the following examples are somewhat variable, with a minority of
speakers rating them fully acceptable:[12]

(69)   ?What did Bush ask whether he could do?

(70)   ?Which man is he wondering whether she's met?

However, as was the case with factive islands, unbounded dependencies
from within wh-clauses are clearly degraded when the dependent element is
an adjunct instead of an argument.

(71)   *When did he ask whether he could eat dessert _?
(on the interpretation that the timing of desert is at issue)

It is clear that the BCI account predicts a wide variety of facts in a straightforward
way: the fact that subjects, definite relative clauses, full noun complements, the
ditransitive recipient argument, presupposed adjuncts, complements of manner-of-speaking verbs, and factive verbs are all islands is predicted. The fact that
unbounded dependencies are sometimes allowed from presentational relative
clauses, (reduced) indefinite relative clauses, non-presupposed adjuncts, and
verbs of saying is also expected. In addition, the fact that direct questions and
exclamative *ah!* is sensitive to islands is also expected on an account that relies on
the discourse properties of the constructions involved.

The first two columns in Table 7.3 summarize the predictive power of the
BCI generalization. Also included, simply for reference and a point of comparison, in the final column are the predictions made by the "subjacency"
constraint that is typically appealed to in generative accounts of island
phenomena. The subjacency constraint is a purely formal generalization that
states that there may not be more than one "bounding node" (NP or S)
between a dependent (filler) and its canonical position (gap).

The BCI generalization arguably has more predictive power than the syntactic subjacency generalization insofar as it allows for finer-grained distinctions than are possible on a purely syntactic account. The BCI generalization

---

[12] Informal judgments were solicited from twelve naive native speakers based on a six-point scale,
where 1 was "terrible" and 6 was "perfect." The average score across all subjects for extraction out of
wh-clauses was 3.2; the average for the grammatical extractions (e.g. *Who did he tell her he met?*) was
4.8; for extraction out of definite relative clauses was 1.75.

TABLE 7.3. Predictions made by BCI generalization and "subjacency" constraint

	Islands	Predicted to be islands by BCI	Predicted to be islands by subjacency constraint
Arguments within subjects	Yes	Yes	Yes
Ditransitive recipient:			No
Active	Yes	Yes	
Passive	No	No	
Adjuncts	Sometimes (when presupposed)	Sometimes (when presupposed)	Yes
Relative clauses and Noun Complements			Yes (except by stipulation)
Definite	Yes	Yes	
Presentational	No	No	
Indefinite:			
"Reduced"	No	No	
Full	Yes	No	
Wh-complements	Yes (marginally)	No	Yes
Sentential Complements:			No (except by stipulation)
say, tell	No	No	
manner-of-speaking verbs	Yes (unless manner-of-speaking verb is made neutral by context)	Yes (unless manner-of-speaking verb is made neutral by context)	
Factive verbs	Yes (marginally)	Yes	

predicts that the active ditransitive recipient argument should disfavor long-distance dependencies, while the passive recipient does not; the BCI also predicts in a principled way the fact that many adjuncts are not islands. Moreover, the BCI generalization predicts, again, in a principled way, the difference between *say* and *tell* on the one hand and manner-of-speaking and factive verbs on the other. It also correctly predicts that presentational relative clauses and "reduced" relative clauses (or complements) of nouns should not be islands, while definite relative clauses should be. The preponderance of the evidence indicates that island constraints exist because backgrounded elements are not available for unbounded dependencies.

At the same time, Table 7.3 includes two mismatches between information structure status and island status: unbounded dependencies from within full indefinite relative clauses are not possible and are only marginal from within wh-complements. These judgments hold despite the fact that neither indefinite relative clauses nor wh-complements are backgrounded according to the negation test. A full account will require an explanatory analysis of these cases. In the case of wh-complements, processing demands have been demonstrated to play a crucial role, as outlined in the following section.

7.10 A critical role for processing demands

Kluender and Kutas (1993) provide compelling experimental evidence that processing demands coupled with lexical factors lie at the root of variable acceptance of unbounded dependencies within wh-complements. To demonstrate a role for lexical factors, they report that judgments are systematically variable, depending on the choice of complementizer, even in yes/no questions that are considered by linguistic theory to be fully and equally grammatical. The relative judgments are indicated in (72)–(74):

(72)   Isn't he sure [that the TA explained it to them in the lab]? >

(73)   Isn't he sure [if the TA explained it to them in the lab]? >

(74)   Isn't he sure [what the TA explained ___ to them in the lab]?
       (Kluender and Kutas 1993)

That is, questions with embedded complements were judged to be less acceptable when the complement clause contained an *if* as compared with *that*, and less acceptable still if they contained *who/what*. Kluender and Kutas observe that the complementizer *that* requires little semantic analysis, whereas the complementizer *if* demands that a hypothetical context be constructed, and the complementizers *who/what* requires that a referent be activated.

There clearly is an extra processing load involved when arguments appear in displaced positions relative to their canonical expression. Just and Carpenter's (1992) Capacity Constrained Comprehension Theory suggests that the system's goal is to release elements from the memory store as quickly as possible (cf. also Gibson 2000; Gibson et al. 2005; Kitagawa and Fodor 2003; Kluender 1998; Kluender and Kutas 1993; Ellefson and Christiansen 2005). Kluender and Kutas (1993) in fact demonstrate a processing cost to holding a filler in working memory before finding its canonical position in the embedded clause (the "gap"). They find a marked decrease in acceptability ratings between (74) above and example (75), even though (75) is supposed to be fully grammatical. That is, while (74) was judged grammatical 90 per cent of the time (with mean acceptability rating of 32/40), (75) was judged grammatical only 55 per cent of the time (with mean acceptability rating of 19/40).

(75)   Who$_a$ isn't he sure [that the TA explained it to _____$_a$ in the lab]? >

(76)   ?Who$_a$ isn't he sure [if the TA explained it to _____$_a$ in the lab]? >

(77)   *Who$_a$ isn't he sure [what the TA explained ___$_b$ to ___$_a$ in the lab]?
       (Kluender and Kutas 1993)

Thus displaced constituents across clause boundaries place a burden on working memory. At the same time, accounts based on simple processing difficulty do not predict the full range of facts in Table 7.3. Processing accounts do not explain *why* it is that clause boundaries should present a problem, nor why clause boundaries involving factive and manner-of-speaking verbs should present more difficulty than clause boundaries of other verbs. Moreover, accounts based on the difficulty of crossing clause boundaries do not explain the facts surrounding the ditransitive, since a strong dispreference for unbounded dependencies exists, but no clause boundary is crossed; i.e. the recipient argument resists being the filler in an unbounded dependency despite the fact that it is an argument of the main clause. Finally, processing accounts also do not account for the fact that direct questions and exclamative *ah!* are sensitive to islands. The present proposal relies on recognizing the functions of the constructions involved in addition to recognizing the existence of processing constraints.

7.11 Cross-linguistic facts

The discourse properties of the constructions involved combine with processing factors to yield the witnessed patterns of acceptability. A critical role for processing demands is evident in languages that allow question words to appear in canonical position (wh-*in-situ* languages). These languages are much freer in their unbounded dependency relations (Huang 1982). For example, the following examples in Japanese (78) and Korean (79) are judged to be acceptable, despite the fact they involve questioning within complex NPs:

Japanese   (examples from Norvin Richards (1999), Japanese Islands, http://web.mit.edu/norvin/www/papers/)

(78)   Nakamura-san-wa   yakuza-ga   dare-o   korosita tatemono-o
       Nakamura-HON-TOP gangster-NOM who-ACC killed   building-ACC
       kaimasita ka?
       bought
       (*)Who did Nakamura-san buy a building [where gangsters killed _]?

Korean (examples from Sung Ho Hong (2000), "A Non-movement approach to wh-*in situ*", http://privatewww.essex.ac.uk/~shong)

(79) Mary-ka [[t$_i$ nwuku-lul bipanha-n] chaek$_i$]-lul choaha-ni?
Mary-NOM what–ACC criticize-REL book-ACC like-Q
Mary likes books [that criticize what]?

The present account predicts that there should be some evidence of the dispreference for asking questions within backgrounded constructions, even in *in situ* languages, since questions within islands should be dispreferred due to the function of the constructions involved. In fact, judgments about wh-words within islands are quite variable in some *in situ* languages. Examples often require special context to be judged acceptable (Kitagawa and Fodor 2003). Thai is an *in situ* language for which I was able to collect judgments from five native speakers; as indicated, there was little agreement among speakers about whether questions within islands are acceptable[13](*=unacceptable; #=requires special context; √=acceptable). All five judgments are indicated below by a string of *s, #s, and √s:

Complex NPs:

(80) ***√√ khaw hen raayngaan thii kiawkap khray?
(s)he see report that about who
She saw that report that was about who?

Subjects:

(81) ****√ kaan thii Mary ruucak khray thamhay John ramkhaan?
NOM that Mary know who make John be-bothered
She knew who bothered him?

Complements of manner-of-speaking verbs:

(82) * #√√√ Mary krasip waa John luum aray?
Mary whisper that John forget what
She whispered that he forgot what?

Presupposed adjuncts:

(83) **√√√ Mary ook caak rongnang phro phuun-phuun kin aray?
Mary exit from theatre because friends eat what
She left the movie because friends were eating what?

13 I thank Theeraporn Ratitamkul for collecting these judgments for me.

Lakhota is another wh-*in-situ* language, and Van Valin and La Polla (1997) report a systematic avoidance of questions from within islands. An example is cited below (Van Valin and LaPolla 1997: 617):

(84)   *Wičháša ki   [[šṵka wa táku φ-φ-yaxáke] ki   le]   wa-o-o-yáka   he?
       Man   the dog   a   3sgU-3sgA-bite   the this 3sgU=3sgA-see Q
       The man saw the dog which bit what?
       (acceptable under yes–no question interpretation)

There are other types of evidence for island effects within other *in situ* languages, as well. For example, while it is possible to have a wh-word within a relative clause in Japanese (85), it is not possible to put *ittai* ("the hell") within the island (86); *ittai* must appear just outside the island (Pesetsky 1987). This is despite the fact that in main clause questions, *ittai* generally appears directly before the wh-word (87) (examples from Pesetsky 1987):

(85)   Mary-wa   ittai   [John-ni nani-o   ageta hito-ni] tatta-no?
       Mary-TOP the.hell John-DAT what-ACC gave man-DAT met-Q
       What the hell did Mary meet the man who gave t to John?

(86)   *Mary-wa [John-ni ittai   nani-o   ageta hito-ni] atta-no?
       Mary-TOP John-DAT the.hell what-ACC gave man-DAT met-Q
       What the hell did Mary meet the man who gave t to John?
       (Pesetsky 1987: 112, 126)

(87)   Taroo-wa Hanako-ni ittai   nani-o   agemasita ka? (main clause:
                                                                non-island)
       Taroo-TOP Hanako-to the.hell what-OBJ gave   Q
       What the hell did Taro give to Hanako?

Quite parallel facts have been cited for Sinhala, another wh-*in-situ* language. The Sinhala question particle *də* cannot appear within an island but must appear just outside as well (Gair 1998; Hagstrom forthcoming).

   Thus I hypothesize that constructions that serve to convey backgrounded information are *dispreferred* for containing question words cross-linguistically, even in *in situ* languages that do permit wh-words within backgrounded constructions. Suggestive evidence comes from the variable Thai judgments, and the data reported on Lakhota by Van Valin and La Polla. Systematic corpus evidence and sentence processing experiments would be required to confirm fully the claim more generally, however. It is predicted that examples of questions within islands are relatively rare as compared with other sorts of questions of similar complexity. It is also expected that there should be an increase in processing load required for comprehending question words within islands. Still, it seems that the pragmatic clash is not necessarily sufficient to result in clear judgments of ungrammaticality unless there is displacement involved. **Displacement from canonical position creates additional processing load and this combines with the pragmatic clash to result in unacceptability.**

On the basis of different data, Deane likewise comes to the conclusion that information structure combines with processing load to result in ill-formedness. He puts the idea this way: "Extraction consists in the establishment of a long-range grammatical relation. An obvious prerequisite to establishing a relation between two concepts is that one be paying attention to both concepts at the same time … But in long-distance extraction, the two concepts to be linked are separated far enough from one another that some means must be provided to focus attention on both. And what means would be more natural than if the two concepts were ones which commanded attention anyway? [i.e. topic and focus]" (Deane 1991).

Hundreds of volumes have been dedicated to island phenomena and I do not pretend to have done the topic full justice here. For insightful discussion of the role of processing and information structure in "superiority" effects, see Arnon et al. (2004); for "that"-trace effects see Homer and Michaelis (2005); and for negative clauses Oshima (2005). For discussion of the complexities involved in parasitic gaps, see Levine and Sag (2003); for a non-syntactic account of certain definiteness effects, see Deane (1991) and Kluender (1998). For arguments that long-distance dependencies receive a natural treatment on monostratal approaches without traces, see Sag and Fodor (1994).

What I hope to have accomplished is to provide some new data and arguments for the idea that information structure properties of the constructions involved combine with processing complexity to account for many island phenomena. For additional arguments see also Deane (1991); Erteschik-Shir and Lappin (1979); and Erteschik-Shir (1998a,b). We now turn to issues related to quantifier scope, where again, we see a critical role for recognizing construction-specific discourse properties.

7.12 Topicality and Quantifier Scope

Quantifier scope plays a role in semantic interpretation when there are two quantifiers of different types. For example, if a sentence contains an existential quantifier (e.g. *a, one, some*) and a universal quantifier (e.g. *all, every, each*), then the existential quantifier may have wide scope over the universal: "There exists (at least) one x, such that all y...”; or the universal quantifier may have wide scope over the existential: “For all y, there exists some x (or other)...” In the first case, the existential quantifier's referent is determined once and for all at the outset; in the latter case, the existential quantifier's referent may vary according to which one of the set of referents referred to by the universal quantifier is considered. It turns out that there are general tendencies that hold across constructions, once the particular discourse functions associated with constructional arguments are understood.

Ioup (1975) long ago observed that relative scope is determined by two interacting hierarchies. One hierarchy, slightly simplified here,[14] is described in terms of grammatical relations (see also Kuno 1991):

Topic   >   subject   >   IO   >   Obl/DO

Greatest inherent tendency for wide scope   >>>   least inherent tendency for wide scope

FIGURE 7.2 Hierarchy of topicality of grammatical relations

The hierarchy is interpretable as a scale of topicality. Topicalized expressions are likely to be informationally topical in that they tend to be related to a frame or set already introduced in the discourse (Chafe 1976; Lambrecht 1994). As noted above, subjects are the default clausal topic (Chafe 1987; Michaelis and Francis forthcoming; Givón 1984; Gundel 1998; Halliday 1967; Lambrecht 1994). Also as discussed in Section 7.3, ditransitive recipients (Ioup's "IO"s) are secondary topics. At the other end of the spectrum, obliques and direct objects are available to be part of the focus domain; they readily accept new or focal information and are generally non-topical (Du Bois 1987; Du Bois, Kumpf, and Ashby 2004).

Ioup provides support for the hierarchy from many diverse languages. It appears that languages generally obey a hierarchy of topicality in determining scope, irrespective of word order. For example, in Arabic and Japanese, a topicalized NP, appearing at the end of the string, necessarily has wide scope (examples from Ioup 1975: 53):

Arabic topicalization:
(88)   Khabaz Hanna li   kol li   binaat feteer.
        Baked   John   for all the girls   cake
        A cake, John baked for all the girls.   a > all

---

[14] Ioup places Oblique arguments above DO in the hierarchy, but for our purposes it is sufficient to assume that they are both at the low end of the wide-scope hierarchy.

Japanese topicalization:

(89) Keiki-o Taro-wa nisannin-no onnanoko-ni tsukuri-mashita.
       cake   Taro   a few girls   for   made
       A cake, Taro made for a few girls.   a > all

(90) Nissanin-no onnanoko-ni Taro-wa keiki-o tsukuri-mashita.
       A few girls   for   Taro   cake   made
       For a few girls, Taro made a cake.   few > a

Similar effects can be seen in English (cf. Kuno 1991):

(91) a. A chocolate cake, John baked for all the girls.   a > all (preferred)
      b. For all the girls, John baked a chocolate cake.   all > a (preferred)

(92) a. All of us have read many of his articles with great enthusiasm.
                                                              all > many
      b. Many of his articles, all of us have read with great enthusiasm
                                                              many > all

The idea that topicality is intimately related to quantifier-scope interpretation can be seen to be intuitive once one examines what it means to have
wide scope. A wide-scope interpretation of a variable is one in which the
variable is given or fixed, and a second variable is interpreted with respect to
it. That is, a variable x that is given a wide-scope interpretation provides the
"anchor." It is within the context provided by the wide-scope operator that
variables with more narrow scope are interpreted. This is clearly reminiscent
of what topics are: the topic is given or fixed, playing the role of an anchor,
while the comment is predicated of it. Chafe notes that topics typically set up
"a spatial, temporal or individual framework within which the main predication holds" (Chafe 1976).

As Francis and Michaelis (forthcoming) point out, it is the scale of topicality that is important, not particular grammatical relations per se. They
observe that particular semantic frames can constrain their arguments to be
more or less topical, with the concomitant differences in scope possibilities.
For example, they account for the following facts this way:

Creation frames:

(93) She made a canoe from it.
       She made a canoe from every log.   every > a

(94) An oak grew out of it.
       An oak grew out of every acorn.   every > a

Transformation frames:

(95)   *She made a log into it.
       *She made a log into every canoe.   *every > a

(96)   *A acorn grew into it.
       *An acorn grew into every oak.   *every > a

While the creation frame allows the material argument to be more topical than the created entity—presumably because a creation scene is typically specified in order to introduce a new entity that is created, the transformation frame requires that the material argument be more topical than the transformed entity, presumably because a scene of transformation is typically specified in order to introduce the new, altered entity into the discourse.

A second interacting factor in determining quantifier scope concerns the particular lexical choices of quantifiers. As Ioup notes, the hierarchy places quantifiers that refer to more members of a given set higher than those that refer to fewer members. A slightly elaborated version of Ioup's quantifier hierarchy is provided in Fig. 7.3.

Each > every > all > most > many > several > a few > at least one > someone or other

Greatest inherent tendency for wide scope   >>>   least inherent tendency for wide scope

FIGURE 7.3 Hierarchy of quantifiers

What is the source of the lexical effects on quantifier scope? The lexical effects are arguably related to topicality as well. An unidentified new referent serves as a poor choice of topic, and correspondingly non-specific quantifiers such as *some x or other* or (non-specific) *a* tend to have narrow scope. On the other hand, universal quantifiers, referring to an identifiable-in-context set of entities are like definites, and are thus relatively more likely to serve as topics. Differences among universal quantifiers stem from lexical semantic differences. For example, *each* is lexically a distributive quantifier, and is therefore a wide-scope operator, since a collective reading is required for narrow scope. See also Carlson (MS) for relevant discussion.

Kuno (1991) suggests two other interacting factors that play a role in quantifier-scope interpretation, both of which are interpretable in terms of topicality in a straightforward way. His factors and illustrative minimal pairs are given in Fig. 7.4.

More discourse-linked Q > Less discourse-linked Q

Many Democrats distrust some of these Republicans. some > many (easier than for b)

Many Democrats distrust some Republicans.

1st or 2nd person pronouns (local) Q > 3rd person (non-local) Q

Many of them know some of us.   some > many (easier than for b)

Many of us know some of them.

FIGURE 7.4 Other factors relevant to topicality and quantifier scope (Kuno 1991)

"Discourse linking" implies that an NP is anchored in the discourse, and is therefore accessible as opposed to brand new; i.e. an NP that is discourse-linked is therefore more given, and givenness is correlated with topicality. First- and second-person pronouns are always available for topic status.[15]

The Ditransitive Construction and Scope facts

In order to put the arguments of the ditransitive construction on a linear scale of relative topicality, the following scale emerges from the characterization of ditransitives given earlier in (20).

Ditransitive topicality hierarchy:

(97)   Agent (subject) >> recipient >> Agent (oblique) >> Theme
       High topicality   >>>   Low topicality

These relative topicality facts predict all of the relevant scope facts that hold of the ditransitive. Since the subject is the primary topic, it should take wide scope over the recipient and theme arguments. This prediction holds:

(98)   Everyone gave a girl a book.   Everyone > a girl (preferred)

(99)   Everyone gave him a book.   Everyone > a book (preferred)

That is, in (98), the preferred reading is that everyone gave some girl or other some book or other.

In passive ditransitives, the recipient argument as subject has wide scope over the agent, since the recipient in the case of passive is the primary topic of the clause. The oblique agent remains more topical than the focal theme argument, and as expected, the former tends to be interpreted as having wider scope over the latter:

---

[15] Further support for the argument made above that the ditransitive recipient is a secondary topic comes from the fact that ditransitive recipients show a marked preference for 1st- and 2nd-person pronouns when compared with recipients expressed pronominally in the prepositional dative (57% for the former as compared with 20% in the latter in a study of the entire parsed Switchboard corpus) (Bresnan and Nikitina MS).

(100)   A girl was given a book by everyone.   A girl > everyone (preferred)

Everyone > a book (preferred)

Moreover, as observed in Section 2.1, the recipient argument of the ditransitive strongly tends to have wide scope over the theme argument, as in (101):

(101)   The teacher assigned one student every problem.   One > every
(Bruening 2001; Ioup 1975; Larson 1990: 604)

The goal argument of the prepositional phrase, on the other hand, need *not* take wide scope over the theme argument, and the following sentence is ambiguous between a reading in which one particular problem was given to all the students and one in which all the students received one problem:

(102)   The teacher assigned one problem to every student. (ambiguous)

Since the recipient argument is more topical than the theme argument in the ditransitive, we predict the scope facts evident in (101). Since the two non-subject arguments of the prepositional paraphrase are not specified for relative topicality, we also predict that sentences such as (102) will be ambiguous with respect to scope assignment.

We saw above that brand-new recipient arguments do not necessarily strike native speakers as ungrammatical. Therefore, the quantifier hierarchy predicts that it should be possible to invert the most prevalent scope interpretation of recipient and theme if the right quantifiers are chosen. This is also the case:

(103)   They gave at least two people each Nobel prize.   Each > a least two
(preferred)

Example (103) is naturally interpreted as meaning that each Nobel prize was awarded to at least two recipients: the theme argument taking wide scope over the recipient argument.

Similarly, as expected, the recipient argument can be interpreted as having wide scope over the subject argument when particular quantifiers are chosen. The phrase "some x or another" encourages a narrow scope reading for x, even in positions that normally have wide scope such as subject position:

(104)   Some person or other gave each child a book.   Each > some or other
(preferred)

Thus the scope properties of the ditransitive construction can be seen to follow naturally from the combination of lexical facts and a topicality scale. Proposals that rely on the structural description of ditransitives for an explanation of scope effects (e.g. Bruening 2001) do not predict the acceptability of the inverse scope in (103) and (104).

To summarize, then, because scope is strongly correlated with topicality, **the information-structure properties of constructions predict their predominant assignment of scope.** Since lexical content also plays a role in scope assignment, it is to be expected that the right choice of lexical elements allows for occasional inverse scope assignment as well.

7.13 Conclusion

In this chapter, we have extended existing accounts that relate apparently syntactic phenomena to the domain of information structure, in order to account for a range of seemingly mysterious facts. By proposing an elaborated version of the insight that unbounded dependencies cannot involve backgrounded elements (Erteschik-Shir 1979; Takami 1989; Van Valin 1998), we have addressed the majority of standard constraints on movement. The discussion surrounding the ditransitive construction provides evidence that a close analysis of the particular constructions involved yields answers to otherwise recalcitrant problems. In particular, we have been able to explain the recipient argument's statistical tendency to resist being involved in unbounded dependencies unless it is the passive subject.

We have also built upon previous observations (particularly that of Ioup, Kuno, and Francis and Michaelis) to offer a general account of how a wide-scope interpretation correlates with topicality. We have demonstrated that an information-structure analysis of the ditransitive predicts the fact that the recipient argument tends to have wide scope over the theme argument (and the fact that it doesn't when it is passivized or when particular lexical items are chosen).

Both explanations benefited from a careful analysis of lexical semantics and the particular constructions involved. Which arguments are backgrounded or topical depends critically on the choice of constructions. Not all sentential complements serve the same function (compare the complement of *say* with the complement of *shout*); neither do all postverbal NPs (compare the direct objects of transitive verbs which are within the potential focus domain with the recipient arguments of ditransitives which are backgrounded). Determining which arguments are topical likewise depends on which constructions one is considering (compare the verbs of creation with the verbs of transformation). FUNCTIONAL EXPLANATIONS REQUIRE REFERENCE TO THE FUNCTION OF THE CONSTRUCTIONS INVOLVED (including the lexical semantics of the words involved).

While the field of information structure is complex and it requires recognizing statistical regularities, a case has been made that information structure and processing are absolutely central to the investigation of issues that lie at the center of linguistic theorizing.

Appendix: Corpus evidence for the proposed information structure of the ditransitive

A replication of earlier findings on the strong tendency for the recipient of ditransitives to be non-new was found in the speech of three mothers, to their children (Nina, Adam, and Eve) in the CHILDES database:

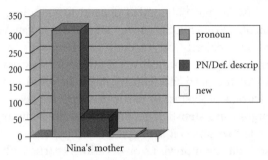

Number of pronouns (given), proper names/definite descriptions (accessible), and indefinite (new) arguments in active recipient position (n = 381) in Nina's mother's speech

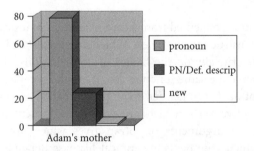

Number of pronouns (given), proper names/definite descriptions (accessible), and indefinite (new) arguments in active recipient position (n = 103) in Adam's mother's speech

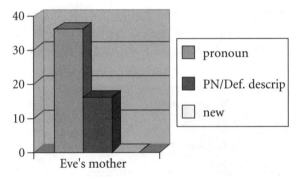

Number of pronouns (given), proper names/definite descriptions (accessible), and indefinite (new) arguments in active recipient position (n = 52) in Eve's mother's speech

The trends are the same across mothers. That is, the distribution of NP types across the three mothers is not significantly different: $\chi^2(4 \ N = 536) = 8.9$, $p = .06$.

Data from Alta Vista is again similar, with the ditransitive recipient showing even more of a tendency to be pronominal than the ditransitive actor argument. The theme argument of the ditransitive, on the other hand, overwhelmingly appears as a lexical NP.

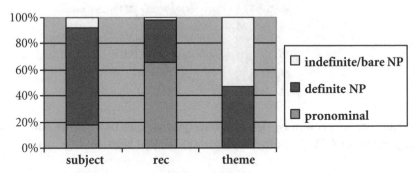

Percentage of various nominal marking in each argument of active ditransitives, found in the first 110 instances involving the verb *give*, gathered on Alta Vista using the Linguists' Search Engine. The distribution of NP types is distinct in subjects and recipients: $\chi^2(2 \ N = 211) = 49, p < .001$; recipients and themes $\chi^2(2 \ N = 181) = 51.5, p < .001$; and themes and recipients $\chi^2(2 \ N = 190) = 106, p < .001$. (N < 220 because not all instances of *give* expressed each argument).

The fact that the prepositional goal argument is not constrained to be given is evident from the frequency of proper names and definite descriptions among the corpora of each mother. The data are given below.

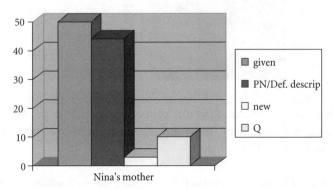

Number of pronouns, definite descriptions, question words, and new arguments of Nina's mother's prepositional goal argument (n = 107)

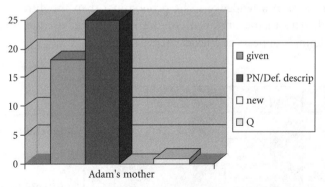

Number of pronouns, definite descriptions, question words, and new arguments of Adam's mother's prepositional goal argument (n = 44)

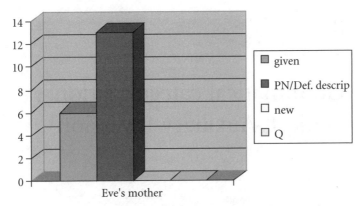

Number of pronouns, definite descriptions, question words, and new arguments of Eve's mother's prepositional goal argument (n = 19)

The trends are again the same across mothers.[16] A comparison of the frequencies of NP types appearing as ditransitive recipient and prepositional goal indicates a significant difference: $\chi^2(3\ N = 706) = 106.6$, p $< .001$.

---

[16] The distribution of NP types across the three mothers is not significantly different: $\chi^2(6\ N = 170) = 9.9$, p $= .13$.

8

Grammatical categorization: Subject–Auxiliary Inversion[1]

8.1 Introduction

A recognition of the general nature of categories can be used to illuminate the functional underpinnings of aspects of grammar that appear at first to be brute syntactic facts. This chapter investigates one such case, that of Subject–Auxiliary Inversion (SAI). SAI is found in a variety of utterances including yes/no questions, non-subject wh-questions, counterfactual conditionals, sentences with initial negative adverbs, exclamatives, comparatives, negative conjuncts, and positive rejoinders:

(1)	Did she go?	Y/N questions
	Where did she go?	(Non-subject) wh-questions
(2)	Had she gone, they would be here by now.	Counterfactual conditionals
(3)	Seldom had she gone there...	Initial negative adverbs
(4)	May a million fleas infest his armpits!	Wishes/Curses
(5)	Boy did she go!	Exclamatives
(6)	He was faster at it than was she.	Comparatives
(7)	Neither do they vote.	Negative conjunct
(8)	So does he.	Positive rejoinder

These, or a subset of these widely varying contexts have been cited as evidence that there is no functional generalization associated with the syntactic pattern (Green 1985); SAI has been used in this context as evidence for the existence of purely syntactic generalizations or autonomous syntax

---

[1] This chapter is based on a jointly authored paper with my undergraduate student at UIUC, Alex Del Giudice (forthcoming), in *The Linguistic Review*. I wish to thank Bill Croft, Seizi Iwata, and Kunie Miyaura for very helpful comments on an earlier draft.

(Newmeyer 2000).[2] SAI therefore provides a strong challenge to the idea that formal patterns are generally associated with and motivated by functions, a claim that distinguishes cognitive and functional approaches from otherwise parallel generative approaches (e.g. Jackendoff 2002).

This chapter builds on previous accounts that have offered insightful generalizations about the function of SAI constructions (Lakoff and Brugman 1987; Lambrecht 1994; Michaelis and Lambrecht 1996a; Diessel 1997). In addition, it is argued that a case that is apparently somewhat exceptional, that of exclamatives (e.g. (5)), is actually strongly motivated as well. Apparently formal restrictions on SAI, are in fact demonstrated to be better accounted for by a functional account. Finally, the particular internal syntactic form of SAI is motivated by appeal to its semantic/pragmatic function. The implication of this work is that synchronic functional motivations often lurk behind seemingly syntactic brute facts and can be used to explain many aspects of grammar that appear otherwise to be wholly idiosyncratic.[3]

The relevant functional categories may only be found if researchers are aware of insights gained from cognitive psychology. In particular, the claim that SAI bears no functional generalization is based on a false assumption about what such a generalization would look like. The implicit assumption is that there should be a single feature or set of features common to the category, and yet, as discussed below, this assumption is widely recognized to be false. As Murphy notes, "The groundbreaking work of Eleanor Rosch in the 1970s essentially killed the classical view [of necessary and sufficient definitions], so that it is not now a theory of any actual researcher in this area" (Murphy 2002: 16).

It is argued below that the set of constructions that exhibit SAI naturally form a coherent functional category of the type familiar from general categorization and lexical concepts.

---

[2] Fillmore (1998) takes a similar stand, providing a detailed discussion of the formal properties of SAI and its various specific subconstructions, but offering no semantic or pragmatic properties to relate the subtypes. He is explicitly agnostic on the question of whether such properties exist (note 11, p. 121) and in fact goes so far as to state that many basic constructions are not pairings of form with function, but are simply formal generalizations. Fillmore's position is somewhat surprising given his central role in the development of Construction Grammar, an approach that is explicitly designed to deal with pairings of form with function.

[3] It should be made clear that the failure to find a unified functional category for SAI or some other pattern would only indicate that certain brute syntactic facts exist that are not synchronically motivated. While I do accept the existence of occasional instances of synchronically unmotivated syntactic facts (normally motivated by diachronic developments), these appear to be the exception rather than the rule.

Newmeyer (2000) claims that SAI is a prime example of a formal generalization with no functional underpinnings. That is, SAI has been claimed to
display unified syntactic properties, but not to be associated with any unified
function. For example, Newmeyer suggests that no instances of SAI, regardless of type, appear in embedded questions or subordinate clauses:

(9)   a. I wondered whether you had been working late.
       b. *I wondered whether had you been working late.

This is claimed to be a *formal idiosyncrasy*—since the same restrictions appear
to hold of each separate use of the structure despite the fact that they are
associated with a range of functions.

The present chapter argues on the contrary that there is a coherent category
of functions associated with SAI, and moreover that there are no unified
syntactic properties, with the exception, of course, of the surface form of SAI
itself, which I will argue is motivated by its function. In this way, the present
chapter makes a case study of SAI, the point being that a focus on form to the
neglect of function is like investigating a human organ such as the liver,
without attending to what the liver does: while this is not impossible, it is
certain to fail to be explanatory.

8.2 A semantic/pragmatic generalization

Several semantic/pragmatic generalizations have been proposed in the literature. Many SAI constructions are framed negatively or at least non-positively
(Lakoff and Brugman 1987). Many SAI constructions in both German and
English are non-declarative or non-assertive speech acts (Lambrecht 1994;
Michaelis and Lambrecht 1996a; Diessel 1997). Finally, many SAI constructions are often narrow-focus or sentence-focus constructions—that is, they
often do *not* have more typical, predicate focus (i.e. topic-comment) information structure (Michaelis and Lambrecht, 1996a).

All of these accounts implicitly or explicitly note that SAI is a deviation
from the prototypical sentence form in one way or another, the prototypical
sentence being a declarative, positive assertion with predicate-focus information structure. Another feature of prototypical sentences is that they may
stand alone and they are not dependent on another clause. We will see that
many SAI constructions differ from prototypical sentences in this respect as
well.

At the same time, no SAI construction simultaneously has all the attributes
of non-prototypical sentences; each SAI construction has its own subset of
the attributes. While this would seem unhappily to lead to too many dis-

junctive characterizations, such a situation is the norm for lexical items and for categorization generally: a subset of attributes that hold of the prototypical case is instantiated in each conventionalized extension (e.g. Lakoff 1987). That is, as we saw in Chapter 3, learners retain quite a bit of item-specific linguistic information at the same time that they form generalizations. As discussed in Chapter 4, instances with high type frequency provide a cognitive anchor or prototype that helps the learner assimilate new cases to the category.

For example, consider the word *home*: prototypically, it evokes a house where an intact family unit lives and sleeps and where children grow into adulthood, and where one feels comfortable and a sense of belonging. Yet it can be used for many of these aspects in isolation from the others (Fillmore 1992):

(10) a. Prototype: 138 FitzRandoph Rd. is Aliza's and Zach's home.
         (house, where they grow up, live with their family, feel comfortable, and belong)
      b. She owns 14 homes.   (houses)
      c. She went home to her dorm room. (place where someone lives and sleeps)
      d. She traveled home to see her family. (place where she grew up)
      e. She's at home in the mountains. (place where one feels a sense of belonging)

Home clearly has a prototypical meaning that can be extended to highlight a particular attribute (or attributes) of the prototypical meaning.

The word *baby* is another example. Prototypically, *baby* refers to a small human, who is cute, needs to be taken care of, is immature emotionally, and is the youngest in the family. Any single one of these attributes can be used as the reference of *baby* in its various senses, however:

(11) a. Prototype: She had a baby (small, human, cute, immature, needs to be taken care of, youngest in a family)
      b. Baby carrots   (small)
      c. Hey, baby!   (cute)
      d. Don't baby me.   (to take care of as a parent would a baby)
      e. He's such a baby.   (emotionally immature)
      f. Mr Platt is the baby in his family (youngest in the family)

Are we to say that the words *home* and *baby* have no meaning? Or that their various senses are unrelated to one another? To assume so would be to claim that it is an accident that all the senses are referred to by the same morpheme. However there exists evidence from processing (Klein and Murphy 2002; Pylkkanen and Murphy 2004) and from language acquisition (Casenhiser 2004) that systematic relationships among senses of a polysemous word are recognized by speakers. It is therefore preferable to view the prototypical sense as extended such that one or more particular attributes are highlighted in each extension.

A natural category relating the various conventionalized uses of "baby" is represented in Fig. 8.1.

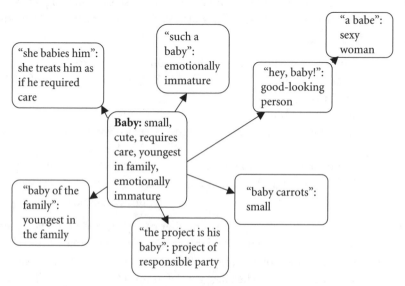

FIGURE 8.1 Polysemous senses of the lexical item "baby"

Each of the links from the prototype can be interpreted as indicating a metonymic relationship whereby an attribute of the prototype is referred to by the same word as the prototype itself.

The function of SAI can be analyzed in similar terms: there are attributes that hold of the prototypical case, and conventional extensions of the prototype systematically differ from the prototype in displaying only a subset of the relevant attributes. On the basis of the distribution of SAI constructions, it is further suggested that the dominant attribute of SAI is NON-POSITIVE; this attribute of SAI constructions serves to motivate the form of the construction.

Questions

Yes/no questions are clearly non-declarative speech acts whose propositional content is non-positive (it does not assert or presuppose the truth of the proposition). For example, (12) does not assert or presuppose that he left. Wh-questions such as (13) do presuppose that he did something, but are non-declaratives.

(12) Did he go?

(13) What did he do?

The fact that (non-echo) *subject* wh-questions do not invert (14) is attributable to the fact that the only way to invert the subject and auxiliary would be to position the auxiliary before the wh-word subject. Yet the wh-question construction requires the wh-word to appear sentence-initially.[4]

(14) *Did who leave?

Counterfactual conditionals

SAI is required in counterfactual conditionals, as in (15a):

(15) a. Had he found a solution, he would take time off and relax.
      b. *He had found a solution, he would take time off and relax.

This construction presupposes (not asserts) a *negative* word-to-world fit— that is, the hypothetical antecedent is presupposed to designate a non-actual state of affairs in the world. Thus this construction involves non-positive, non-asserted propositional content. The inverted clause is also not a stand-alone sentence, but instead is dependent on the following clause. Thus counterfactual conditionals have three attributes of non-prototypical sentences: they are non-positive, non-asserted, and dependent.

Initial Negative Adverbs

SAI can be seen to be obligatory with initial adverbs that are construed negatively, as demonstrated in (16) (see also Green 1985; Lakoff and Brugman 1987):

(16) a. Not until yesterday did he take a break.
      b. *Not until yesterday he did take a break.

---

[4] In a default inheritance hierarchy making use of a usage-based model of grammar, these facts are naturally accounted for since the non-subject question construction, as expected, inherits from both the general wh-construction and the SAI construction. The conflict between the two constructions is accounted for by the non-subject wh-question construction, which specifies that its order is [Wh$_{subj}$] [VP].

At the same time it may not appear with a positively framed adverb such as in (17 a-b):

(17)   a. *Everywhere has he found a solution.
        b. *Yesterday did he take a break.

The negative implication conveyed by SAI can be seen by comparing (18a) and (18b). Example (18a) implies that even with money offered as incentive she would not quit, while (18b) expresses that she would quit with the slightest incentive (Jackendoff 1972; Lakoff and Brugman 1987; Newmeyer 2000):

(18)   a. For no money would she leave. (she wouldn't)
        b. For no money she would leave. (she would)

Example (19) can be used to demonstrate that what is important is not the factual word-to-world fit in determining whether SAI is appropriate, but instead whether the propositional content is *construed* positively or not. That is, (19a) is logically equivalent to (19b), and yet (19b), since it is framed positively, cannot be phrased with SAI (19c):

(19)   a. Not until yesterday did he   (SAI: framed non-positively)
           take a break.
        b. He took a break yesterday   (positively framed equivalent
           and not before.   proposition)
        c. *Did he take a break yesterday (SAI with positively framed
           and not before.   proposition)

May you live to be 100!

SAI also appears in utterances like (20).

(20)   May a million flies infest his armpits!

This special type of statement is an appeal to some unspecified forces about some uncontrollable event. Thus this pattern, like other uses of SAI we have seen, is not a declarative speech act, but rather a curse or wish (an "expressive" speech act in Searle's (1979) terminology). Moreover, no positive state of affairs is asserted or presupposed: whether or not the curse or wish will be fulfilled is left open.

The use and function of statements such as that in example (20) are quite limited. The only auxiliary that can be placed in this construction is "may":

(21)   a. May you live a good life!
        b. *Should you live a good life!

In addition, this construction differs from other uses of SAI in that it doesn't provide a negative polarity context:

(22)   *May you ever lift a finger!

Thus this case must be listed as a special subconstruction (see also Fillmore 1998). No general syntactic account would predict these idiosyncrasies without stipulation. At the same time, the construction obeys the generalization that utterances with SAI are non-declarative and non-positive. Thus its existence is motivated.

Exclamatives: making sense of a recalcitrant case

The exclamative construction seems to pose the greatest threat to a functional account of SAI, since instances of this construction can be positively framed with topic-comment information structure. It has been observed that exclamatives are at least non-assertive in that they presuppose, rather than assert the truth of the propositional content, and in that way have one feature associated with SAI (Diessel 1997; Michaelis 2001).

It is possible to motivate further the use of SAI in the exclamative construction by observing that exclamatives are closely related to a subtype of questions: rhetorical questions. This is not the received wisdom. While Lambrecht (1994), for example, suggests a functional restriction on SAI, namely that utterances with SAI are not declaratives, he nonetheless suggests there is no direct relationship between questions and exclamatives (p. 30). Fillmore (1999) likewise states without qualification that exclamatives "are clearly not questions" (p. 122). This chapter argues that it is possible to relate exclamatives to questions in a quite strong, direct way, therefore more strongly motivating the fact that exclamatives, like questions, are expressed with SAI. Exclamatives can be seen to be closely related to rhetorical questions: that they should have the form of questions is therefore unremarkable.

Cross-linguistically, exclamatives and questions often bear formal similarities (Zanuttini and Portner 2003). Note that many exclamative utterances are at the same time rhetorical questions, as indicated by the phrase *or what* which is generally restricted to appear with rhetorical yes/no questions:

(23)   a. Do you want to go?   (request for information)
        b. Do you want to go or what? (rhetorical question: it is assumed
                                        that you want to go)

(24)   Boy, are you tired or what?!

Moreover, there is evidence that speakers sychronically perceive a relationship between exclamatives and questions. Alex Del Giudice collected examples of SAI using the Google Search Engine, searching for the following randomly selected four instances of <expletive aux pronoun> as exact phrases (that may or may not continue)(Goldberg and Del Giudice forthcoming):

(25)   a. "boy is this"
        b. "boy are you"
        c. "wow does this"
        d. "man does this"

Irrelevant cases such as instances of the string that crossed sentence boundaries (e.g. *First Boy: Is he doing that on purpose?*) were ignored. The first fifty instances of exclamatives returned by Google for each of the four strings were combined into a master list of 200 attested tokens. A full 13 per cent (26/200) of the exclamative sentences included the specific phrase *or what*. A few examples of these are given below. All spelling and punctuation have been preserved:

(26)   a. "Boy, is this the summer of angst-ridden Australian tough guys, or what?"
        b. Boy is this a bit more involved than I expected, or what?!
        c. Boy, is this an awesome picture or what?!?
        d. Hoo boy, are you dropped into a pot of boiling water or what.
        e. "Wow! Does this guy own stock in Microsoft or what?"

That this many examples should bear the specific lexical phrase *or what* is quite striking and can be taken as evidence that speakers relate exclamatives to rhetorical questions. In fact positively framed exclamatives in general are compatible with the phrase *or what*, just as positively framed rhetorical questions are, indicating that an even greater number of instances may have been construed as rhetorical questions, even though they were not explicitly marked as such.[5]

Thus exclamatives are actually strongly motivated by the fact that they are a minimal extension from rhetorical questions. Rhetorical questions are well suited to being used as exclamatives because rhetorical questions are by

---

[5] Notice also that exclamatives that do not have subj–auxiliary inversion are not compatible with *or what?*

(i)   What a big boy he is! (exclamative, no SAI)
(ii)   *What a big boy he is or what?!

definition questions that are posed that require no response because the answer is already clear. Exclamatives likewise are used to express states of affairs that are clearly true (and remarkable).

Comparatives

SAI optionally occurs in comparatives, in a formal or archaic register:

(27)   a. He has read more articles than have his classmates.
       b. He has read more articles than his classmates have.

Unless the subject is a full lexical NP, inversion sounds decidedly archaic, and it is downright unacceptable with pronominal *it* as subject:

(28)   a. (archaic) He has read more articles than have they.
       b. *Our library has more articles than has it.

The preference for lexical NP subjects in comparatives follows from the fact that comparatives with SAI require a narrow focus on the subject argument, instead of the more typical topic-comment interpretation.

The use of SAI in comparatives may be motivated independently by a tendency to position heavier or longer constituents clause finally (see, e.g., Hawkins 1994; Wasow 2002). In support of this idea is the fact that SAI is only used in comparatives when there is VP ellipsis in the inverted clause, thus allowing the lexical subject to appear clause-finally:

(29)   a. *He has read more articles than have his classmates read.
           (cf. He has read more articles than his classmates have read.)
       b. He has read more articles than have his classmates.

The inverted clause in comparatives is dependent on the preceding clause and cannot stand alone as an independent sentence. Thus SAI in comparatives is used to mark dependent clauses that have narrow focus on the subject argument: two characteristics of non-prototypical sentences.

Nor is this one unmotivated

Sentences beginning with *neither* or *nor* require SAI:

(30)   a. Neither is this construction unexpected.
       b. *Neither this construction is unexpected.

Such sentences are negatively framed. They are also pragmatically dependent on another contextually given proposition, insofar as *neither* and *nor* are conjunctions and thus require reference to a second conjunct. Thus these cases have two attributes of non-prototypical sentences: they are non-positive and they are dependent.

So is this one

A final use of subject–auxiliary inversion to be discussed here is found immediately after initial conjunct "so/as/likewise," as in:

(31)   Context: "His girlfriend was worried."
       a. So was I.
       b. *So I was.

These are distinct from the negative conjuncts just discussed in that they must involve VP ellipsis, as in:

(32)   *So was I worried.

These cases are positively framed assertions. But they have two features associated with prototypical SAI: they have narrow focus on the subject argument as opposed to topic-comment information structure, and they are pragmatically dependent on another evoked proposition.

The majority of constructions that license SAI have at least two features of non-prototypical sentences. The case of exclamatives is additionally motivated by its close relationship with rhetorical questions, and wh-questions are also motivated by their close relationship to yes/no questions as well.

A functionally motivated category of SAI is diagrammed in Fig. 8.2. Independent evidence for the naturalness of this category comes from the fact that several of the most central functions have been found to cluster together in cross-linguistic work on an entirely different construction: indefinite pronouns (Haspelmath 1997). Haspelmath finds a tendency for indefinite pronouns to be expressed alike in questions, conditionals, comparatives, and indirect negations. In the case of SAI constructions, the following are roughly analogous: questions, counterfactual conditionals, comparatives, initial negative adverbs, and negative rejoinders: i.e. extensions A,B,C,D,E,G, as indicated in Fig. 8.3.

The SAI category proposed and the category for the senses of *baby* described above are quite similar in having conventionalized extensions radiating out from a central core. One important difference between them, however, is that the prototype suggested for SAI: "non-prototypical sentence," is actually a generalization that is not directly instantiated (as indicated by the dashed circle in Figure 8.2.) That is, while we frequently encounter prototypical sentences, we do not encounter "non-prototypical sentences" as instances

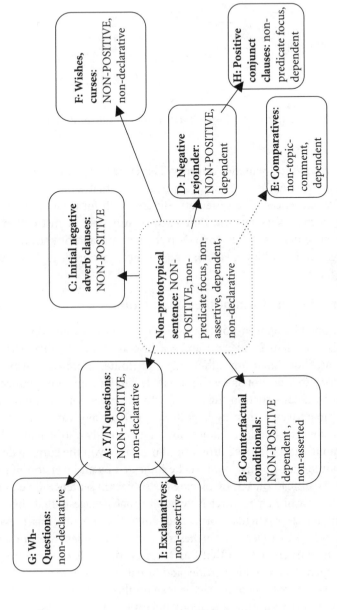

FIGURE 8.2 Functional category of SAI constructions with "non-prototypical sentence" as its prototype

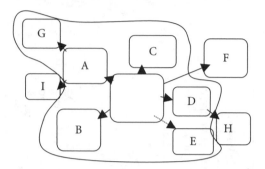

FIGURE 8.3 SAI functions that cluster together in indefinite pronouns

of a non-prototypical sentence category. Therefore it is possible to reconstrue the category of SAI as a halo of constructions that stand in *contrast* to prototypical sentences. The systematic difference in form (subject–auxiliary inversion) signals a systematic difference in function (a distinction from prototypical sentences). This analysis recognizes an additional link-type to those suggested in Goldberg (1995): a markedness link, indicated by a curved link in Fig. 8.4.

8.3 Motivating the form of the construction

The attribute of being non-positive is the dominant feature of SAI constructions. This is evident in Fig. 8.2 and 8.4 insofar as more subconstructions have this attribute than any other single attribute. Moreover, each of the constructions that do not share this attribute can be seen to be immediately motivated by a construction that does, with the exception of comparatives. SAI in comparatives is then by hypothesis the least motivated, and it turns out, is also the least stable. As noted above, it is strictly optional and slightly archaic sounding. It may well drop out of use entirely in the coming decades.

Why should non-positive contexts be indicated by an inversion of subject and auxiliary instead of, say, by placing the subject in sentence-final position or some other arbitrary feature? Newmeyer (2000) suggests that there is no motivation for its particular form, and notes that no one has previously suggested one. Moreover, he further suggests that unless we are able to motivate the particular form that SAI takes on the basis of some proposed function, then this would provide additional evidence for the thesis of autonomous syntax (2000: 46). Let us take up this challenge.

Auxiliaries carry information about polarity as well as tense and aspect (Langacker 1991). By positioning the auxiliary in a non-canonical position,

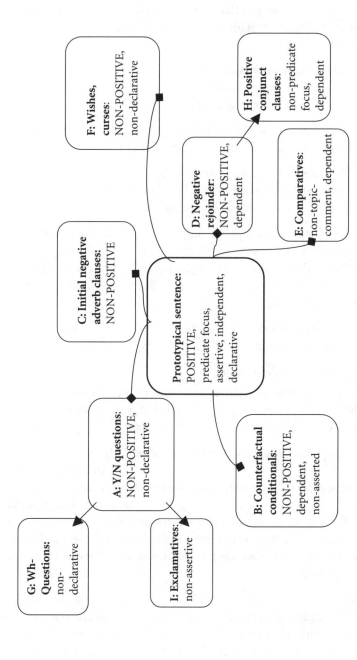

FIGURE 8.4 Functional category of SAI constructions with prototypical sentence as its prototype and markedness links motivating each of the extensions from the prototype

the construction conveys that the polarity involved is not the canonical, positive polarity; i.e. no positive word-to-world fit is asserted. This motivation can be used to account for the fact that only the first auxiliary is inverted (Newmeyer 2000: 48):

(33) a. Have you been working late?
　　　 b. *Have been you working late?
　　　 c. *Could have been you working late?

Only the first auxiliary serves to indicate polarity of a sentence; the broad-scope negative, for example, can only appear after the first auxiliary:

(34) a. You couldn't have been working late.
　　　 b. You could have not been working late.
　　　 c. You could have been not working late.

   Examples (34b,c) are acceptable only under the narrow-scope reading in which *not* predicates the word or phrase immediately following, and not the entire sentence: that is, only (34a) is paraphrasable by "It's not the case that you could have been working late." Notice that *not* can only cliticize on the first auxiliary (as in 34a):

(35) a. *You have been't working late.
　　　 b. *You could haven't been working late.

Putative Main Clause Restriction

Is SAI actually uniformly restricted to main clauses, as has been suggested (Emonds 1970; Newmeyer 2000)? It turns out it is not (Hooper and Thompson 1973; Green 1976; Bolinger 1977b), as the examples in (36) illustrate:

(36) a. They knew that *had she* left on time, she'd be here by now.
　　　　　　　　　　　　　　　　　　　　(counterfactual conditional)
　　　 b. She reflected to herself that *never had she* seen such a beautiful sight.
　　　　　　　　　　　　　　　　　　　　(clause-initial negative adverb)
　　　 c. Junie B. knew that *boy, was she* in trouble!　　　(exclamative)
　　　 d. I knew that they would spend millions on defense, but I knew equally that *not one cent would* they give for tribute. (Bolinger 1977b: 515)　　　　　　　　　　　　(Negative NP preposing)

   Certain uses of SAI are restricted to convey particular non-declarative speech acts, including, in particular, questions and wishes/curses. Even these SAI constructions can appear in subordinate clauses, but only when the main speech act is conveyed by the subordinate clause, as in examples (37a,b) (from Green 1976: 385):

(37) a. I guess John didn't come in, did he?   (tag question)
      b. We ought to assign Postal, because who can understand *Aspects?*
                                                            (rhetorical question)

There are many subtleties related to which subordinate clauses can appear
with SAI, but the restrictions have been widely argued to be pragmatic, not
syntactic. (For more specific formulations of where putative main clause
phenomena can occur, see Hooper and Thompson 1973; Green 1976; Bolinger
1977a.)[6] As a first approximation, the following generalization holds: (**Only**)
**SAIs that are restricted to conveying particular speech acts are restricted to
main clauses, or to subordinate clauses that convey speech acts.**

Cross-linguistic rarity

The use of subject–auxiliary inversion to indicate a non-prototypical sentence
is rare cross-linguistically. This fact raises a challenge to an autonomous
syntax account, at least as traditionally construed by generative grammarians:
if SAI were based on a universal system of syntactic knowledge, one should
presumably expect the generalizations to be universal or at least common
cross-linguistically. On the present account, on the other hand, SAI is a
motivated device for indicating deviations from prototypical sentences, particularly for non-positive expressions. It is certainly not the only possible
device: overt negatives, discourse particles, and other special constructions
could do the job equally well. Once we recognize that SAI and its range of
conventional uses are learned on the basis of positive input by each new
generation of speakers, there is no expectation that it should necessarily be
common across languages.

8.4 Conclusion

Given parallel evidence for radial categories in the concepts designated by
words (*home, baby*) and grammatical categories, and the convergent understanding of how human categories are formed generally, the type of category
of functions exhibited by SAI can be seen to be quite natural.

   The implication of this chapter is that functional motivations often underlie seemingly idiosyncratic facts of grammar. The distribution of SAI in

---

   [6] Hooper and Thompson suggest that SAI can appear in subordinate clauses that are asserted as
opposed to presupposed. Green similarly argues that SAI can appear in subordinate clauses in which
the speaker appears to agree with the proposition expressed by the subordinate clause. Bolinger
observes additional idiosyncratic pragmatic facts about the appearance of SAI constructions in
subordinate clauses.

subordinate clauses and its restriction to the first auxiliary, are explained by attention to the functions that SAI conveys. In contrast, a purely syntactic account of the phenomenon can only stipulate the form of SAI—that subject and first auxiliary are inverted—without making any accurate further predictions or generalizations. The formal account would moreover still have to stipulate a list of all of the subconstructions that require or allow SAI (and whether each requires or allows SAI), as well as each of the constructions' other special properties, without motivating the existence of SAI in English in any way. It is fair to say that while the formal approach may be descriptively adequate, it does not, in the case of SAI, have any explanatory force.

In seeking out functional categories we need to be cognizant of the sort of categories we should expect to find. Categories of language, like most human categories, are much more flexible than those defined rigidly by necessary and sufficient conditions.

9

Cross-linguistic generalizations in argument realization

In Chapters 4–6, it was argued that argument structure constructions are learnable, but I acknowledged that we needed an account of the cross-linguistic tendencies that exist. If the mappings between form and meaning were universal and *not* attributable to general cognitive mechanisms, then one could legitimately argue that while they are learnable, they are not learned.

Claims that linking rules are universal are widespread (Baker 1988; Pinker 1989; Gleitman 1994; Levin and Rappaport Hovav 1995). The implication has been that universal aspects of language are innate, proposed specifically to solve the apparent "poverty of the stimulus" problem (Chomsky 1957, 1965). Pinker (1989: 248), for example, suggests that "Linking rules...seem to be near-universal in their essential aspects and therefore may not be learned at all.... Linking rules can be universal and innate in the current theory..." He offers a very explicit proposal for the mappings from semantic roles to surface syntactic positions, as follows (Pinker 1989: 74):

1. Link the agent to SUBJECT
2. Link the patient to OBJECT
3. Link the theme argument (first argument of BE or GO) to SUBJECT unless SUBJECT is already linked; to OBJECT otherwise
4. Link the goal to an OBLIQUE (prepositional phrase) argument
5. Link the theme argument in a CAUSE TO HAVE predicate to the second object in a ditransitive construction

Naigles, Gleitman, and Gleitman (1993: 136–7) suggest that "there is sufficient cross-linguistic similarity in these linking rules to get the learning procedure started.... [T]here is an overwhelming tendency, cross-linguistically, for agents to appear as subjects and themes as direct objects, with other arguments appearing in oblique cases." In the same vein, Gleitman (1994: 203) suggests that "at least some of the mapping rules [between syntax and semantics] have to be in place before the verb meanings are known, or else the whole game is over."

Levin and Rappaport Hovav (1995: 21–2) make a similar claim as follows: "We assume, in addition, that the information in a verb's argument structure, together with the Projection Principle and the Theta-Criterion, determine the syntactic configuration that a verb is found in. Thus, the relation between argument structure and the D-structure syntactic representation is viewed as 'trivial.'" Baker (1996: 1) echoes a similar theme: "One central task for any theory of grammar is to solve the so-called 'linking problem': the problem of discovering regularities in how participants of an event are expressed in surface grammatical forms."

In this chapter, we focus on several concrete proposals for universals of linking generalizations. What we find is that the "universals" are only tendencies, and each tendency is argued to be a result of general cognitive, pragmatic, or processing attributes of human cognition. Therefore, given that argument structure constructions are demonstrably learnable (cf. Chapters 4–6), and given that the cross-linguistic generalizations that do exist are (*a*) not exceptionless, and (*b*) motivated by non-linguistic generalizations, we conclude that generalizations about the linking between form and function provides no evidence for a genetically determined "universal grammar" related to argument structure generalizations.

9.1 Actors and Undergoers are expressed in prominent syntactic slots

What are the cross-linguistic generalizations about how arguments are linked to syntactic positions? Dowty (1991) proposed linking generalizations that are now widely cited as capturing the cross-linguistic universals. But in fact his generalizations were quite modest. He observed that in simple active clauses, *if* there's a subject and an object, *and if* there's a proto-agent and proto-patient, then the proto-agent role is expressed by the subject, and the proto-patient argument is linked to object position. (This generalization also corresponds to the first two of Pinker's proposed universals.) Properties of proto-agents (Actors) and proto-patients (Undergoers) are listed in Fig. 9.1.

Contributing properties for Actor role
— Volition; sentience (and/or perception); causes event; movement
Contributing properties for Undergoer role
— Change of state (including coming-to-being, going-out-of-being); incremental theme (i.e. determinant of aspect); causally affected by event; stationary (relative to movement of proto-agent)

Figure 9.1 Protypical properties of Actors and Undergoers (cf. Dowty 1991)

Dowty notes that the linking of Actor to subject and Undergoer to object holds *except* when the linking is the *opposite* in syntactically ergative languages. When stated in this way, it is clear that it is not a terribly strong claim.

Yet even this generalization is oversimplified in that languages with ergative properties are typically "split ergative" in that only, for example, perfective clauses or third-person clauses are expressed ergatively—the generalizations do not hold across the board for all constructions in a given language (Silverstein 1976; Cooreman, Fox, and Givón 1984; Du Bois 1987; Dixon 1994; Manning 1996; Lemmens 1998; Siegel 2000). Moreover, within every language, there are particular constructions that violate the generalizations: e.g. passives, anti-passives.

A fair generalization, nonetheless, can be rephrased as follows:

The Salient Participants in Prominent Slots Generalization (SPPS): Actors and Undergoers are expressed in prominent syntactic slots.

This generalization allows for languages for which the notion of "subject" is not clearly relevant, or not clearly parallel to more familiar cases (Schachter 1977; Gil 1994; Morris and Cottrell 1999; Croft 2001; Donahue MS; Foley forthcoming). Potential subjects, or "pivots" in a language are sometimes only definable in terms of particular constructions within a given language (Van Valin and LaPolla 1997; Croft 2001; Donahue MS; Foley forthcoming).

The SPPS generalization also accounts for the fact that an Actor argument without an Undergoer, and an Undergoer without an Actor are also expressed in a prominent syntactic position; in this way the third of Pinker's generalizations is also captured. Finally, this generalization has the added advantage that it follows directly from well-documented aspects of our general cognition as described below.

Actors are salient

There is a large literature documenting the fact that entities that initiate actions are highly cognitively "accessible." Fisher et al. (1994), for example, have shown an "agent bias" in the choice of verb used in free descriptions of events; for example, a scene of a girl chasing a boy could be construed as a "chasing" scene or a "fleeing" scene, but speakers overwhelmingly choose to describe it as "chasing." More generally, events that could be coded with or without mentioning an agent strongly tend to be construed as agentive.

Humans' attention is naturally drawn to actors, even in non-linguistic tasks. For example, visual attention tends to be centered on the Actor in an event, during and after an action is performed (Robertson and Suci 1980).

Infants as young as nine months have been shown to attribute intentional behavior to even inanimate objects that have appropriate characteristics (e.g. motion, apparent goal-directedness) (Csibra et al. 1999); infants habituated to a scene in which a computer-animated circle jumped over an obstacle and contacted another circle, expected the first circle to take a direct route when the obstacle was removed from the scene. Children as young as sixteen months can distinguish intentional versus accidental actions (Carpenter, Akhtar, and Tomasello 1998). Thus, the characteristics of Actors: volition, sentience (and/ or perception), and movement are closely attended to by prelinguistic infants in visual as well as linguistic tasks. The role of causal forces and effects are also highly salient to infants and result in focused attention on both Actors and Undergoers in events.

Undergoers are salient

The Undergoer in an event is generally the end point of some sort of force (Talmy 1976; Langacker 1987a; Croft 1991). End points are generally better attended to than onsets in both non-linguistic and linguistic tasks. For example, Regier and Zheng (2003) note that subjects are better able to discriminate between events that have distinct end points than distinct onsets; in addition, subjects use a wider range of more specific verbs to describe end-point-focused actions (such as putting a key in a lock) than onset-focused actions (such as taking a key out of a lock); see also Landau (2003). Pourcel (2004) has demonstrated that goal-directed paths are salient attributes in scenes, in that speakers of both French and English are more likely to mention goal-directed paths of motion than atelic paths of motion when describing video clips portraying motion events.

The tendency to attend closely to one particular type of end point, that of change of state, begins as early as six months. Woodward's (1998, 1999) studies demonstrate that six-month-old infants attend more to changes of state than to changes of motion without corresponding state change. Jovanovic et al. (forthcoming) replicated Woodward's study and also demonstrated that six-month-old infants attend to changes of state even if the means of achieving the change of state is unfamiliar (in this case a pushing-over effect is caused by means of a hand outstretched, palm outward) (see also Csibra et al. 1999; Bekkering, Wohlschlager, and Gattis 2000). It has been hypothesized that *effects* of actions are the key elements in action-representations both in motor control of action and in perception (Prinz 1990, 1997).

Thus the observation that Actors and Undergoers tend to be expressed in prominent slots follows from general facts about human perception and attention.

9.2 Number of arguments = Number of complements

A strong tendency that has been cited as evidence for a universal form–function mapping is the tendency for the number of overtly expressed complements to equal the number of semantic participants. For example, a recent article by Lidz, Gleitman, and Gleitman (2003: 169) concludes with the fact that "Noun phrase number is a privileged source of information as to the semantic structure of predicates." This article purports to demonstrate the viability of a universalist mapping between syntax and semantics as opposed to an "emergentist" view of the mapping, attributed to Goldberg (1999) and Tomasello (2000).

Lidz, Gleitman, and Gleitman (2003) performed an experiment involving the Dravidian language, Kannada, based on the methodology of Naigles, Gleitman, and Gleitman (1993). They presented to children (mean age 3;6) familiar verbs in familiar and unfamiliar (ungrammatical) contexts. Unfamiliar contexts included intransitive verbs presented in transitive frames and/or with causative morphology, and transitive verbs presented in intransitive frames with or without causative morphology. Children were then encouraged to act out a scene corresponding to the sentence they had heard using a set of toy animals. Of particular interest is the degree to which the children, when faced with an intransitive verb in an ungrammatical context, relied on causative morphology as compared with the transitive syntax in their interpretations.

The authors observe that in Kannada, the causative morpheme is reliably associated with a causative interpretation. They further note that the transitive construction involving the overt expression of two arguments is associated with a wider range of interpretations than causation (as is also the case in English—cf. transitive clauses with the verbs *know, see, want, owe*).

They suggest that any emergentist theory that claims that argument structure is learned from the input, would predict that subjects should rely more on the causative morpheme as a predictor of a causative interpretation than the number of semantic participants expressed. They suggest that the "universalist" position on the other hand, predicts that the appearance of two linguistically expressed participants should better predict a causative interpretation. For this, they invoke the "theta criterion" (Chomsky 1981), or what we will refer to more transparently as the Isomorphic Mapping Hypothesis: "noun phrase number lines up as simply as possible with argument number" (Lidz et al. 2003: 154). They suggest that the Isomorphic Mapping Hypothesis is an aspect of "universal grammar": i.e. part of a set of hard-wired principles that are specific to language and are not the result of empirical experience.

Lidz et al. found that subjects rely on the number of linguistically expressed noun phrases to a much greater extent than they rely on the causative morpheme, concluding that the evidence supports their universalist position.

The authors suggest that the emergentist versus universalist debate is akin to the long-standing empiricist versus rationalist debate implying that those who eschew the Universal Grammar Hypothesis believe that humans are born blank slates, willing and able to learn anything at all. However, the emergentist position, as laid out in Elman et al. (1996), Tomasello (2003), MacWhinney (1999), and Lakoff (1987), for example, very explicitly relies on various sorts of constraints that may well be specific to humans. Human beings are biologically determined to have a particular perceptual/conceptual apparatus (as well as a particular type of physiology) that is distinct from that of dogs, chimps, and chinchillas. Possibly critical aspects of the general, human conceptual apparatus include the fact that humans appear to be particularly adept at imitation, and at reading others' intentions and realizing that they are able to alter them (Tomasello 1999).

The question is not, therefore, whether anything at all is specific to human beings and/or hard-wired into the brain, but rather, whether there exist rules that are specific to human language and not a result of our general conceptual/perceptual apparatus together with experience in the world.

As explained below, it is agreed that learners can be expected to pay attention to the number of nouns expressed as an indication of the propositional meaning being conveyed (see also Fisher 1996, 2000). It is necessary to question, however, an interpretation of the facts that relies on an innate "universal grammar," specific to language.

Note first that the Isomorphic Mapping Hypothesis is far from being universally valid as a generalization about the surface structure that is available to children. For example, it is systematically violated in many particular constructions within English where the number of linguistically expressed participants ("complements") differs from the number of central semantic participants ("arguments") in the scene. Examples are provided in Table 9.1.

The situation can be seen to be even more complex when one considers other languages. For example, in Ewe, many verbs that are expressed intransitively in English, obligatorily appear transitively with an NP object. For example, "run" is expressed *fú du*, literally "verb course"; "swim" is *fú tsi*, literally "verb water"; "blow" is *gbɔ ya*, literally "breath air" (Essegbey 1999, forthcoming; Ameka forthcoming). In Lao, various specialized constructions are required to convey three semantic participants—at most two full NPs are allowed for a single verb (Enfield forthcoming).

TABLE 9.1. Various systematic exceptions to the Isomorphic Mapping Hypothesis

Construction Type	Number of linguistically expressed NPs (complements)	Number of central semantic participants in the scene (arguments)
Short Passives[1] (e.g. *Pat was killed*)	1: (*Pat*)	2: (Pat, Pat's killer)
The Deprofiled Object construction[2] (e.g. *The tiger killed again*)	1: (*the tiger*)	2: (tiger, tiger's prey)
Semantic "Incorporation" constructions[3] (e.g. *Pat buttered the toast*)	2: (*Pat, the toast*)	3: (Pat, toast, the spread)
Cognate Object construction (e.g. *Pat laughed a hearty laugh*)	2: (*Pat, a hearty laugh*)	1: (Pat)
Certain idioms[4] (*e.g. Pat kicked the bucket; Pat gave a salute*)	2: (*Pat, the bucket/a salute*)	1: (Pat)

A universalist claim that the Isomorphic Mapping Hypothesis is true would presumably expect the generalization to be universally valid, and yet we see that it is systematically violated both within and across languages.

A more robust generalization is a weaker, pragmatic generalization: that the referents of linguistically expressed NPs are assumed to be directly *relevant* to the semantic interpretation conveyed. This generalization follows from Gricean pragmatic principles. Grice observed that human interactions generally, not just those that are specifically linguistic, are governed by a cooperative principle: one is assumed to make his/her contribution sufficient but not excessive, at the stage at which it occurs, by the accepted purpose or direction of the exchange in which s/he is engaged. For example, if I am in the middle of building a treehouse and I point to a hammer out of my reach, I do not expect you to hand me a screwdriver; I also do not expect you to run away, to throw nails at me, to begin to eat a kumquat, or to hand me a dozen hammers, assuming we are engaged in a communicative exchange. I expect you to recognize that my pointing gesture is directly relevant to the information I am trying to convey, and I expect you to hand me a single hammer.

---

[1] See Mouner and Koenig (2000) for evidence that an agent argument is conceptually evoked by passives without the "by" phrase.

[2] See Goldberg (forthcoming).

[3] See Mithun (1984).

[4] See Nunberg, Wasow, and Sag (1994).

The cooperation principle implies that any information supplied must be *relevant* to the communication at hand. In the case of language, for example, linguistically expressed participants must be relevant to the message being conveyed. This is captured by the generalization in (A) below. Moreover the generalization in (B) is also valid, following from the Gricean requirement that sufficient information be indicated for the intended message (e.g. if I do not mention, point, or gaze at the hammer, I cannot expect you to realize that I want it).

Pragmatic Mapping Generalizations:

(A) The referents of linguistically expressed NPs are interpreted to be *relevant* to the message being conveyed.

(B) Any semantic participants in the event being conveyed that are *relevant* and *non-recoverable* from context must be overtly indicated.

The difference between (A) and (B), on the one hand, and the Isomorphic Mapping Hypothesis, on the other, is that (A) does not specify exactly how the referents of linguistically expressed NPs should be integrated semantically, nor does (B) specify exactly how semantic participants may be indicated. This allows for the possibility that different languages and different constructions obey the principles (A) and (B) in different ways; some of this expected variation is in fact found in Table 9.1. Each of the constructions in Table 9.1 links form with function in a slightly different way (see references cited in table for discussion).

Note that (B) makes no predictions about semantic participants that are recoverable or irrelevant. This is important because different languages (and indeed, different constructions within languages) do different things in these circumstances. In Kannada, as well as perhaps the majority of the world's languages, recoverable arguments are regularly omitted (cf. discussion below). This is also the case in "incorporation" constructions cross-linguistically, in which one argument is indicated by the verb (or part of the verb) and is therefore recoverable. In English, in the majority of constructions, even recoverable arguments must be expressed as long as they are deemed relevant.

When arguments are irrelevant and non-recoverable (that is, non-recoverable except in the most general of ways as determined by the lexical semantics of the verb), languages also allow differing options. In English, the argument can be unexpressed as in the Deprofiled Object construction (1), or it can be expressed as in (2):

(1) The tiger killed again.
(2) The tiger killed someone/something again.

The same scene can be described by either (1) or (2) and yet the number of overtly expressed NPs differs in the two examples.

Why do children rely on the number of nouns expressed to determine the semantic transitivity of novel expressions, as Lidz et al. found? The universalist position claims that it is a result of a general universal principle; however, we have just seen that there exist empirical problems with the idea that the generalization is universally valid within or across languages.

The pragmatic generalization in (A), namely that the referents of linguistically expressed NPs are interpreted to be relevant to the message being conveyed, predicts that subjects should be strongly motivated to try to integrate each linguistically expressed participant in some way. Moreover, three-and-a-half-year-olds are old enough to recognize the transitive construction, both by means of language-specific word order (Subject Object Verb) and by the morphological case markers specific to Kannada's transitive construction, indications that were provided in the input to the experimental subjects. In addition, the simple transitive construction is presumably more frequent in Kannada than any other possible mappings of two NPs. Finally, the referents of the two NPs would rule out possible cognate object, idiomatic, or other specialized constructions. For all these empirical reasons, a two-participant interpretation is to be expected.

Lidz et al. suggest that subjects tended to act out overtly *causative* scenes despite the fact that the transitive construction is used to convey a broader range of meanings in Kannada. It is not clear why a universal principle should predict this, however. Most accounts of transitive constructions cross-linguistically have allowed for a broader range of meanings, although emergentists have emphasized that causation is perhaps the prototypical interpretation (Hopper and Thompson 1980; Kemmer and Verhagen 2002). In fact, it is not clear that subjects ignored other possible interpretations of the transitive construction; the coding scheme developed by Naigles et al. and used by Lidz et al. would count as causative a situation in which a child picked up two animals in one hand and simply waved them around.

How does the pragmatic account explain that two NPs should serve as a *better* indication of a two-participant message than the causative morpheme? Critically, the causative morpheme does not tell the child which entity should be chosen as the second argument.[5] This source of indeterminacy would leave

---

[5] The causative morpheme in itself also does not directly indicate whether two or three major participants will be involved, since it is used both with simple and complex causatives (Lidz et al. 2003: n. 5). While direct causation is entailed when the morpheme appears with two participants, indirect causation is entailed when the morpheme appears on an inherently causative verb such as *open*:

children in a quandary: how should they incorporate a causative meaning without knowing which entities are involved? There is a strong indication that this indeterminacy in what was expected of them led children to under-produce transitive actions. In particular, the three-year-olds were *no more likely* to produce semantically transitive actions when presented with nor-mally transitive verbs causatively marked, with a single overt argument (including *rub, hit, hug, lift, pinch, pull*) than they were to produce causative actions for causatively marked semantically *in*transitive verbs in the same single-argument context (see Lidz et al. 2003: 164, Fig. 1). This is despite the fact that Kannada readily allows arguments to be omitted as long as they are recoverable in context. Because the arguments were *not* recoverable in context in the experimental setting, children were at a loss to decide which entity should play the role of the second argument.

More specifically, note that Grice's cooperative principle implies that if there exists important information that is relevant and not known to the listener, it must be indicated by the speaker ((B) above). This implies that semantic arguments may not be omitted unless they are either irrelevant or recoverable, since semantic arguments, by definition, are normally important to an event being conveyed. Thus omitting an argument that is neither irrelevant nor recoverable in context is a violation of (B). To counter the violation, children in the experiment chose to avoid presupposing that a second argument was involved unless a second argument was expressed.[6]

Another factor that may have been relevant is the following. While it is true that the causative morpheme implies a causative interpretation, the converse is not true: a causative interpretation does not necessitate the appearance of the causative morpheme. As Lidz et al. note, lexical causatives appear transitively without the causal morpheme. That is, while the causal morphology may well have perfect *cue validity* as a predictor of causal meaning, it is far from having perfect *category validity* (probability that the causative meaning involves the causative morpheme): many causal utterances do not contain the morpheme.

(i)   Hari naan-inda baagil-annu terey-IS-id-a   (Lidz et al. 2003: 159 n. 5 ii)
      Hari I-INSTR   door-ACC   open-CAUSE-PST-3SM
      'Hari made me open the door.'

(ii) naanu   barf-annu   karg-IS-id   (Lidz et al. 2003: 158, 7c)
      I   ice-ACC   melt-CAUSE-PST-3SM
      'I melted the ice.'

---

[6] Adults were somewhat more bold in guessing which second entity to use in acting out a scene with a verb that was known to be transitive (and with a verb with the causative morpheme). This is probably due to the fact that adults are better at imagining scenarios in which the unidentified argument is somehow inferable from the context. Still even adults performed transitive act-outs move often for verbs expressed with two complements than those expressed with one, regardless of causative morphology or lexical meaning.

At the same time, in contexts in which neither participant is recoverable, the simple transitive has perfect category validity for a two-participant causative meaning: whenever a two-participant causative meaning is expressed in a context in which neither argument is recoverable (as in the experimental context), the transitive construction is used. Thus the starting assumption of Lidz et al. (2003), that causal morphology in Kannada is more strongly correlated with a two-participant interpretation than the transitive construction, is flawed.

It is interesting that the debate has shifted away from the traditional claim, that specific syntactic mappings of particular semantic roles to fixed syntactic positions or relations are universal and hard-wired into the brain (Pinker 1989; Grimshaw 1990; Gleitman 1994). That is, Lidz et al. do not claim that what is universal are traditional linking rules—they do not claim that children are born with the expectation, for example, that agents will appear as subjects, a claim that necessitates not only an innate representation for the notion grammatical subject but also some universal way of identifying a particular language's subject (for critiques of such a suggestion, see Bates and Mac-Whinney 1987; Bowerman 1996; Morris and Cottrell 1999; Tomasello 1992, 2000, 2003; Croft 2001; Goldberg, Casenhiser, and Sethuraman 2004).

To mention just one study that is relevant in this context, Sethuraman, Goldberg, and Goodman (1997) replicated the original experiment that Naigles et al. had done with English speakers, with one difference: instead of using known verbs, nonsense verbs were used. This was done in order to disentangle the effects of experience with verbs from knowledge of syntactic frames. As in the Naigles et al. (1993) and Lidz et al. (2003) studies, subjects were asked to act out scenes corresponding to the sentences they heard. Act-outs were coded as being either "frame compliant" (consistent with the semantics associated with the syntactic frame) or not frame compliant (inconsistent with the semantics associate with the frame). Sethuraman, Goldberg, and Goodman found increasing frame compliance as a function of subjects' age, and decreasing frame compliance as a function of syntactic complexity. Both of these findings indicate that the mappings between syntax and semantics are learned, with learners showing more facility with constructional patterns the simpler the patterns are and the greater experience with language that subjects have.

The current Lidz et al. (2003) study focuses not on the mapping of semantic roles to particular syntactic positions or relations, but simply on the number of linguistically expressed participants. As we have seen, a pragmatic explanation for their findings is at least as plausible as one based on a Universal Grammar Hypothesis.

Lidz and Gleitman (2004) have responded to the counterproposal just out-lined. They begin by accurately noting that the abstract categories and mechan-isms posited by generative grammar are so "far removed from the surface form of a sentence" that it is difficult to see how they could be learned. Unacknowledged, however, are non-generative proposals for what the end state of grammar looks like. These proposals make language a less daunting system to learn (Langacker, 1987a, 1991; Goldberg 1995; Tomasello 2003; Culicover and Jackendoff 2005).

Lidz and Gleitman offer other sorts of generalizations that seem to require recourse to universal grammar, other than the notion that noun phrase number lines up with number of semantic participants that their original article was about. To this end, they cite Kayne's (1981) claim that preposition stranding occurs only in languages with exceptional case marking, citing English as one language that has both and French as a language that has neither. However, it seems that preposition stranding only exists in Germanic languages, and not as far as we know among any of the other hundreds of language families. Therefore it is an odd candidate for a universal parameter of variation. Moreover, as Sugisaki and Snyder (forthcoming) point out, Kayne's parameter crucially depends on the notion of "government," a con-struct that has been abandoned within current Minimalist theory (Chomsky 1995), rendering Kayne's proposal without theoretical support. Lidz and Gleitman also cite certain coreference facts, and suggest that there are no non-generative proposals for accounting for them. See, however, Van Hoek (1995) for such a proposal.

In the latter part of their article, Lidz and Gleitman critique the Pragmatic Mapping principles as being based on "vague" notions like recoverability and relevance. They assert that "this alternative kind of explanation at present seems too informally stated even to evaluate." At the same time that the pragmatic explanation is dismissed, however, Lidz and Gleitman suggest that when learning languages that omit arguments, a learner must "modulate her hypotheses accordingly" about how the overt number of complements expressed lines up with the number of semantic arguments. But in order to modulate her hypotheses, the child has to recognize the factors of relevance and recoverability, since these are just the factors that are well recognized to condition omissibility in all languages (Resnik 1993; Cote 1996; Allen 1997, 1999, 2000; Haspelmath 1999; Allen and Schroeder 2000; Goldberg 2000; Ratitamkul, Goldberg, and Fisher 2005). Let us now turn to further illustra-tions of this final point, that argument omission is conditioned by relevance and recoverability.

9.3 Discourse-conditioned argument omission

We noted above that the Pragmatic Mapping Generalizations suggested do not predict whether arguments that are recoverable need to be expressed. In fact, there is a clear motivation from conversational pragmatics for often leaving such arguments unexpressed, e.g. Horn's (1984) R Principle or Grice's (1975) Maxim of Quantity: say no more than you must. When topical arguments are recoverable, there is no need to utter them. Many, perhaps the majority of languages in the world, readily allow recoverable arguments, both subjects and objects, to be routinely omitted. These languages include, for example, Japanese, Korean, Thai, Hungarian, Russian, Hindi, and Lao. Typical dialogues come from Russian in (3) and Korean in (4):

(3)   Q: Did you introduce Ivan to Masha?
      A: Da, pedstavil.
      "Yes, (I) introduced (him) (to her)"   (Franks 1995)

(4)   A: I ran across a big fat bug this morning
      B: kulayse, cwuki-ess-e?
           So kill-PAST-SENTENTIAL. ENDING
      "So, did [you] kill [it]?"
      A: Ani, tomanka-key   naypelie twu-ess-e
      No, run away-COMP   leave   let-PAST-SENTENTIAL.ENDING
      "No, [I] let [it] run away" (W. Nahm, personal communication,
      Feb. 16, 1999)

While omissability generalizations are motivated by non-conventional pragmatics in this way, omissability is clearly conventional in that languages differ in whether or not recoverable arguments can be omitted. In Hindi, all continuing topics and backgrounded information can be dropped (Butt and King 1997). In Hebrew, discourse topics, whether subjects or objects, can be omitted, but other recoverable arguments cannot generally be (Uziel-Karl and Berman 2000). In Brazilian Portuguese, a combination of discourse and lexical semantic factors seem to be at play in argument omission (e.g. Farrell 1990): e.g. omitted objects must be topics and are predominantly inanimate or third-person animate, i.e. first- or second-person objects are not readily omitted, even when they are topical. In Thai, we find that nicknames are often used instead of pronouns (including first- and second-person pronouns) in contexts of intimacy and respect (e.g. among friends, from children to parents), even though the language readily allows argument omission (Theeraporn Ratitam-kul, personal communication). English generally requires all arguments to be overtly expressed, unless lexically specified for object omission (Fillmore 1986). Since the pragmatic mapping generalizations do not determine whether arguments that are recoverable are necessarily expressed, we expect just this kind of variation in conventionalized options.

9.4 A case of argument omission in English

Interestingly enough, all languages allow omitted arguments in certain constructions, even when they generally require all relevant arguments to be expressed. The existence of such constructions in these languages further motivates the claim that the underlying motivation for the expression of arguments is at root pragmatic. An illustrative case comes from English, a language that, in relation to most of the world's languages, rarely allows argument omission. Even in English, a particular confluence of discourse properties can result in object omission, even for verbs that normally require that their objects be expressed. The following examples illustrate this phenomenon:

(5)   a. The chef-in-training chopped and diced all afternoon.
      b. Tigers only kill at night.
      c. Pat gave and gave, but Chris just took and took.

As in all cases of argument omission, the semantic requirement of recoverability must be satisfied. In addition, a further discourse condition seems to be necessary to license these examples:

(6)   **Principle of Omission under Low Discourse Prominence:**
Omission of the patient argument is possible when the patient argument is construed to be de-emphasized in the discourse vis-à-vis the action. That is, omission is possible when the patient argument is not topical (or focal) in the discourse, and the action is particularly *emphasized*. (Goldberg 2005).

"Emphasis" is intended as a cover term for several different ways in which an action is construed to be especially prominent in the discourse. The following examples illustrate the phenomenon with various types of emphasis labeled on the right:

(7)   Pat gave and gave but Chris just took and took.   Repeated action

(8)   He was always opposed to the idea of murder, but in the middle of the battlefield, he had no trouble killing.   Discourse topic

(9)   She picked up her carving knife and began to chop.   Narrow focus

(10) Why would they give this creep a light prison term!? He murdered!
                                                    Strong affective stance

(11)   "She could steal but she could not rob." (from the Beatles song "She
        Came in through the Bathroom Window")   Contrastive focus

The generalization in (6) is paralleled by Brown's (2002) finding that children
and adult speakers of Tzeltal realize the object argument lexically less often
when the verb is semantically rich than when it is semantically general. For
example, object arguments are more often omitted for verbs like *k'ux* "eat
mush stuff" than for verbs like *tun* "eat (anything)." The finding is reminiscent of the Quantity generalization (only one new mention per clause)
proposed by Givón (1975), Chafe (1987), and DuBois (1987): in both cases,
there is a trade-off in terms of how much is expressed per clause. However,
unlike the facts motivating the Quantity generalization, it is not clear that
emphasizing a predicate makes it preferable to omit the object, only that it
makes it possible.

9.5 Generalizations about reduced forms cross-linguistically

As was discussed in Chapter 3, highly frequent words and collocations tend to
be reduced in online production and over time, the reduced forms often
become conventionalized (Bybee 1985; Losiewicz 1992; Resnik 1993; Bybee,
Perkins, and Pagliuca 1994; Bybee and Hopper 2001; Jurafsky et al. 2001). One
reason for the reduction may well be that it is more economical to produce
shorter utterances if the same informational content can be conveyed (Bolinger 1963; Lindblom 1990). That is, high frequency is correlated with predictability. Thus the tendency to reduce highly frequent strings may be motivated
in the same way that omission of recoverable arguments is motivated: by the
pragmatic dictum of economy: say no more than is necessary. Another
motivation for the reduction of highly frequent strings is based in the
motor control of the speaker: highly practiced sequences tend to become
"routinized" and thus abbreviated (Bybee 1985; Bybee, Perkins, and Pagliuca
1994; Thompson and Fox 2004).

Motivating coreferential "equi deletion"

Haspelmath (1999) notes that there is a strong cross-linguistic tendency
for "want" constructions to omit the subject pronoun in same-subject complements, citing thirty-one languages from nineteen languages families
that omit such subjects. This is true, for example in English (compare (12)
with (13)):

(12)   *I want to play.*

(13)   *I want her to play.*

Haspelmath (1999) notes that not all languages allow the coreferential lower clause subject to be omitted; for example, Standard Arabic and Modern Greek obligatorily express the coreferential argument. Clearly, then, this is a cross-linguistic tendency that should be motivated, but not predicted by linguistic theory. Haspelmath argues that the lower clause subject omission is motivated because it is statistically predictable—we tend to talk more about a person's wishes about their own actions. The statistical likelihood of the lower clause subject being coreferential with the main clause subject allows the complement clause to be abbreviated.

In Malagasy, which has an unusual VOS word order, it seems that the higher clause subject can come after the reduced lower clause, as in (14). In this case, the lower clause subject is available for reduction not because it is predictable in the sense of being predicted during online processing, but because it is semantically recoverable by the end of the main clause.

(14)   nanandrana [namono ny akoho]   Rabe (Polinsky and Potsdam 2004:
                                                                           ex. 6a)
        try.ACT   [kill.ACT the chicken] Rabe
        Rabe tried to kill the chicken.

The idea that the complement clause can be abbreviated when it follows statistical biases would suggest that the message might be abbreviated in other ways as well. In fact, Haspelmath notes that in Maltese and Chalcatongo Mixtec, the complementizer, not the subject, is omitted in same-subject complement clauses. In Hopi and Mupun, the complementizer is shorter when the lower clause subject is coreferential with the main subject (e.g. in Hopi: -*ge* versus –*gat*). In Panansese, Boumaa-Fijian, and Samoan, a different, shorter verb "want" appears in same-subject constructions (Haspelmath 1999). Thus there is evidence of another independently motivated universal of linguistic expression: highly frequent or predictable combinations tend to undergo reduction.

9.6 The role of analogy: motivating the form–function pairing of the ditransitive

Many languages in addition to English have a ditransitive form with the recipient immediately postverbal and without preposition, followed by the theme argument, where this ditransitive form is associated with a meaning of "transfer." These include, for example, the Bantu languages Swahili, Kinyar-wanda, and Chilunda; Mandarin Chinese; Vietnamese; Twi, a Kwa language; Itonama, a Macro-Chibchan language; Huasteca Nahuatl, an Uto Aztecan language; Puluwat, a Micronesian language; Hausa, a Chadic language; Nengone of New Caledonia; Lango of Uganda; Fulani, a West Atlantic lan-guage; and Igbo, a Niger-Congo language (Dryer 1986, forthcoming; Foley forthcoming).

Since constructionists argue that constructions are learned pairings of form and function, it is necessary to explain why this generalization exists across unrelated languages. The first thing to observe is that the formal pattern typically has a somewhat wider or narrower range of meaning associated with it. For example, in Mandarin, the ditransitive pattern is as likely to be associated with the meaning "taking away from" as "to give to" (Ahrens 1994; Zhang 1998). The translation of a sentence such as "She stole him a book" could equally well mean "She stole a book for him" or "She stole a book from him." In Bantu languages, the ditransitive form can be used for a much wider array of meanings, leading researchers to coin a new term, "applicatives," to refer to the construction. For example, in Kinyarwanda, the ditransitive (applicative) form is used to encode possession (without transfer), patient + instrument, and cause + patient roles.

Still, even in languages that have applicatives, there is reason to suspect that "transfer" is a relevant notion. For example, in Kinyarwanda, Polinsky and Kozinsky (1992) note that verbs designating transfer such as "give," "show," "offer," "send," "teach," and "promise" are unmarked in the sense that they require no verbal marking, whereas other verbs require an applica-tive affix.

The recurrence of this pattern in unrelated languages leads us to ask why this is a natural form to use to express meanings related to transfer. Part of the explanation lies in the fact that in the semantics of transfer, the recipient argument is a prototypical Undergoer, a causee, since it is caused to receive (or lose) the theme argument. At the same time, the theme argument is a different type of Undergoer in that it undergoes a change of ownership. Thus the SPPS generalization suggested above motivates both arguments being expressed in prominent slots. In order further to motivate the fact that recipient argument strongly tends to come before the theme argument in ditransitive constructions, it is important to recognize that the recipient argument has certain *subject*-like properties vis-à-vis the theme argument, and subjects appear before objects in all the languages that have ditransitive constructions cited above. Semantically, the recipient is animate, as are the great majority of subjects. It strongly tends to be already given or topical in the discourse and is typically expressed pronominally, as are subjects. As discussed in Chapter 7, the recipient in a ditransitive is a "secondary clausal topic." The term evokes an analogy to subjects, which are primary clausal topics (Givón 1979, 1984; Dryer 1986). Cross-linguistically, if only one post-verbal NP is marked by agreement morphology, it is the recipient argument (Dryer 1986; Foley forthcoming). Verbal agreement is of course typical for subject arguments as well.

Thus the syntactic expression of the recipient argument of ditransitives is based on simultaneous analogies with causee-objects and possessor-subjects (thus accounting for Pinker's fifth proposed linking universal). This idea appears to be supported by a cross-linguistic trend for languages that have ditransitive constructions to be languages that express simple possession with the possessor in subject position, e.g. with a lexical verb, such as *have* (Harley 2002). That is, languages that express possession exclusively with a "<Possessed> belong to <possessor>" construction or a "<possessed> is with/at/by/to <possessor>" type construction, in which the possessed, not the possessor, is the subject of the clause, apparently do not have ditransitive constructions (Harley cites Scots Gaelic and Navajo Diné). It thus appears that only languages that can express possessors as subjects in simple clauses are candidates for having a ditransitive construction (e.g. English and list given above).

Harley claims that there is a stronger universal generalization, namely that the correlation is perfect, and that all languages with possessor-subjects also have a double object construction in the sense that they have a "cause-to-have" construction in which the recipient argument c-commands the theme argument.

TABLE 9.2. Relationship between languages that have possessor-as-subject construction and the ditransitive construction

	Have simple possessor as subject construction (e.g. "have")	Doesn't have simple possessor as subject construction (has, e.g., "belong to")
Has double object construction	English, Kunama	
Doesn't have double object ditransitive (has, e.g., prepositional dative construction)	Italian, French, Spanish, Persian	Scots Gaelic, Navajo Diné (according to Harley 2002)

However, familiar languages such as Italian, French, and Spanish contradict such a claim; these languages do have verbs that mean "to have," and yet they do not have ditransitive constructions. Harley suggests that they do actually have ditransitive constructions, using as evidence not surface form, but certain scope properties: whenever the recipient argument tends to have wide scope over the theme argument, Harley claims that the construction in question is a ditransitive. This is because scope is assumed to be determined by c-command relations: if the recipient has wide scope over the theme argument, then it must c-command the theme argument. However, we saw in Chapter 8 that the scope phenomena related to ditransitives are more naturally treated in terms of topicality. We need not claim that languages that have possessor-subjects *necessarily* have ditransitive constructions. This allows Romance languages' prepositional dative constructions to be what they look like: prepositional datives.[7]

For our purposes, the generalization can be restated as follows: **the existence of possessor-subjects in a language** *motivates* **the existence of a causative construction in which the possessor is expressed formally like a subject vis-à-vis the theme argument** via an analogical process.

9.7 Word-Order Generalizations

It has been noted that languages in which verbs canonically appear before their non-subject complements tend to have prepositions and postnominal complements, whereas languages in which verbs canonically appear clause-finally tend to have postpositions and postnominal modifiers as represented below:

(15)   Head-initial languages: $_{VP}[V\ldots]$, $_{NP}[N\ldots]$, $_{PP}[P\ldots]$
       Head-final languages: $_{VP}[\ldots V]$, $_{NP}[\ldots N]$, $_{PP}[\ldots P]$

This "head-direction parameter" is often cited as an example of a purely syntactic generalization which requires appeal to universal grammar (Jackendoff 1977; Chomsky 1981). However, the generalization, like other generalizations discussed above, is not exceptionless. Persian, for example, is a language in which adpositions come before their objects while verbs come after their objects (Hawkins, 1979), and the language has stably remained in this state for hundreds of years. This fact casts doubt on the idea that a "head-direction parameter" is hard-wired into our genome. Moreover, the "paucity of the stimulus" argument clearly does not apply to this generalization.

---

[7] I thank Heidi Harley and Malka Rappaport Hovav for discussion.

Children have to learn each of the particular verbs, prepositions, and nouns involved. As they do so, the order of arguments is apparent in the input.

Explanations for the tendency for heads to align have been proposed. The most robust aspect of the generalization across languages is the fact that verbs and adpositions tend to appear in the same order relative to their objects (notice that even in English, adjectival modifiers appear before nouns while relative clauses follow nouns). But the close relationship between verbs and adpositions is likely a consequence of the fact that adpositions typically evolve from verbs diachronically. Hawkins in addition offers a processing explanation for the tendency, suggesting that the statistical likelihood of processing difficulty can lead to the conventionalized preferred ordering of constituents (Hawkins 1990, 1994).

The popular press[8] recently claimed that evidence of a different kind of word-order generalization had been found on the basis of a paper by Sandler et al. (2005). Sandler et al. observe that a new sign language discovered in Israel—Al-Sayyid Bedouin Sign Language (ABSL)—has come to have a fixed SOV word order. As the authors note, however, a fixed word order is strongly motivated by communicative demands, since the language does not have case endings that would allow speakers to keep track of who did what to whom based on morphology. That is, without a fixed order, it would be impossible to distinguish "She bit the duck" from "The duck bit her" except by contextual cues. In a commentary on the Sandler et al. article, Goldin-Meadow suggests that there may be something universal about SOV order in sign languages, insofar as the homesign systems she has investigated also tend to display OV order (Goldin-Meadow 2005). Clearly, however, SOV order is not a candidate for a hard-wired syntactic universal, given that roughly 50 per cent of languages do not have SOV order (Greenberg 1963). The tendency for sign languages to display SOV order apparently comes from the fact that the same tendency exists in a non-linguistic domain, that of gesture; Goldin-Meadow et al. have found that hearing adults who know no sign language also use OV order when gesturing without words (Goldin-Meadow, Yalakik, and Gershkoff-Stowe 2000). The same basis in gesture has been argued to underlie the tendency for sign languages to develop verbal agreement, indicated by a fixed handshape that is moved from one abstract referent to another (Casey 2003).

---

[8] The subheading on the front of the *Science Times* read "A preference for a specific word order seems to be innate" (Nicholas Wade, *New York Times*, Feb. 1, 2005).

9.8 Iconicity

Iconicity has been much maligned in the literature as an explanatory factor, but there are a few robust generalizations that seem readily interpretable as iconic. Generally, a tight semantic bond between items tends to be represented by a correspondingly tight syntactic bond (Haiman 1983; Bybee 1985; Givón 1991; Wasow 2002). Givón (1991) described the generalization, which he terms the Proximity Principle, this way:

(*a*)   Entities that are closer together functionally, conceptually, or cognitively will be placed closer together at the code level, i.e. temporally or spatially.

(*b*)   Functional operators will be placed closest, temporally or spatially at the code level, to the conceptual unit to which they are most relevant.

Examples of this generalization are often so intuitively natural that they are easy to overlook. For example, grammatical operators (e.g. plural markers, determiners, case markers, classifiers) are expressed near their operands in the linear string. Notice that on this view, the most "natural" situation is one in which semantic scope and syntactic structure are aligned. In the same spirit, Baker's Mirror Principle (Baker 1988) effectively claims that morphological scope should mirror syntactic scope. While the principle is stated as a relation between morphology and syntax, not morphology and semantics, on Baker's view, syntax is assumed to be isomorphic to semantics. Therefore, the principle can be construed as capturing a relation between morphology and semantics. This same idea is made in explicitly semantic terms by Bybee (1985).

Goldberg (2003) discusses the strong preference in Persian and other languages for treating various kinds of complex predicates as single, syntactically integrated predicates. It is suggested that this is motivated iconically by the complex predicates' status as a semantically integrated predicate.

9.9 Conclusion

In Chapter 7 we discussed certain universal tendencies that can be explained in terms of information-structure generalizations: scope phenomena and island constraints. In this chapter we have analyzed several proposed universals of argument realization. Actors and Undergoers tend to be expressed in prominent positions because they are highly salient. The number of semantic arguments tends to align with the number of overt complements because rational communicators express as much as and not more than is necessary. It is natural to express the meaning of transfer with a ditransitive form because of simultaneous parallels between recipients and patient–objects on the one hand, and possessor–subjects on the other. Predictable, recoverable, or highly frequent information tends to be reduced in order to make expressions more economical. Languages tend to have stable head orders due to diachronic processes and processing preferences. Languages tend to develop fixed word order or case marking in order to avoid rampant ambiguity; the fact that sign languages appear to prefer OV order and directional agreement appears to have its roots in non-linguistic gesture.

We have seen that generalizations typically capture tendencies, not hard and fast constraints. It is therefore advantageous to explain universal tendencies by appeal to independently motivated pragmatic, semantic, and processing facts, since these would not be expected to be perfectly exceptionless. Explanations in terms of broader cognitive facts thus allow us to avoid simply stipulating universals as if they were arbitrary and exceptionless.

10

Variations on a constructionist theme

Section 10.1 addresses a subset of mainstream generative grammar approaches that will be referred to here as Syntactic Argument Structure theories (**SAS**); subsequent sections focus on more closely related first cousins of the framework developed in this book.

10.1 A comparison with mainstream Generative Grammar proposals

Certain mainstream generative grammar frameworks share the basic idea that some type of meaning is directly associated with some type of form, independently of particular lexical items (e.g. Borer 1994, 2001; Hale and Keyser 1997; Marantz 1997). To the extent that syntax plays a role in contentful meaning, these other approaches are "constructionist," and they are occasionally referred to that way in the literature. However, the approaches are fundamentally different from the type of constructionist approaches outlined in Chapters 1 and 2, in that these mainstream generative analyses fail to share basic tenets with constructionist approaches. The major differences are given below:

1. Syntactic Argument Structure (SAS) accounts do not adopt a non-derivational (monostratal) approach to syntax.
2. They do not emphasize speaker construals of situations; the emphasis is rather on rough paraphrases.
3. On SAS accounts, "constructions" are pairings of underlying form and coarse meaning instead of surface form and detailed function.
4. On SAS accounts, only certain syntactic patterns are viewed as instances of constructions; words or morphemes are assumed to be stored in a separate component, and most syntactic generalizations are assumed to make no reference to semantics or function.
5. According to SAS accounts, constructions are assumed to be universal and determined by Universal Grammar.

6. SAS accounts have not addressed language-internal generalizations across distinct but related constructions.

7. On SAS accounts, constructions are assumed to be compatible with Minimalist architecture and assumptions instead of providing an alternative way to view our knowledge of grammar.

In what follows we consider in turn proposals made by Hale and Keyser, Borer, and Marantz. The discussion focuses on issues that relate to the first three differences listed above, differences whose impact cannot be underestimated.

Hale and Keyser (1997)

As an example of the SAS approach, let us focus first on a particular analysis proposed by Hale and Keyser (1997). This approach emphasized a central theoretical role for certain denominal verbs. In particular, verbs such as *dance, shelve, laugh, sneeze, corral, box, saddle, blindfold, bandage, clear, narrow, lengthen* are hypothesized to involve syntactic incorporation. The approach assumes an underlying structure exists for these predicates such that the morphological form originates as a noun in a nominal position as in (1):

(1)   *Dance*$_v$ is derived from the noun *dance* by incorporating *dance*$_N$ into V1:

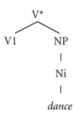

(2)   *Corral*$_v$ is derived by incorporating *corral*$_N$ into P and then into V2 and finally into V1 (Hale and Keyser 1997: 32):

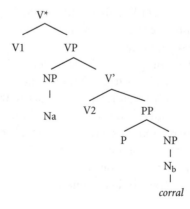

This idea is extended to other verbs as well, such that Hale and Keyser ultimately claim, "No ordinary verbal lexical item . . . consists solely of a head and the associated category V" (1997: 29). In particular, they suggest that possibly every verb has an internal argument.

At the same time, Hale and Keyser recognize that the nouns and their verbal counterparts typically do not have meanings that exactly correspond to one another. The verb *shelve* means something slightly different than to put on a shelf (cf. also e.g. Jackendoff 2002; Kiparsky 1996). That is, there is, as Hale and Keyser put it, "an additional increment of meaning" (p. 42). If one shelves sand, the sand must be in a container; if one shelves a box of books, the books must be individually placed upright on the shelf. Moreover, no actual shelf need be involved at all. In fact, it is quite possible to shelve books on a windowsill or on top of a bookcase. In light of these facts, Hale and Keyser suggest that each denominal verb has an "adverbial" component and a "referential" component. The "referential" component is what is claimed to come from the syntactic derivation; that is, what comes from the referent of the noun *shelf*. The "adverbial" component captures the notion of placing items upright on something shelf-like.

Given the adverbial semantic component, it is not clear what role the "referential" component actually plays. That is, the adverbial component seems to capture the entire meaning of *shelve*.[1] The syntactic derivation from one form to another, however, effectively subverts any attempt to account for the adverbial component. That is, it cannot come from the lexicon since *shelve* is not supposed to be listed in the lexicon. It cannot be attributed to the syntactic derivation, since the derivation is supposed to be general across verbs and there is no way to reference peculiar interpretations of specific words. In fact Hale and Keyser candidly note, "we cannot say how it is that a denominal verb acquires its adverbial increment" (1997: 42) . . . it is "totally mysterious to us at this point" (1997: 44).

Also troubling for the incorporation account is the fact that while the position from which incorporation takes place is expected to be occupied

---

[1] It might be suggested that the "referential" aspect of meaning relating to the noun *shelf* comes into play if an alternative to a shelf is unspecified. That is, in an expression like *We shelved the books*, it is assumed that the books were put on an actual shelf. However, this assumption can be seen to be only an implication; notice it is cancelable: *We shelved the books. By that I mean we lined them up on the top of the file cabinet.* The implicature arguably follows from the Gricean principle of Quantity. Listeners assume the location argument is a shelf unless there is reason to infer otherwise. That is, as Goldberg and Ackerman (2001) have argued, normal implications of predicates and modifiers are not redundantly stated. Therefore an additional prepositional phrase only appears if the speaker wants to make clear some refinement on the "shelf-like" entity.

by a trace, not by an overt nominal; overt nominals are in fact allowed in that position as seen in the following (Jackendoff 1997a):

(3)   a. She shelved her books on the windowsill.   (Hale and Keyser 1997: 41)
       b. I shelved the books on the highest shelf.

In the face of this data, Hale and Keyser make a suggestion that all normal effects of the derivation can be *eliminated*. Specifically they claim that:

> the referential component is represented by the chain defined by head movement... Let us assume that the derivation of the verb *to shelve*, or of any such verb, regularly involves incorporation as we have suggested. And let us assume also, that it is possible to delete the index from the chain defined by incorporation. This, we propose, essentially eliminates, or at least subordinates, the referential increment of the verb, leaving the adverbial increment as predominant. Syntactically, all vestiges of the chain are removed, leaving, in place of the original noun, a syntactic variable representing the argument, to be realized through lexical insertion in the formation of d-structure. (1997: 42)

That is, Hale and Keyser suggest that all evidence of a derivation vanishes along with the "referential" meaning whenever either a real shelf is not involved (as in (3a)) or when a real shelf is involved but it is overtly specified (as in (3b)). In place of the trace appears the mysterious "adverbial increment" of meaning, along with an otherwise unexpected place-holder that the overt expression fills.

This move appears only to be motivated by a desire to save the analysis in the face of what many would consider to be strong counterevidence. It is appropriate to ask what motivation for the original analysis was so strong that we should be convinced to accept the proposal? The central piece of evidence used to justify the proposal is the claim that external arguments cannot incorporate: only internal arguments can. That is, it is widely accepted that the X^0 must properly govern any head that incorporates into it (Baker 1988). Because this was originally stated as a syntactic generalization, a syntactic incorporation account is assumed. The generalization, at first blush, appears to account for when nouns have verbal counterparts (e.g. (4b) and (5b)) and when they do not ((4c) and (5c)):

(4)   a. A cow had a calf.
       b. A cow calved.
       c. *It cowed a calf.

(5)   a. Dust made the horse blind.
       b. Dust blinded the horses.
       c. *It dusted the horses blind.   (Hale and Keyser 1997: 31)

However, it is possible to state the same generalization about incorporation in semantic terms, namely that only patient, instrument, or location arguments can be named by the verb (Mithun 1984). Or alternatively that only roles that are prototypically filled by inanimates can be named by the verb (Evans 1997).

Before trying to choose between one of these formulations, and before attempting to seek a deeper explanation for the facts, it is worth asking, are these roughly equivalent generalizations about denominal verbs accurate, for example, in English? In fact, it is not at all clear that they are. Consider the following expressions:

(6)   a. The cook made dinner.
      b. He cooked dinner.

(7)   a. The staff worked the table.
      b. They staffed the table.

(8)   a. The judge reviewed the case.
      b. He judged the case.

Admittedly, the interpretation of noun and verb in these cases is not identical. However, we have already seen that this is also the case with verbs that name non-agentive arguments (or non-external arguments) such as *shelf* and *to shelve* as well. While the noun has a referential meaning, the verb in all cases refers to a type of event and does not pick out an individual. Just as one can cook a meal without being a cook and one can judge a case without being a judge, one can shelve a book on something other than a shelf. The relationship between *cook/cook* and *staff/staff* is arguably just as close as that between *shelf/shelve*. Thus the generalization that all deverbal nouns correspond to non-external arguments in the corresponding paraphrases is cast into doubt.

Returning to Hale and Keyser's original motivation again, we might ask, why *is* there no verb *cow* to mean, to reproduce as a cow does (recall (4c))? Again, before we assume that there is a general deep explanation for this fact, we should note that there is also no verb corresponding to "calf" for many other animals:

(9)   a. A cow had a calf. A cow calved. (cf. (4a,b))
      b. A woman had a baby. *A woman babied.
      c. A kangaroo had a joey. *A kangaroo joeyed.
      d. A chicken laid an egg. *A chicken egged.

That is, some denominal verbs are far more conventional than others. This fact alone should make one wary of a general syntactic account, which would predict full productivity.

To summarize, the problems for this account run deep. The proposal does not account for the meaning of denominal verbs (the "adverbial component"), offers an ad hoc stipulation to account for the fact that overt arguments may appear in places that should be occupied by a trace, and is, in the first place, based on questionable empirical generalizations.

This analysis would not have gotten off the ground if the second foundational tenet of constructionist approaches had been adhered to. In particular, since constructionist approaches emphasize speaker construals of situations, the difference in meaning between denominal verbs and their corresponding nouns could not be ignored.

Borer (2001)

Borer, working in what she terms a "neo-constructionist" paradigm, also proposes to assign meaning directly to skeletal syntactic forms. Adopting a derivational, autonomous view of syntax nominally couched within the Minimalist framework, she suggests that grammatical category information and the interpretation of arguments is derived entirely from syntactic structure. That is, she claims that open-class words (at least what are normally thought of as nouns and verbs)[2] are stored in an "encyclopedia" and do not contain any reference to grammatical categories or argument structure. These open-class words are referred to as "encyclopedic items" (EIs).

Let us consider how category information and argument structure properties in turn are to be determined. Grammatical categories are thought to arise from allowing EIs to "merge" with grammatical features. For example, when a sound–meaning pairing such as *dog* combines with a feature such as past tense <pst> it becomes the verb, *dogged*. Another such example offered is the pair *sink/sink*; if the single EI *sink* combines with a noun phrase ("DP"), it appears as a noun; if the same word combines with a verbal feature, it appears as a verb (Borer 2001).

This account falls prey to the same major problem that the Hale and Keyser account does: it does not account for lexical meaning. The noun *dog* and the verb *dog* do not mean the same thing; neither do the noun *sink* and the verb *sink*. In fact, in these particular cases, the differences in meaning are rather striking. To dog someone means to follow them in an annoying manner or to an excessive degree; it is related to the noun *dog* insofar as dogs are prone to

---

[2] Adjectives, according to Borer, are not category-less EIs, because any conversion between A and N or V requires overt morphology (2001: 6, n. 6). Of course there also exists verbalizing and nominalizing morphology in English and in other languages as well; why this should not deter one from positing category-less EIs for what most would consider Ns and Vs is not explained.

dog their owners, but it has a meaning all its own. Likewise the meaning of the verb *sink* is only remotely, if at all, related to the meaning of the noun *sink*. The former refers to the event of becoming submerged in water whereas the latter refers to a concave fixture devised for washing hands and dishes that is found in kitchens and bathrooms. Since on the account there is only a category-neutral meaning of each word stored in the encyclopedia, where do these distinctions in meaning between noun and verb come from? This question goes unaddressed.

Borer adopts a version of the traditional idea that the lexicon is the realm of the idiosyncratic while the syntax is a fully productive, regular, computational system (Wasow 1977). Argument structure is viewed as entirely general and close to fully productive (pp. 2–3), and thus is entirely within the domain of syntax. However this vastly underappreciates the amount of lexical idiosyncrasy that exists (see Chapter 3). Since, according to the account, words are assumed to be listed with only their encyclopedic meanings and nothing else, they cannot specify a number or type of obligatory arguments. Thus the account appears unable to account for well-known differences among *dine, eat, devour*. *Dine* is intransitive, *eat* may be transitive or intransitive, and *devour* is obligatorily transitive.

It is standardly assumed that agent arguments are expressed as subjects or "external arguments." Borer proposes instead the converse generalization: that all external arguments must be interpreted as agents (p. 2). While the traditional generalization is quite robust, at least in syntactically accusative languages, and excepting passives and middles for principled reasons, the proposed generalization is faced with a multitude of counterexamples. To mention just a few, none of the following transitive expressions involve agent subjects:

(10) a. The coma victim underwent the operation.
      b. She received a package.
      c. Water filled the tub.
      d. Heights frightened the child.
      e. The book cost a fortune.
      f. The brick weighed a ton.

It must be recognized that meaning cannot simply be *read off* syntactic trees (Goldberg and Jackendoff 2004; Sorace 2000). Verbs and arguments make very real contributions to the most basic of semantic interpretations, such as whether an agent is involved. Borer's proposal greatly reduces the role of the lexicon, rather than greatly expanding it as constructionist approaches discussed in the rest of this book do.

Distributed Morphology (Marantz 1997)

A closely related proposal, identified as "Distributed Morphology" (DM), is also motivated by the existence of productive, compositional processes of word formation. DM proposes that all words are formed syntactically, by combining roots with affixes (Marantz 1997). Roots are to be listed in an "Encyclopedia," which is presumed for the most part to involve real world meaning and not linguistic knowledge. The same root is assumed to be represented by √WALK when it appears as a noun and as a verb; that is, category information is not associated directly with roots. Instead, whether a root appears as an N or V is determined by its surrounding syntactic environment.

As already discussed with respect to *dog* and *sink* (and *shelf* and *shelve*), many words sharing a root differ semantically in various ways. To take one more example, the verb, *bake*, can be used to refer to the activity of cooking various things including potatoes as well as desert items. Yet the noun, *bakery*, refers to an establishment where baked goods are sold—one does not expect to be able to purchase potatoes.

Unlike the accounts discussed above in this chapter, DM attempts to account for this type of idiosyncrasy or non-compositionality. The theory allows roots to make reference to a meaning associated with a certain syntactic configuration within the Encyclopedia. This solution constitutes a necessary retreat from the idea that the Encyclopedia contains only world knowledge and not linguistic knowledge; it effectively makes the Encyclopedia more like the traditional, familiar lexicon, at least for roots that have meanings that are not totally compositional.

Yet the proposal makes a clear prediction: a *second* affix must be compositionally related to the corresponding word with a single (innermost) affix. That is, there shouldn't exist words in which the second affix adds any idiosyncratic meaning. This is because there would be nowhere at all to put the idiosyncratic meaning that comes with a second affix (Marantz, personal communication, Jan. 11th, 2003).

Admittedly, such words are relatively rare. However, their rarity is likely a result of their relative infrequency, since words need to be used with some regularity in order to acquire or retain non-compositional meanings. Still, it is possible to find exceptions to the generalization, exceptions that call into question the overall architecture of the theory. For example the word *derivational* would presumably be formed by combining √DERIVE with TION and then with AL. Any possible non-compositionality relating to *derivation* could be noted in the Encyclopedia in a pointer from the root to the affix. But a non-compositional relationship between *derivation* and *derivational* is predicted to be impossible. And yet it is clear that *derivational* as used in *derivational morpheme* has for many, a non-compositional meaning. One need not ascribe to derivational theories of morphology or even know about them to have learned the distinction between "derivational" and "inflectional" morphology: the former being meaning changing, possibly idiosyncratic, closer to the root, etc. Other exceptions include *impressionable* (IMPRESS + ION + ABLE) which is non-compositional in two ways. First *able* is normally attached to verbs, not nouns, and secondly because it means "naive" and not simply "able to be make an impression." *Actionable* (ACT + ION + ABLE) does not mean simply "able to do an action on" but instead means something like "giving just cause for legal action."

To summarize, and oversimplify only slightly, the problem with all the approaches outlined in Section 10.1 is that they have effectively legislated the idiosyncratic out of existence.

On the present proposal, each distinct verb sense lexically specifies the number and semantic type of arguments it has, and which of those arguments are obligatory ("profiled"), along with its rich frame semantic meaning. Each argument structure construction specifies its formal properties, its semantic and information-structure properties, and how it is to combine with verbs and arguments. For example, constructions specify whether the verb can stand in a manner relation with the constructionist meaning or whether it may only stand in a means relation (Goldberg 1997). Constructions also specify which if any arguments they contribute. Usage-based constructionist approaches recognize a cline of productivity and regularity (see Chapters 3 and 5). According to constructionist approaches, the role of the lexicon is greatly expanded to include phrasal patterns with their own idiosyncratic syntactic or semantic properties. It is the interaction of the argument structure of verb and construction that gives rise to interpretation.

10.2 A comparison of more closely related constructionist approaches

The following approaches differ sharply from the Syntactic Argument Structure approaches just discussed, and instead are much more closely aligned with the constructionist approach outlined in brief in Chapter 1:

1. **UCxG:** Unification Construction Grammar (Fillmore 1999; Fillmore, Kay, and O'Connor 1988; Fillmore et al. forthcoming; Kay 2002a,b; Kay and Fillmore 1999)

2. **CG:** Cognitive Grammar (e.g. Langacker, 1987a, 1987b, 1988, 1990, 1991, 1992, 2003)
3. **RCxG:** Radical Construction Grammar (Croft 2001)
4. **CCxG:** Cognitive Construction Grammar (e.g. Lakoff 1987; Goldberg 1995; Bencini and Goldberg 2000)

Various researchers have carved out their own theoretical versions of a constructionist approach, that share much in common with these four approaches (Boas 2000; Booij 2002c; Ginzburg and Sag 2000; Gleitman et al. 1996; Iwata 2000; Jackendoff 2002; Lamb 2002; Lambrecht 1994; Michaelis 2004; Michaelis and Lambrecht 1996ab; Nakamura 1997; Riehemann 1997; Sailer 2002; Schmid 2001; Van Valin 1998; Webelhuth and Ackerman 1998; Wierzbicka 1988; Zadroxny and Ramer 1995; Zwicky 1994). The approach proposed in Goldberg (1995) and further developed in the present book will be referred to in this section as COGNITIVE CONSTRUCTION GRAMMAR to distinguish it from other constructionist proposals (cf. also Lakoff 1987). Construction Grammar as developed by Paul Kay, Charles Fillmore, Ivan Sag, and Laura Michaelis will be referred to here as UNIFICATION CONSTRUCTION GRAMMAR (Fillmore et al. forthcoming). It was Fillmore and Kay who first coined the term, "Construction Grammar." Their early work on idioms and idiomatic phrasal patterns such as *let alone, even,* and *What's X doing Y?* laid the foundation for many of the variations of Construction Grammar that have since developed.

Yet, Unification Construction Grammar (UCxG) has developed quite distinctly from other construction grammars, including the present Cognitive Construction Grammar (CCxG), Cognitive Grammar (CG), and Radical Construction Grammar (RCxG) (e.g. Langacker 1987ab, 1991; Lakoff 1987; Goldberg 1995; Croft 2001; Lamb 2002). Several key differences include whether aspects of the grammar are redundantly specified in various constructions, whether the model is more generally usage-based or not, whether motivation is sought for the relationship between form and function, and whether or not unification is adopted as the formal means for representing constructions. The positions that UCxG takes on these issues are represented in Table 10.1. Each difference is explained below.

10.3 Usage-Based or Maximal Generalization Only

UCxG, in line with most generative frameworks, aims to account for generalizations in language without redundancy. Patterns or expressions that are predictable from other generalizations are assumed not to be part of a

TABLE 10.1. Similarities and differences between Cognitive Grammar, Cognitive Construction Grammar, and Radical Construction Grammar on the one hand, and Unification Construction Grammar on the other

	CG, CCxG, RCxG	UCxG
Constructions	Learned pairings of form and function	Learned pairings of form and function
Role of constructions	Central	Central
Non-derivational	Yes	Yes
Inheritance	Default	Default (previously monotonic)
Usage-based	Yes	Not uniformly
Formalism	Notation developed for ease of exposition only	Heavy focus on unification-based formalism
Role of "motivation"	Central	None
Emphasis on	Psychological plausibility	Formal explicitness; maximal generalization

speaker's knowledge of language. The frequencies of particular grammatical patterns are also not explicitly represented within UCxG. Instead a strict division between grammar and the use of the grammar is made.[3]

On the other hand, **CG, CCxG, and RCxG are all usage-based frameworks.** The aim of these frameworks is to represent grammatical knowledge in such a way that it can interface transparently with theories of processing, acquisition, and historical change. This desideratum has led to the recognition that even fully regular patterns may be stored if such patterns occur with sufficient frequency. The merits of a usage-based account are the topic of Chapter 3.

10.4 Formalism: Unification or Diagramatic or Other

Although generative linguistic theories are often referred to as "formal theories," few of them actually employ any systematic formalization. As Geoff Pullum once put it in one of his memorable Topic/Comment columns, "The extent to which most of today's 'generative grammar' enthusiasts have abandoned any aspiration to a formal orientation...can only be described as utter" (Pullum 1991: 49).

Exceptions to the dearth of formalization in linguistic theory typically involve those theories that have close ties to computational linguistics (e.g.

---

[3] Although this is true of the collaborative work of Fillmore et al. (forthcoming), it is not true of independent work by, e.g., Michaelis (Brenier and Michaelis 2005; Francis, Gregory, and Michaelis 1999; Gregory and Michaelis 2004; Michaelis 1994, 2001; Michaelis and Lambrecht 1996b).

TAG grammar: Joshi, Levy, and Takahashi 1975). HPSG, with its strong computational component, is one of the leaders in linguistic formal architecture, using a unification-based formalism (Pollard and Sag 1987, 1994). With its close ties to HPSG, and to the FrameNet project of Fillmore, Unification Construction Grammar also adopts a unification-based formalism, as the label used here suggests.[4]

Unification is a feature-based system in which each construction is represented by an Attribute-Value Matrix (AVM). Each attribute can have at most one value. Attributes may be n-ary, or may be feature structures themselves. Any pair of AVMs can be combined to license a particular expression, just in case there is no value conflict on any attribute. When two AVMs unify, they map onto a new AVM, which has the union of attributes and values of the two original AVMs. As Zaenen and Uszkoreit (1996: 3.3) note, the strength of unification grammar formalisms stems from the ease with which they lend themselves to engineering applications. Another reason for formalization is simply for the sake of clarity and explicitness.

At the same time that it offers an explicit representational system, there are arguably certain drawbacks to using the unification-based approach. One drawback is that unification-based approaches are not sufficiently amenable to capturing detailed lexical semantic properties. As many have observed, real meaning is not easily captured by a fixed set of features (Bolinger 1965; Fodor and Lepore 1999). Fillmore himself (1975) has been a leading critic of feature-based systems for representing semantics, arguing that we need instead to recognize *frame*-based or encyclopedic knowledge. In practice, Unification Construction Grammar uses constants (e.g. A, B, C) that are intended to represent rich frame semantic meaning, which allows one to avoid decomposing meaning into a fixed set of features. Arguably, however, the formalism serves to overemphasize syntactic elements insofar as it is primarily these features that recur, and it is the recurrent features that are most relevant to the unification mechanism.

Use of a fixed set of features or tools for even formal aspects of constructions is at odds with Croft's (2001) position that grammatical categories and roles are not general across constructions but are only defined with respect to particular constructions (see also Foley and Van Valin 1984).

Thus as a matter of practicality, if one wishes to concentrate on subtle differences in meaning between different constructions, or on subtle differ-

---

[4] In the heyday of GB Theory, Annie Zaenen wryly dubbed rival unification-based theories springing up at Stanford and Berkeley "BG Grammars" for Bay area Grammars. These include LFG, HPSG, and Unification Construction Grammar.

ences in syntactic patterning across different constructions, it is not clear that a feature-based system such as unification is the best method.

Beyond the issue of the extent to which construction-specific syntax and semantics can be naturally represented using unification is a different kind of practical issue. To linguists unfamiliar with the formalism, unification can appear dauntingly opaque and cumbersome. Each complex category must be defined in terms of features and each feature must be defined using prose. To the extent that the features and categories of languages are numerous—and constructionist approaches generally argue that they are—the formalism quickly becomes unwieldy. For these reasons, the present framework does not adopt the unification formalism.

10.5 To Motivate or to Stipulate

[T]he issue is not whether grammars have functional motivation, but where and how much, and the centrality of focusing on this motivation in one's research program. (Newmeyer 2003: 687)

Cognitive Construction Grammar seeks to provide *motivation* for each construction that is posited.[5] Motivation aims to explain why it is at least possible and at best natural that this particular form–meaning correspondence should exist in a given language.[6] Motivation is distinct from prediction: recognizing the motivation for a construction does not entail that the construction *must* exist in that language or in any language. It simply explains why the construction "makes sense" or is natural (cf. Haiman 1985; Lakoff 1987; Goldberg 1995). Functional and historical generalizations count as explanations, but they are not predictive in the strict sense, just as parallel generalizations in biology are not predictive. That is, language, like biological evolution, is contingent, not deterministic. Just as is the case with species, particular constructions are the way they are not because they *have* to be that way, but because their phylogenetic and ontogenetic evolution was motivated by general forces.

Non-linguistic examples of general functional and general historical explanations are given below:

---

[5] One systematic exception is that the particular phonological forms that a language chooses to convey particular concepts need not be motivated but generally are truly arbitrary (Saussure 1916), except in relative rare cases of phonaesthemes (Bergen 2004).

[6] An account that *fully* motivates a given construction is ultimately responsible for demonstrating how the construction came to exist and how it can be learned by new generations of speakers.

General-Functional explanation

Q: Why do lizards change colors?
A: Many animals display camouflage—it protects them from prey.

General-Historical explanation

Q: Why does the male peacock have such a huge beautiful tail?
A: It provides an advantage in sexual selection since males with impressive apparatus are more likely to get mates and thus are more likely to produce offspring.

Cognitive Construction Grammar attempts to motivate each construction in an effort to constrain the theory and make it explanatorily adequate (Lakoff 1987). Goldberg (1995) suggests the following Principle of Maximized Motivation:

The Principle of Maximized Motivation: if construction A is related to construction B formally, then construction A is motivated to the degree that it is related to construction B semantically (cf. also Haiman 1985; Lakoff 1987). Such motivation is maximized.

Consider a few concrete examples. All English words that refer to lower-trunk-wear are grammatically plural, e.g. *pants, shorts, knickers, kulots, leggings, stockings, trousers, khakis* (Williams 1994). As Langacker (1987a) points out, this type of grammatical plurality is motivated by the fact that the referents involved all have bipartite structure. Lower-trunk-wear all have two parts, one for each leg. Notice *skirt* and *wrap* are non-bipartite and as expected are also not grammatically plural.

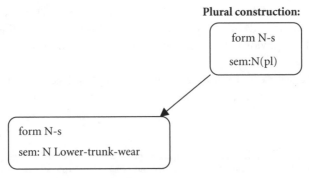

FIGURE 10.1 The lower-trunk-wear construction as a motivated extension of the plural construction

The general, productive plural construction and the lower-trunk-wear plural construction share the same form and have related meaning. Because the formal similarity indicates a semantic relationship, the lower-trunk-wear construction is motivated.

Number terms are likewise motivated (Saussure 1916). For example, "Thirty-one" is generated by the "thirty-n" construction. The "thirty-n" construction is strongly motivated by both the "thirty" construction and the "Twenty-n" (also "Forty-n", "Fifty-n"—not drawn) constructions, since the similarity in form indicates a similarity in meaning and the difference in form indicates the relevant numerical difference. The relationships are diagramed in Fig. 10.2.[7]

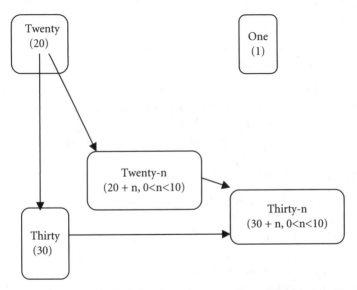

FIGURE 10.2 A subset of the English numeral system as a motivated network

Unification Construction Grammar, on the other hand, eschews "motivation" as failing to make any testable predictions. However, this is a misinterpretation. While motivation is distinct from prediction insofar as a motivated construction *could have been otherwise*, it typically could not have had the opposite values of the properties claimed to provide motivation. For example,

---

[7] Anecdotal evidence that speakers are aware of these motivations come from an innovation made by Aliza (6;11): "What's 80 + 20?" (100), "Nope! Tendy!" Also, it seems that the number *fifteen* is occasionally omitted by children when they learn to count (in the case of my own son and one other unrelated child); this may stem from the fact that *fifteen* is less clearly motivated than the other teens. surrounding it, which retain the unit without phonetic alternation (*four-teen; six-teen; seven-teen;* etc.).

while it is quite possible that terms referring to lower-trunk-wear would be grammatically singular, it is predicted to be *im*possible that, for example, only clothing articles without bipartite structure would be labeled with grammatically plural terms, while clothing articles that had bipartite structure were grammatically singular. Moreover positing the link predicts, not that *every* language has the same construction, but that *some* other language also marks entities with bipartite structure as grammatically plural.

The final difference between UCxG and CCxG is one of emphasis. Both approaches intend the grammars proposed to be psychologically valid, and both strive to be explicit and to capture relevant generalizations. Still, arguably CCxG ranks the desideratum of psychological validity higher than the goal of being explicit or maximally general, whereas UCxG generally has the opposite priorities.

10.6 Cognitive Grammar

In a recent paper, Langacker, the major architect of Cognitive Grammar, compares and contrasts Cognitive Grammar with both CCxG and RCxG (Langacker 2003). His points are discussed in this section. The influence of Cognitive Grammar upon Cognitive Construction Grammar is hard to overestimate. Langacker (2003) provides a long list of tenets that CxG, RCxG, and CG all agree upon:

(11)   a. Constructions (rather than "rules") are the primary objects of description.
   b. The frameworks are non-derivational.
   c. Lexicon and grammar are not distinct components, but form a continuum of constructions.
   d. Constructions are form–meaning pairings.
   e. Information structure is recognized as one facet of constructionist meanings.
   f. Constructions are linked in networks of inheritance ("categorization").
   g. Regularities (rules, patterns) take the form of constructions that are schematic relative to instantiating expressions.
   h. Apart from degree of specificity/schematicity, expressions and the patterns they instantiate have the same basic character.
   i. Linguistic knowledge comprises vast numbers of constructions, a large proportion of which are "idiosyncratic" in relation to "normal," productive grammatical patterns.

j. A framework that accomodates "idiosyncratic" constructions will easily accommodate "regular" patterns as a special case (but not conversely).

k. Well-formedness is a matter of simultaneous constraint satisfaction.

l. Composition is effected by "unification" ("integration").

At the same time Langacker takes issue with a few aspects of Cognitive Construction Grammar (CCxG) and Radical Construction Grammar (RCxG), including the following:

1. The alleged adoption by CCxG of autonomous syntax;
2. The fact that RCxG and CCxG are non-reductionist and do not adopt Cognitive Grammar's essentialist definitions of grammatical categories and functions;
3. The too-restrictive definition of construction in Goldberg (1995);
4. The fact that Goldberg (1995) allows the construction itself to be the profile determinant of the clause instead of universally requiring the verb to be the profile determinant.

The first critique is based on a misconception. References to "Subj," "Obj," "N," and "V" in CCxG (e.g. Goldberg 1995) are not an endorsement of strongly autonomous syntax, whereby these labels refer to irreducible grammatical primitives without corresponding meanings or functions. Rather, the labels simply capture a relevant level of description: they are used to capture the form of particular constructions using easily recognizable terms. I essentially endorse Croft's (2001) position that these labels are metageneralizations over construction-specific categories (cf. also Morris and Cottrell 1999). The appeal to grammatical categories and relations in defining the constructions readily allows for functional characterizations of the grammatical relations themselves (Goldberg 1995: 48–9). Therefore the use of grammatical category and relation labels should be understood to appeal to a relevant level of description, not to atomic, purely syntactic, universal categories.

The misinterpretation arises because Langacker seems to make the assumption that if "subject" and "object" or "noun" and "verb" are referred to in grammatical descriptions, then they must refer to fundamental, atomic syntactic features. This raises a fundamental difference between CxG (both Radical and Cognitive) and CG. Cognitive Grammar is explicitly reductionist. As Langacker puts it, "Grammar exists and has to be described as such. Like water (a particular configuration of hydrogen and oxygen atoms), it is however reducible to something more fundamental (configurations of semantic structures, phonological structures, and symbolic links)" (Langacker 2003: 8).

CCxG and RCxG, on the other hand, are both non-reductionist approaches. In some sense, water *is* clearly reducable to hydrogen and oxygen; however, no reductionist account of water is going to explain why water is wet, nor why it is used the way it is: to bathe in, to drink, etc. If our question is one about reservoirs, a discussion of hydrogen and oxygen will not be helpful. Reductionism assumes that the finest-grained level of analysis is somehow privileged. Yet even the existence of predictive reductionist analyses are often questionable, even within the "hard" sciences such as physics (Anderson 1972; Laughlin 2005; Laughlin and Pines 2000).

In accord with the non-reductionist nature of CCxG and RCxG, both approaches emphasize that there are often interactions between parts that lead to emergent properties that can only be described at the level of the whole. Moreover, the pieces of many constructions are unique to those constructions and thus can only be described with reference to those constructions.

Goldberg (1995) emphasized construction-specific properties of semantic roles, whereas Croft (2001) emphasizes construction-specific properties of grammatical categories and relations. For example, Goldberg (1995) notes that the "recipient" argument and corresponding complement is unique to the ditransitive: the argument has some properties of typical direct objects but not all (e.g. it only rarely can control depictive predicates), and it is the only construction in which an argument with "recipient" semantics is expressed by a postverbal NP. Likewise *participant roles* are defined as roles that are specific to particular verbs such as *kicker* and *kickee*. They only make sense relative to a particular semantic frame named by the verb.

Croft emphasizes the frequently construction-specific properties of linguistic entities that are often assumed to be purely syntactic: "Syntactic roles must be defined construction-specifically, and the patterns of distribution that they define are varied both within and across languages. Terms such as "subject" and "object" do not define some fixed category or syntactic structure ... Both syntactic and semantic characterizations are heterogeneous, varying within and across languages" (Croft 2001: 170; Barðdal forthcoming; Dryer 1997).[8]

In contrast, Langacker's definitions of Subject as primary focal point, Object as secondary focal point, N as "thing," and V as "relation" are claimed

---

[8] Langacker appears sympathetic with this view when he notes "[a given construction] might occur in a variety of structural frames, each reinforcing its cognitive status, *so that* its categorization is to some degree autonomous, i.e., independent of any particular structural context...It is *only* by occurrence in a variety of frames, whose differing specific features cancel out, that any notion of a context-independent lexeme can ever arise" (2003: 27, emphasis added). Yet in an apparent turn around, he asks rhetorically, "Does it matter that the augmented unit is confined to a particular symbolic assembly, where it occurs in combination with a certain constructional schema? No it does not" (2003: 27).

to provide necessary (and implicitly, sufficient) conditions for the relevant categories. Langacker puts it this way: "a particular, schematic conceptual factor is part of every such extension [to each grammatical category], constituting an invariant conceptual characterization of each category" (Langacker 2003: 29).[9] He suggests that these essentialist definitions are defined simply at a more abstract level than the prototype definitions.

Neither CCxG nor RCxG have adopted these essentialist definitions. They may be correct, but independent evidence for them (in the form of reliable speaker intuitions or psycholinguistic experimentation) is so far lacking. Critically, as Croft (2001) notes, there is no consistent cross-linguistic distributional pattern that can be used to provide independent evidence for a shared conceptual representation.

There is additional reason to be skeptical of an essentialist definition of grammatical entities: essentialist definitions for *non*-linguistic categories are the exception not the norm, particularly for inductive, empirical generalizations. To the extent that we wish to say that linguistic categories are like other categories, we would *not expect* them to be definable by necessary and sufficient conditions (recall the discussion in Chapter 8). Murphy, a leading expert on general categorization, acknowledges the intuitive appeal and lasting influence of the essentialist or "classical" view of categories:

Why are writers so interested in saving [the classical view]? To some degree, I believe that it is for historical reasons. After all, this is a view that has a long history in psychology, and in fact has been part of Western thinking since Aristotle. (Aristotle!) If this were a theory that you or I had made up, it would not have continued to receive this attention after the first 10 or 20 experiments showing it was wrong..... Another reason is that there is a beauty and simplicity in the classical view that succeeding theories do not have. It is consistent with the law of excluded middle and other traditional rules of logic beloved of philosophers ... Unfortunately, the world appears to be a sloppy place.... [W]e must conclude that this theory is not a contender. (Murphy 2002: 39–40)

At the same time, the non-essentialist view does not entail that there are no linguistic generalizations: there necessarily are. The system accrues less cost to the extent that the formal trappings of particular constructions are shared. Formal patterns (morphology, word order) are extended and reused for

---

[9] Although Langacker appears to suggest that CxG accepts autonomous syntax, he notes that "While practitioners of the two frameworks would not deny that these grammatical constructs tend to correlate with certain meanings or functions, there is no definite claim that such constructs are fully definable conceptually, nor even any inclination to consider this a possibility worth exploring". (2003: 9). This quote suggests that the only non-autonomous syntax recognized is one in which all grammatical categories and relations are understood to have essentialist definitions.

related but distinct functions. That is, languages do not indicate each and every possible semantic difference with a unique form.

There are also cross-linguistic generalizations. For example, most if not all languages appear to make a grammatical category distinction with Things on one side and Relations on another, differentiating the "what" from the "where" (Chang 2002; Kaas and Hackett 1999). Arguably recurrent archetypes across languages are based on universal functional pressures (Croft 2001; cf. also the discussion of conceptual archetypes in Langacker 1991: 295). Examples of certain cross-linguistic tendencies and their likely cognitive motivations were discussed in Chapter 9.

Langacker takes issue with the idea that Goldberg (1995: 4), following Fillmore, Kay, and O'Connor (1988), defines a construction to be any not strictly predictable pairing of form and function, instead of any learned pairing of form and function that is mentally represented, whether or not it is compositionally derivable from other constructions. In earlier work, I had adopted the not strictly predictable formulation because it was conservative methodologically—we know we must mentally represent a construction if there is anything not strictly predictable about it. The same work was implicitly usage-based insofar as knowledge of the way particular verbs were used in particular constructions was required to account for partial productivity (1995: ch. 5). The present proposal is more explicitly and uniformly usage-based (cf. Chapter 3), in line with CG and RCxG.

Another point to be considered is whether there is reason to believe that the verb is always the semantic head of the clause, determining, in effect, who did what to whom. Goldberg (1995) offers several arguments against this assumption, including that it entails the existence of ad hoc, implausible verb senses. At the same time, I readily agree that it is part of our knowledge of English, for example, that we know that *bake* appears in the ditransitive construction (cf. discussion in Goldberg 1995: ch. 5; present volume, Chapter 3). However, knowing that two elements co-occur is not the same thing as knowing that the two things mean the same thing. For example, we may know that the verb *want* regularly appears with *something to eat*, but we don't assign the meaning of *something to eat* to *want*. We parcel out the responsibility for meaning among the various elements in a sentence. (This is not to say that there is never redundancy in language, but only that it is not rampant.) Thus given the prototypical meaning of *bake*, and the prototypical meaning expressed by the ditransitive, it is more natural to assume that the learner parcels out the meaning such that the construction in this case, not the verb, determines who did what to whom— that is, the construction is the semantic head. This allows us to avoid the idea that learners have a representation of the word *bake* that means "someone intends to give someone something that they bake."

One additional difference between CG on the one hand, and CCxG and RCxG on the other, is that the former does not emphasize the role of language-internal contrast in fixing the meaning or function of a construction; instead, the function is believed to inhere in the form. Cross-linguistic differences in the conventional expression of bodily sensations, for example, are assumed to reflect Whorfian differences in construal, albeit relatively inconsequential differences. CCxG, on the other hand, embraces the structuralist notion that each construction is understood as one potential option among others. The meaning assigned to one construction on this view is not necessarily an inherent aspect of the form the construction takes, but may be in part a pragmatic inference made upon the rejection of other alternatives (Levinson 1983).

Thus CG and CCxG share a great deal, although there are a few fairly important distinctions which distinguish the two approaches.

10.7 Construction Grammar and Radical Construction Grammar (Croft 2001)

Radical Construction Grammar extends work in Construction Grammar by investigating in detail the cross-linguistic divergences among what many assume are atomic, universal syntactic categories and relations. Noting, for example, that words that translate into English as nouns, adjectives, and adverbs, as well as verbs are inflected for person, aspect, and mood in Makah, a native American language, and that no words are inflected for these categories in Vietnamese, Croft points out that tense-mood-aspect inflection cannot be taken as criterial for determining the category of V cross-linguistically (unless of course one is willing to say that all words are verbs in Makah and no words are verbs in Vietnamese). Croft goes on to point out that no syntactic test will pick out all and only entities that one might wish to call verbs, nouns, adjectives, subjects, objects, and so on across all languages. Moreover, Croft observes, that even within a single language, a given criterion often only applies to certain constructions. For example,

If one takes passivizability as the criterion for Direct Object in English, then one's conclusions will tell us something about the Passive, not about some allegedly global category Direct Object. CONSTRUCTIONS, NOT CATEGORIES OR RELATIONS, ARE THE BASIC, PRIMITIVE UNITS OF SYNTACTIC REPRESENTATION ... THIS IS RADICAL CONSTRUCTION GRAMMAR. (Croft 2001: 46, emphasis in the original)

At the same time, Croft does not deny that there are generalizations within or across languages. But the generalizations that exist are determined by the functional purpose that each language's constructions serve.

The present approach is in agreement with Croft's point. Variation within and across languages is embraced on the current Cognitive Construction Grammar approach. Yet at the same time, we retain the more traditional emphasis on trying to capture and motivate generalizations, imperfect though we recognize them to be. This is in fact the main theme of the present work.

11

Conclusion

Speakers' knowledge of language consists of systematic collections of form–function pairings that are learned on the basis of the language they hear around them. This simple idea forms the heart of the constructionist approach discussed in this book. Two major questions are addressed:

1. How do learners acquire generalizations such that they can produce an open-ended number of novel utterances based on a finite amount of input?
2. Why are languages the way they are?

A usage-based model of grammar is required to account for speakers' full knowledge of language (see Chapter 3 for an overview), including both instances (represented at a level of abstraction due to selective encoding) and generalizations. The usage-based model of grammar is supported not only by linguistic facts, but also by what we know about how non-linguistic categories are represented; they, too, involve both knowledge of instances and generalizations over instances. Far from being an arbitrary collection of stipulated descriptions, our knowledge of linguistic constructions, like our knowledge generally, forms an integrated and motivated network.

Children bring to the task of language learning a host of pragmatic and cognitive abilities which they employ to great effect. These include the ability to make statistical generalizations, and the ability to use semantics and pragmatics to help guide interpretation and generalization (see also Tomasello 1999, 2003). Children are experts at observing statistical correlations and making predictions on the basis of them, and they are also experts at interpreting others' intentions. Constructions can be learned, and learned quickly, on the basis of the input (Chapter 4). The experiments summarized here are the first to train subjects on pairings of novel forms and novel meanings, while testing learners' ability to generalize beyond the input. Skewed input that provides an anchor point facilitates generalizations; and just such skewed input is common in the input children receive. Clearly work in this area has just begun. For example, it remains to be seen how much input is required before learners are willing to use a new construction productively, and how learners are able to integrate their newly acquired knowledge of a construction with their prior knowledge of other constructions.

Mainstream generative grammar has emphasized the fact that children do not reliably receive explicit feedback about their utterances; it has therefore appeared to be quite mysterious how children are able to avoid or recover from overgeneralizations. However, children do receive indirect negative evidence in the form of statistical preemption. Their generalizations are also constrained by general principles of induction that depend on the range of examples witnessed (see discussion in Chapter 5).

The question of *why* constructional generalizations are learned is not a question that has commonly even been formulated. But if we do away with the notion of "universal grammar"—innate syntactic knowledge that simply kicks in upon hearing fixed-in-advance triggers in the environment—the question clearly arises. The answer, or at least a substantial part of the answer, derives from the fact that constructions are highly valuable both in predicting meaning, given the form, and in predicting form, given the message to be conveyed. These two tasks form the *raison d' être* for linguistic communication: to understand and produce utterances. Constructions are also primed in production, simplifying the task of using a language (Chapter 6).

The variety of constructions within a given language exists to enable speakers to package information in useful ways. Ignoring the information-structure properties of constructions is like trying to account for evolution without reference to natural selection. Information structure is responsible, at least in part, for many important syntactic phenomena such as constraints on long-distance dependencies (i.e. "island" constraints). That is, Island constraints strongly correlate with the information-structure properties of the constructions involved. In particular, (sub)constructions that are neither the primary topic nor within the focus domain are not eligible for long-distance dependencies. These correlations, while imperfect, are at least as strong as the purely syntactic generalizations that have been widely taken for granted (see Chapter 7).

Constructionist approaches emphasize the individual functions that constructions serve. While purely formal generalizations may exist, they are much less common than is often assumed. Subject–auxiliary inversion had been argued to be a prime example of a purely syntactic generalization, but in fact, a purely syntactic account has no predictive power beyond stipulating the mere fact that subject–auxiliary inversion exists in English. An account of the distributional properties of subject–auxiliary inversion requires recourse to the particular functions of the constructions involved. The form of the inversion in addition is motivated by its function (Chapter 8).

Embracing a constructionist approach to language does not, of course, relieve us of the burden of explaining cross-linguistic generalizations (Chapter 9; see also Croft 2001). Quite the contrary, it encourages explanations that go beyond a restatement of the facts. General pragmatic, processing, historical, iconic, and analogical facts, ultimately buttressed by experimental data, shed light on issues related to why languages are the way they are. There has been precious little work explicitly relating well-known findings in cognitive psychology to phenomena in language, and the discussion here also only scratches the surface. But explanations that appeal to facts that are independently motivated beyond language are more satisfying than appeals to mysterious, hard-wired linguistic knowledge.

What have we learned about the nature of generalization in language? Generalizations are best described by analyzing surface structure instead of positing an underlying level of representation (Chapter 2). The generalizations of language, like generalizations in other cognitive domains, are formed on the basis of instance-based knowledge that is retained (Chapter 3). Children are able to learn certain kinds of generalization quite quickly, with skewed input like that commonly found in natural language playing a facilitory role (Chapter 4). Generalizations can be constrained by the indirect negative evidence children receive involving statistical preemption of non-occuring patterns (Chapter 5). Generalizations at the level of argument structure are made because they are useful, both in predicting meaning and in online production (Chapter 6). Classic island and scope phenomena can be accounted for by recognizing the discourse function of the constructions involved (Chapter 7). Generalizations that appear to be purely syntactic are at least sometimes better analyzed in terms of constructions insofar as a pattern's distribution is typically conditioned by its functional role (Chapter 8). Cross-linguistic generalizations can often be accounted for by appealing to pragmatic, cognitive, and processing facts that are independently required, without stipulations that are specific to language (Chapter 9).

Mainstream generative theorists have asserted that constructions are epiphenomenal, apparent only because of an interacting set of universal, fixed principles with parameters selected on a language-particular basis. In the Principles and Parameters framework, grammatical constructions are "taxonomic artifacts, useful for informal description perhaps but with no theoretical standing" (Chomsky 2000). This idea is motivated by the view that "the [apparent] diversity and complexity [of languages] *can* be no more than superficial appearance" (Chomsky 2000: 7, emphasis added). The diversity and complexity can only be apparent, because it has been taken for granted that such diversity and complexity cannot be learned on the basis of the input together with general cognitive processes. Most mainstream generative grammarians thus conclude, with Chomsky, that "the search for explanatory adequacy *requires* that language structure *must be* invariant, except at the margins" (Chomsky 2000: 7; emphasis added).

This book aims to reframe the debate. Constructions exist, and if we allow them to account for the "periphery" or "residue" of language, there is no reason not to appeal to them to account for the "core" of grammar as well. Language is learnable. The task is to detail exactly how it is learned and why it is the way it is.

References

Abbott-Smith, K., Lieven, E., and Tomasello, M. (2001), "What preschool children do and do not do with ungrammatical word orders", *Cognitive Development* 16: 679–92.

—— —— —— (2004), "Training 2;6-year-olds to produce the transitive construction: the role of frequency, semantic similarity and shared syntactic distribution", *Developmental Science* 7: 48–55.

Abeillé, A. and Godard, D. (1997), "French word order and the word phrase distinction". Stanford University.

Ackerman, F. and Webelhuth, G. (1998), *A Theory of Predicates* (Stanford, CA: CSLI Publications).

Ahrens, K. (1994), "Double-object construction in Chinese: off-line evidence". Paper presented at the Third Conference on Chinese Linguistics, City Polytechnic of Hong Kong.

Akhtar, N. (1999), "Acquiring word order: evidence for data-driven learning of syntactic structure", *Journal of Child Language* 26: 339–56.

—— and Tomasello, M. (1997), "Young children's productivity with word order and verb morphology", *Developmental Psychology* 33: 952–65.

Alishahi, A. and Stevenson, S. (forthcoming), "A Probabilistic Model of Early Argument Structure Acquisition", *Proceedings of the Cognitive Science Society.*

Allen, S. E. M. (1997), "A discourse-pragmatic explanation for the subject-object asymmetry in early null arguments: the principle of informativeness revisited", *Proceedings of GALA*: 10–15.

—— (1999), *Learning About Argument Realization in Inuktitut and English: Graduate Development in the Use of Non-Ellipsed Forms.* Unpublished manuscript, Max Planck Institute for Psycholinguistics.

—— (2000), "A discourse-pragmatic explanation for argument representation in child Inuktitut", *Linguistics* 38: 483–521.

—— and Schroeder, H. (2000), "Preferred argument structure in early Inuktitut speech data," in J. DuBois, L. Kumpf, and W. Ashby (eds.), *Preferred Argument Structure: Grammar as Architecture for Function* (Amsterdam: John Benjamins), 301–38.

Alsina, A. and Mchombo, S. A. (1990), "The syntax of applicatives in Chichewa: problems for a theta-theoretic asymmetry", *Natural Language and Linguistic Theory* 8: 493–506.

Ameka, F. K. (forthcoming), "He died old dying to be dead right: transitivity and semantic shifts of *die* in Ewe", in M. Bowerman and P. Brown (eds.), *Crosslinguistic Perspectives on Argument Structure: Implications for Learnability* (Hillsdale, NJ: Lawrence Erlbaum).

Anderson, J. R. (1991), "The adaptive nature of human categorization", *Psychological Review* 98: 409–29.

Anderson, P. W. (1972), "More is different", *Science* 177: 393–6.

Anderson, S. R. (1971), "On the role of deep structure in semantic interpretation", *Foundations of Language* 6: 197–219.

Anh, W.-K. and Medin, D. L. (1992), "A two-stage model of category construction", *Cognitive Science* 16: 81–121.

Argaman, V. and Pearlmutter, N. J. (2002), "Lexical semantics as a basis for argument structure frequency biases", in P. Merlo and S. Stevenson (eds.), *The Lexical Basis of Sentence Processing: Formal, Computational and Experimental Perspectives*, (Amsterdam: John Benjamins), 303–24.

Ariel, M. (1990), *Accessing NP Antecedents* (London: Routledge).

Arnold, J. E. (MS), "Marking salience: the similarity of topic and focus". Unpublished manuscript, University of Rochester.

Arnold, J. E., Wasow, T., Losongco, A., and Ginstrom, R. (2000), "Heaviness vs. newness: the effects of structural complexity and discourse status on constituent ordering", *Language* 76: 28–55.

Arnon, I., Estigarribia, B., Hofmeister, P., Jaeger, T. F., Pettibone, J., Sag, I. A., and Snider, N. (2005), "Long-distance dependencies without island constraints". Poster presented at the HOWL 3: Hopkins Workshop on Language, Johns Hopkins University.

Aronoff, M. (1976), *Word Formation in Generative Grammar* (Cambridge, MA: MIT Press).

Avrahami, J., Kareev, Y., Bogot, Y., Caspi, R., Dunaevsky, S., and Lerner, S. (1997), "Teaching by examples: implications for the process of category acquisition", *Quarterly Journal of Experimental Psychology* 50A: 586–606

Baayen, H., Burani, C., and Schreuder, R. (1997), "Effects of semantic markedness in the processing of regular nominal singulars and plurals in Italian", in G. Booij and J. v. Marle (eds.), *Yearbook of Morphology* (Dordrecht: Kluwer), 13–34.

Baker, C. L. (1979), "Syntactic theory and the projection problem", *Linguistic Inquiry* 10: 533–81.

Baker, M. (1988), *Incorporation: A Theory of Grammatical Function Changing* (Chicago: University of Chicago Press).

—— (1996), "On the structural positions of themes and goals", in J. Rooryck and L. Zaring (eds.), *Phrase Structure and the Lexicon* (Dordrecht: Kluwer), 7–34.

—— (1997), "Thematic roles and syntactic structure", in L. Haegeman (ed.), *Elements of Grammar* (Dordrecht: Kluwer), 73–137.

—— (2004), *Verbs, Nouns, and Adjectives: Their Universal Grammar* (Cambridge: Cambridge University Press).

Baltin, M. (1982), "A landing site for movement rules", *Linguistic Inquiry* 13: 1–38.

Barðdol, J. (1999), "Case in Icelandic—a construction grammar approach", *Tijdschrift voor Skandinavistiek* 20 (2): 65–100.

—— (forthcoming), "The Oblique Experiencer First Construction in Icelandic and German", *Cognitive Linguistics*.

Barlow, M. and Kemmer, S. (2000), *Usage-Based Models of Grammar* (Stanford, CA: CSLI Publications).

Barsalou, L. W. (1983), "Ad hoc categories", *Memory and Cognition* 11: 211–27.

Bates, E., Bretherton, I., and Snyder, L. (1988), *From First Words to Grammar: Individual Differences and Dissociable Mechanisms* (New York: Cambridge University Press).

—— and Goodman, J. (1997), "On the inseparability of grammar and the lexicon: evidence from acquisition, aphasia, and real-time processing", *Language and Cognitive Processes* 12 (5/6): 507–86.

—— —— (1998), "Grammar from the lexicon", in B. MacWhinney (ed.), *The Emergence of Language* (Hillsdale, NJ: Lawrence Erlbaum), 197–212.

—— and MacWhinney, B. (1987), "Competition, variation, and language learning", in B. MacWhinney (ed.), *Mechanisms of Language Acquisition* (Hillsdale, NJ: Lawrence Erlbaum), 157–93.

Bekkering, H., Wohlschlager, A., and Gattis, M. (2000), "Imitation of gestures in children is goal-directed", *Quarterly Journal of Experimental Psychology* 53A: 153–64.

Bencini, G. M. L. (2002), "The representation and processing of argument structure constructions". Unpublished Ph.D. dissertation, University of Illinois.

—— Bock, K., and Goldberg, A. E. (in prep.), "How abstract is grammar?" Hunter College.

—— and Goldberg, A. E. (2000), "The contribution of argument structure constructions to sentence meaning", *Journal of Memory and Language* 43: 640–51.

Bender, L. M. (1996), *Kunama* (Munchen-Newcastle: Lincom Europa).

Bergen, B. (2004), "The psychological reality of phonaesthemes", *Language* 8: 290–311.

Boas, H. C. (2000), "Resultative constructions in English and German". Unpublished Ph.D. dissertation, University of North Carolina at Chapel Hill.

Bock, K. J. (1986), "Syntactic persistence in language production", *Cognitive Psychology* 18: 355–87.

—— and Griffin, Z. M. (2000), "The persistence of structural priming: transient activation or implicit learning?" *Journal of Experimental Psychology-General* 129: 177–92.

—— and Loebell, H. (1990), "Framing sentences", *Cognition* V: 1–39.

—— —— and Morey, R. (1992), "From conceptual roles to structural relations: bridging the syntactic cleft", *Psychological Review* 99: 150–71.

Bolinger, D. (1963), "Length, vowel and juncture", *Linguistics* 1: 5–29.

—— (1965), "The atomization of meaning", *Language* 41: 555–73.

—— (1977a), "Another glance at main clause phenomena", *Language* 53: 511–19.

—— (1977b), *Meaning and Form* (London: Longman).

Booij, G. (2002a), "Constructional idioms and periphrasis: the *aan het* infinitive construction in Dutch". Paper presented at the Periphrasis and Paradigms Workshop, University of California, San Diego, April 12–13.

—— (2002b), "Constructional idioms, morphology and the Dutch lexicon", *Journal of Germanic Linguistics* 14: 301–29.

—— (2002c), "The balance between storage and computation in phonology", in G. Nooteboom, F. Weerman, and F. Wijnen (eds.), *Storage and Computation in the Language Faculty* (Dordrecht: Kluwer), 115–38.

Borer, H. (1994), "The projection of arguments", in E. Benedicto and J. Runner (eds.), *University of Massachusetts Occasional Papers in Linguistics* (Vol. 17).

—— (2001), "Exo-skeletal vs. endo-skeletal explanations: syntactic projections and the lexicon". Paper presented at the Explanations in Linguistics Conference, San Diego, CA.

Borkin, A. (1974), "Problems in Form and Function". Unpublished Ph.D. dissertation, University of Michigan.

Borovsky, A. and Elman, J. (MS), "Language input and semantic categories: a relation between cognition and early word learning". University of California, San Diego.

Bowerman, M. (1973), *Early Syntactic Development: A Cross-Linguistic Study with Special Reference to Finnish* (Cambridge: Cambridge University Press).

—— (1982), "Reorganizationnal processes in lexical and syntactic development", in E. Wanner and L. R. Gleitman (eds.), *Language Acquisition: The State of the Art* (New York: Cambridge University Press), 319–46.

—— (1988), "The 'no negative evidence' problem: how do children avoid constructing an overly general grammar?" in J. Hawkins (ed.), *Explaining Language Universals* (Oxford: Blackwell), 73–101.

—— (1996), "Argument structure and learnability: is a solution in sight?" *Berkeley Linguistic Society* 22: 454–68.

—— and Choi, S. (2001), "Shaping meanings for language: universal and language-specific in the acquisition of spatial semantic categories", in M. Bowerman and S. C. Levinson (eds.), *Language Acquisition and Conceptual Development* (Cambridge: Cambridge University Press), 475–511.

Braine, M. D. S. (1976), *Children's First Word Combinations*, Vol. 4 (1) (Monographs of the Society for Research in Child Development).

—— and Brooks, P. (1995), "Verb argument structure and the problem of avoiding an overgeneral grammar", in M. Tomasello and W. E. Merriman (eds.), *Beyond Names for Things: Young Children's Acquisition of Verbs* (Hillsdale, NJ: Lawrence Erlbaum), 353–76.

Branigan, H. P., Pickering, M. J., Liversedge, S. P., Stewart, A. J., and Urbach, T. P. (1995), "Syntactic priming—investigating the mental representation of language", *Journal of Psycholinguistic Research* 24: 489–506.

Brenier, J. and Michaelis, L. A. (2005), "Optimization via syntactic amalgam: syntax-prosody mismatch and copula doubling", *Corpus Linguistics and Linguistic Theory* 1: 45–88.

Bresnan, J. (1982), *The Mental Representation of Grammatical Relations* (Cambridge, MA: MIT Press).

—— (1994), "Locative inversion and universal grammar", *Language* 70: 72–131.

—— and Nikitina, T. (MS). *On the Gradience of the Dative Alternation*. Unpublished manuscript, Stanford University.

Brooks, P. and Tomasello, M. (1999), "How children constrain their argument structure constructions", *Language* 75: 720–38.

—— —— Lewis, W., and Dodson, K. (1999), "Children's tendency to overgeneralize their argument structure constructions: the entrenchment hypothesis", *Child Development* 70: 1325–37.

Brown, P. (forthcoming), "Verb specificity and argument realization in Tzeltal child language", in M. Bowerman and P. Brown (eds.), *Crosslinguistic Perspectives on Argument Structure: Implications for Language Acquisition* (Hillsdale, NJ: Lawrence Erlbaum).

Bruening, B. (2001), "QR obeys superiority: frozen scope and ACD", *Linguistic Inquiry* 32: 233–73.

Brugman, C. (1988), *The Story of "over": Polysemy, Semantics and the Structure of the Lexicon* (New York: Garland).

Bruner, J. S., Goodnow, J. J., and Austin, G. A. (1956), *A Study of Thinking* (New York: Wiley).

Bryant, J. (2005). *Towards Cognitive, Compositional Construction Grammar*. Unpublished manuscript, University of California, Berkeley.

Butt, M. and King, T. H. (1997), "Null elements in discourse structure". In K. V. Subbarao (ed.), *Papers from the NULLS seminar* (Delhi: Motilal Banarasidas).

Bybee, J. L. (1985), *Morphology: A Study of the Relation between Meaning and Form:* (Amsterdam: John Benjamins).

—— (1995), "Regular morphology and the lexicon", *Language and Cognitive Processes* 10: 425–55.

—— (2000), "The phonology of the lexicon: evidence from lexical diffusion", in M. Barlow and S. Kemmer (eds.), *Usage-Based Models of Language* (Stanford, CA Center for the Study of Language and Information).

—— and Hopper, P. (eds.), (2001), *Frequency and the Emergence of Linguistic Structure* (Amsterdam: John Benjamins).

—— and McClelland, J. (2005). *Alternatives to the Combinatorial Paradigm of Linguistic Theory based on Domain General Principles of Human Cognition*. Unpublished manuscript, University of New Mexico and Carnegie Mellon University.

—— and Moder, C. L. (1983), "Morphological classes as natural categories", *Language* 59: 251–70.

—— Perkins, R., and Pagliuca, W. (1994), *The Evolution of Grammar: Tense, Aspect, and Modality in the Languages of the World* (Chicago: University of Chicago Press).

—— and Slobin, D. I. (1982), "Rules and schemas in the development and use of the English past tense", *Language* 58: 265–89.

Cameron-Faulkner, T., Lieven, E., and Tomasello, M. (2003), "A construction-based analysis of child-directed speech", *Cognitive Science* 27: 843–73.

Campbell, A. and Tomasello, M. (2001), "The acquisition of English dative constructions", *Applied Psycholinguistics* 22: 253–67.

Carlson, G. (MS). *Weak Indefinites.* Unpublished manuscript, University of Rochester.

Carpenter, P., Akhtar, N., and Tomasello, M. (1998), "Fourteen-through-18-month-old infants differentially imitate intentional and accidental actions", *Infant Behavior and Development* 21: 315–30.

Carroll, J., Davies, P., and Richman, B. (1971), *Word Frequency* (New York: Houghton Mifflin).

Casenhiser, D. (2004), "Soft constraints on learning form-meaning mappings". Unpublished Ph.D. dissertation, University of Illinois, Urbana.

—— and Goldberg, A. E. (2005), "Fast mapping of a phrasal form and meaning", *Developmental Science.*

Casey, S. (2003), "'Agreement' in gestures and signed languages: the use of directionality to indicate referents involved in actions". Unpublished Ph.D. dissertation, University of California, San Diego.

Chafe, W. L. (1976), "Giveness, contrastiveness, definiteness, subjects, topics and point of view", in C. Li (ed.), *Subject and Topic* (New York: Academic Press), 25–56.

—— (1987), "Cognitive constraints on information flow", in R. Tomlin (ed.), *Coherence and Grounding in Discourse* (Amsterdam: John Benjamins), 21–50.

—— (1994), *Discourse, Consciousness and Time: The Flow and Displacement of Conscious Experience in Speaking and Writing* (Chicago: University of Chicago Press).

Chang, F. (2002), "Symbolically speaking: a connectionist model of sentence production", *Cognitive Science* 26: 609–51.

—— Bock, J. K., and Goldberg, A. E. (2003), "Can thematic roles leave traces of their places?" *Cognition* 90(1): 29–49.

—— Dell, G. S., Bock, K., and Griffin, Z. M. (2000), "Structural priming as implicit learning: a comparison of models of sentence production", *Journal of Psycholinguistic Research* 29: 217–29.

Chidambaram, V. (2004), *Verb of Motion Ellipsis in Russian.* Unpublished manuscript, Princeton University.

Childers, J. B. and Tomasello, M. (2001), "The role of pronouns in young children's acquisition of the English transitive construction", *Developmental Psychology* 37: 739–48.

Choi, I. (2003), "A constructional approach to English and Korean tough constructions". Paper presented at the Chicago Linguistic Society.

Choi, S. (1999), "Early development of verb structures and caregiver input in Korean: two case studies", *International Journal of Bilingualism* 3: 241–65.

Chomsky, N. (1957), *Syntactic Structures* (The Hague: Mouton).

—— (1965), *Aspects and the Theory of Syntax* (Cambridge, MA: MIT Press).

—— (1970), "Remarks on nominalization", in R. A. Jacobs and P. S. Rosenbaum (eds.), *Readings in English Transformational Grammar* (Waltham, MA: Ginn), 184–221.

—— (1980), "The linguistic approach", in M. Piatelli-Palmarini (ed.), *Language and Learning* (Cambridge, MA: Harvard University Press), 109–30.

—— (1981), *Lectures on Government and Binding* (Dordrecht: Foris Publications).

—— (1982), *Some Concepts and Consequences of the Theory of Government and Binding* (Cambridge, MA: MIT Press).

—— (1988), *Language and Problems of Knowledge: The Managua Lectures* (Cambridge, MA: MIT Press).

—— (1995), *The Minimalist Program* (Cambridge, MA: MIT Press).

—— (2000), *New Horizons in the Study of Language and Mind* (Cambridge, MA: Cambridge University Press).

Chung, S. and McCloskey, J. (1983), "On the interpretation of certain island facts in GPSG", *Linguistic Inquiry* 14: 704–13.

Chung, Y.-S. (2001), "Tough constructions in English: a construction grammar approach". Unpublished Ph.D. dissertation, University of California, Berkeley.

Cinque, G. (1990), *Types of a'-Dependencies* (Cambridge, MA: MIT Press).

Clark, E. V. (1978), "Discovering what words can do", *Chicago Linguistic Society* 14: 34–57.

—— (1987), "The principle of contrast: a constraint on language acquisition", in B. MacWhinney (ed.), *Mechanisms of Language Acquisition* (Hillsdale, NJ: Lawrence Erlbaum).

—— (1996), *Early Verbs, Event Types and Inflections*, Vol. 9 (Mahwah, NJ: Lawrence Erlbaum).

—— and Clark, H. H. (1979), "When nouns surface as verbs", *Language* 55: 767–811.

Clausner, T. C. and Croft, W. (1997), "Productivity and schematicity in metaphors", *Cognitive Science* 21: 247–82.

Cole, P., Harbert, W., Sridhar, S., Hashimoto, S., Nelson, C., and Smietana, D. (1977), "Noun phrase accessibility and island constraints", in P. Cole and J. M. Sadock (eds.), *Syntax and Semantics Vol. 8: Grammatical Relations* (New York: Academic Press), 27–46.

Collett, T. S., Fauria, K., Dale, K., and Baron, J. (1997), "Places and patterns: a study of context learning in honeybees", *Journal of Comparative Physiology*, A 181: 343–53.

Collins, P. (1995), "The indirect object construction in English: an informational approach", *Linguistics* 33: 35–49.

Comrie, B. (1984), "Subject and object control: syntax, semantics, and pragmatics", *Berkeley Linguistic Society* 10: 450–64.

Cooreman, A., Fox, B., and Givón, T. (1984), "The discourse definition of ergativity", *Studies in Language* 8: 1–34.

Cote, S. A. (1996), "Grammatical and discourse properties of null arguments in English". Unpublished Ph.D. dissertation, University of Pennsylvania.

Croft, W. (1991), *Syntactic Categories and Grammatical Relations: The Cognitive Organization of Information* (Chicago: Chicago University Press).

—— (2001), *Radical Construction Grammar* (Oxford: Oxford University Press).

Csibra, G., Gergely, G., Bíró, S., Koós, O., and Brockbank, M. (1999), "Goal attribution without agency cues: the perception of 'pure reason' in infancy", *Cognition* 72: 237–67.

Culicover, P. W. (1999), "*Syntactic Nuts: Hard Cases, Syntactic Theory and Language Acquisition* (Oxford: Oxford University Press).

Culicover, P. W. and Jackendoff, R. (1999), "The view from the periphery: the English correlative conditions", *Linguistic Inquiry* 30: 543–71.

—— —— (2005), *Simpler Syntax* (Oxford: Oxofrd University Press).

—— and Wexler, K. (1973), *An Application of the Freezing Principle to the Dative in English*, Social Sciences Working Paper 39 (University of California, Irvine).

Daugherty, K. and Seidenberg, M. S. (1995), "Beyond rules and exceptions: a connectionist approach to inflectional morphology", in S. Lima, R. Corrigan, and G. Iverson (eds.), *The Reality of Linguistic Rules* (Amsterdam: John Benjamins).

Davidse, K. (2000), "A constructional approach to clefts", *Linguistics* 38: 1101–31.

Davies, L. (2005), "A construction-grammatical analysis of impersonalization in Russian". Unpublished Ph. D. dissertation, Princeton University.

Deacon, T. W. (1997), *The Symbolic Species: The Co-Evolution of Language and the Brain* (New York: W. W. Norton).

Deane, P. (1991), "Limits to attention: a cognitive theory of island phenomena", *Cognitive Linguistics* 2: 1–63.

—— (2003), "Co-occurrence and constructions", in L. Lagerwerf, W. Spooren, and L. Degand (eds.), *Determination of Information and Tenor in Texts: Multidisciplinary Approaches to Discourse* (Amsterdam: Stichting Neerlandistiek, and Muenster: Nodus Publikationen).

Dell'Orletta, F., Lenci, A., Montemagni, S., and Pirrelli, V. (forthcoming, 2005), "Climbing the path to grammar: a maximum entropy model of subject/object learning".

Denison, D. (1993), *English: Historical Syntax: Verbal Constructions* (New York: Longman).

Dennis, S. and Kruschke, J. K. (1998), "Shifting attention in cued recall", *Australian Journal of Psychology* 50: 131–8.

De Villiers, J. G. (1985), "Learning how to use verbs: lexical coding and the influence of the input", *Journal of Child Language* 12: 587–95.

Diessel, H. (1997), "Verb-first constructions in German", in M. Verspoor, K. D. Lee, and E. Sweetser (eds.), *Lexical and Syntactical Constructions and the Construction of Meaning* (Amsterdam: John Benjamins), 51–68.

—— (2001), "The development of complex sentence constructions in English. A usage-based approach". Habilitation thesis, University of Leipzig.

—— and Tomasello, M. (2001), "The acquisition of finite complement clauses in English: a usage-based approach to the development of grammatical constructions", *Cognitive Linguistics* 12: 97–141.

DiSciullo, A.-M. and Williams, E. (1987), *On the Definition of Word* (Cambridge, MA: MIT Press).

Dixon, R. M. W. (1994), *Ergativity* (Cambridge: Cambridge University Press).

Dominey, P. F. and Inui, T. (MS), "Miniature language learning via mapping of grammatical structure to visual scene structure in English and Japanese", ms.

Donahue, M. (MS). *The Ingredients of Grammatical Functions: Sorting Subjects and Pivots in Tukang Besi*. Unpublished manuscript, National University of Singapore.

Dowty, D. (1991), "Thematic proto-roles and argument selection", *Language* 67: 547–619.

Dryer, M. S. (1986), "Primary objects, secondary objects and antidative", *Language* 62: 808–45.

—— (1997), "Are grammatical relations universal?" in J. Bybee, J. Haiman, and S. A. Thompson (eds.), *Essays on Language Function and Language Type* (Amsterdam: John Benjamins), 115–43.

—— (forthcoming), "Clause types", in T. Shopen (ed.), *Clause Structure, Language Typology and Syntactic Description*, Vol. 1 (Cambridge: Cambridge University Press).

Du Bois, J. W. (1987), "The discourse basis of ergativity", *Language* 63: 805–55.

—— Kumpf, L. E., and Ashby, W. J. (eds.), (2004), *Preferred Argument Structure: Grammar as Architecture for Function*, (Philadelphia: John Benjamins).

Elio, R. and Anderson, J. R. (1984), "The effects of information order and learning mode on schema abstraction", *Memory and Cognition* 12: 20–30.

Ellefson, M. R. and Christiansen, M. H. (2005), "Subjacency constraints without Universal Grammar: evidence from artificial language learning and connectionist modeling". Unpublished manuscript, Department of Psychology, University of Coventry, Warwick.

Elman, J. L. (1990), "Finding structure in time", *Cognitive Science* 14: 179–211.

—— (forthcoming), "A different view of the mental lexicon", *Trends in Cognitive Sciences*.

—— Bates, E., Johnson, M., Karmiloff-Smith, A., Parisi, D., and Plunkett, K. (1996), *Rethinking Innateness: A Connectionist Perspective on Development* (Cambridge, MA: MIT Press).

Emonds, J. (1970), "Root- and structure-preserving transformations", Ph.D. dissertation, MIT.

Enfield, N. J. (forthcoming), "Expression of three-participant events in Lao", in P. Austin, J. Bowden, N. Evans, and A. Margetts (eds.), *Three-Participant Events*.

Erteschik-Shir, N. (1979), "Discourse constraints on dative movement", in S. Laberge and G. Sankoff (eds.), *Syntax and Semantics*, Vol. 12 (New York: Academic Press), 441–67.

—— (1998a), *The Dynamics of Focus Structure* (Cambridge: Cambridge University Press).

—— (1998b), "The syntax-focus structure interface", in P. Culicover and L. McNally (eds.), *Syntax and Semantics 29: The Limits of Syntax* (New York: Academic Press), 211–40).

—— (2002), "What's what". Paper presented at the Conference on Gradedness, Potsdam University, October 21–23.

—— and Lappin, S. (1979), "Dominance and the functional explanation of island phenomena", *Theoretical Linguistics* 6: 41–85.

Essegbey, J. (1999), "Inherent complement verbs revisited: towards an understanding of argument structure in Ewe". Unpublished Ph.D. dissertation, Max Planck Institute, Nijmegen.

—— (forthcoming), "Intransitive verbs in Ewe and the unaccusative hypothesis", in M. Bowermann and P. Brown (eds.), *Crosslinguistic Perspectives on Argument Structure: Implications for Learnability* (Hillsdale, NJ: Lawrence Erlbaum).

Estes, W. K. (1986), "Array models for category learning", *Cognitive Psychology* 18: 500–48.

Evans, N. (1997), "Role or cast? Noun incorporation and complex predicates in Mayali", in A. Alsina, J. Bresnan, and P. Sells (eds.), *Complex Predicates* (Stanford, CA: CSLI Publications), 397–430.

Farrell, P. (1990), "Null objects in Brazilian Portuguese", *Natural Language and Linguistic Theory* 8: 325–46.

Fillmore, C. J. (1965), *Indirect Object Constructions in English and the Ordering of Transformations* (The Hague: Mouton).

—— (1975), "Against checklist theories of meaning", in C. Cogen (ed.), *Proceedings of the First Annual Meeting of the Berkeley Linguistics Society* (Berkeley, CA: Berkeley Linguistics Society), 123–31.

—— (1977), "Topics in lexical semantics", in R. Cole (ed.), *Current Issues in Linguistic Theory* (Bloomington: Indiana University Press), 76–138.

—— (1986), "Pragmatically controlled zero anaphora", in V. Nikiforidou, M. VanClay, M. Niepokuj, and D. Feder (eds.), *Berkeley Linguistic Society*, Vol. 12 (Berkeley, CA: Berkeley Linguistic Society), 95–107.

—— (1992), "'Corpus linguistics' vs. "computer-aided armchair linguistics'". Paper presented at the 1991 Nobel Symposium on Corpus Linguistics, Stockholm.

—— (1999), "Inversion and constructional inheritance", in G. Webelhuth, J.-P. Koenig, and A. Kathol (eds.), *Lexical and Constructional Aspects of Linguistic Explanation* (Stanford, CA: CSLI Publications).

—— Kay, P., Michaelis, L., and Sag, I. (forthcoming), *Construction Grammar* (Stanford, CA: CSLI Publications).

—— —— and O'Connor, M. C. (1988), "Regularity and idiomaticity in grammatical constructions: the case of *let alone*", *Language* 64: 501–38.

Fiser, J., and Aslin, R. N. (2002), "Statistical learning of new visual feature combinations by infants", *Proceedings of the National Academy of Sciences, USA*, 99: 15822–6.

Fisher, C. (1996), "Structural limits on verb mapping: the role of analogy in children's interpretations of sentences", *Cognitive Psychology* 31: 41–81.

—— (2000), "From form to meaning: a role for structural alignment in the acquisition of language", *Advanced Child Development Behavior* 27: 1–53.

—— Gleitman, H., and Gleitman, L. R. (1991), "On the semantic content of subcategorization frames", *Cognitive Psychology* 23: 331–92.

—— Hall, D. G., Rakowitz, S., and Gleitman, L. (1994), "When it is better to receive than to give—syntactic and conceptual constraints on vocabulary growth", *Lingua* 92: 333–75.

Fodor, J. and Lepore, E. (1999), "The Emptiness of the Lexicon: Critical Reflections on J. Pustejovsky's *The Generative Lexicon*", *Linguistic Inquiry* 30: 445–53.

Foley, W. A. (forthcoming), "Typology of information packaging in the clause", in T. Shopen (ed.), *Clause Structure, Language Typology and Syntactic Development*, Vol. 1 (Cambridge: Cambridge University Press).

—— and Van Valin, R. (1984), *Functional Syntax and Universal Grammar* (Cambridge: Cambridge University Press).

Ford, M., Bresnan, J., and Kaplan, R. M. (1982), "A competence-based theory of syntactic closure", in J. Bresnan (ed.), *The Mental Representation of Grammatical Relations* (Cambridge, MA: MIT Press), 727–96.

Francis, E. J. (2005), "Syntactic mimicry as evidence for prototypes in grammar", in S. S. Mufwene (ed.), *Multifaceted and Interdiscplinary Linguistics: Jim McCawley's Legacy*, 161–81.

Francis, H. S., Gregory, M. L., and Michaelis, L. A. (1999), "Are lexical subjects deviant?" *Proceedings of the 35th Regional Meeting of the Chicago Linguistic Society* 1: 85–97.

Franks, S. (1995), *Parameters of Slavic Morphosyntax* (New York: Oxford University Press).

Fraser, B. (1971), "A note on the spray paint cases", *Linguistic Inquiry* 2: 604–7.

Freund, Y. and Schapire, R. E. (1999), "A short introduction to boosting", *Journal of Japanese Society for Artificial Intelligence* 14: 771–80.

Fried, M. (2002), "Issues in Representing Flexible Word Order: Beyond Information Structure" Presentation at ICCG2 confernce in Helsinki.

—— (forthcoming), "A frame-based approach to case alternations: the *swarm*-class verbs in Czech", *Cognitive Linguistics*.

Friederici, A. D., Schriefers, H., and Lindenberger, U. (1998), "Differential age effects on semantic and syntactic priming", *International Journal of Behavioral Development* 22: 813–45.

Gahl, S. and Garnsey, S. M. (2004), "Probabilistic Form Variation and Knowledge of Grammar", *Language* 80: 748–75.

Gair, J. (1998), *Studies in South Asian Linguistics: Sinhala and other South Asian languages* (New York: Oxford University Press).

Garnsey, S. M., Pearlmutter, N. J., Myers, E., and Lotocky, M. (1997), "The contributions of verb bias and plausibility to the comprehension of temporarily ambiguous sentences", *Journal of Memory and Language* 37: 58–93.

Garry, J. and Rubino, C. (eds.) (2001), *Facts About the World's Languages: An Encyclopedia of the World's Major Languages Past and Present* (New York: H. W. Wilson).

Gentner, D. (1982), "Why nouns are learned before verbs: linguistic relativity versus natural partitioning", in S. A. Kuzcaj II (ed.), *Language Development, Vol. 2: Language, Thought, and Culture* (Hillsdale, NJ: Lawrence Erlbaum), 301–34.

—— Loewenstein, J., and Hung, B. T. (2002). *Comparison Facilitates Learning Part Names.* Unpublished manuscript, Northwestern University.

—— and Medina, J. (1998), "Similarity and the development of rules", *Cognition* 65: 263–97.

Gergely, G., Bekkering, H., and Kiraly, I. (2002), "Rational imitation in preverbal infants", *Nature* 415: 755.

Gerken, L., Wilson, R., and Lewis, W. (2005). "Infants Can Use Distributional Cues to Form Syntactic Categories." Unpublished manuscript, University of Arizona.

Gibson, E. (2000), "The dependency locality theory: A distance-based theory of linguistic complexity", in A. Marantz, Y. Miyashita, and W. O'Neil (eds.), *Image, Language, Brain: Papers from the First Mind Articulation Project Symposium* (Cambridge, MA: MIT Press), 95–126.

—— Desmet, T., Grodner, D., Watson, D., and Ko, K. (2005), "Reading relative clauses in English", *Cognitive Linguistics* 16(2): 313–53.

Gil, D. (1994), "The structure of Riau Indonesian", *Nordic Journal of Linguistics* 17: 179–200.

Ginzburg, J. and Sag, I. (2000), *Interrogative Investigations: The Form, Meaning and Use of English Interrogatives* (Stanford, CA: CSLI Publications).

Giurfa, M. E. A. (1996), "Symmetry perception in an insect", *Nature* 382: 458–61.

—— Zhang, S., Jenett, A., Menzel, R., and Srinivasan, M. V. (2001), "The concepts of sameness and difference in an insect", *Nature* 410: 930–3.

Givón, T. (1975), "Focus and the scope of assertion: some Bantu evidence", *Studies in African Linguistics* 6: 185–205.

—— (1979), *On Understanding Grammar* (New York: Academic Press).

—— (1984), *Syntax. A Functional-Typological Introduction*, Vol. 1 (Amsterdam: John Benjamins).

—— (1991), "Isomorphism in the grammatical code: cognitive and biological considerations", *Studies in Language* 1: 85–114.

—— and Ute Language Program, Ignacio, Colorado. (1980), "The binding hierarchy and the typology of complements", *Studies in Language* 4: 333–77.

Gleitman, L. (1994), "The structural sources of verb meanings", in P. Bloom (ed.), *Language Acquisition: Core Readings* (Cambridge, MA: MIT Press), 174–221.

—— Henry, G., Miller, C., and Ostrin, R. (1996), "Similar and similar concepts", *Cognition*: 321–76.

Goldberg, A. E. (1992), "The inherent semantics of argument structure: the case of the English ditransitive construction", *Cognitive Linguistics* 3: 37–74.

—— (1993), "Another look at some learnability paradoxes". In E. Clark (ed.) *Proceedings of the 25th Annual Stanford Child Language Research Forum*, (Stanford, CA: CSLI Publications).

—— (1995), *Constructions: A Construction Grammar Approach to Argument Structure* (Chicago: Chicago University Press).

—— (1996), "Optimizing constraints and the Persian complex predicate", *Berkeley Linguistic Society* 22: 132–46.

—— (1997), "Relationships between verb and construction", in M. Verspoor and E. Sweetser (eds.), *Lexicon and Grammar* (Amsterdam: John Benjamins), 383–98.

—— (1999), "The emergence of the semantics of argument structure constructions", in B. MacWhinney (ed.), *The Emergence of Language* (Hillsdale, NJ: Lawrence Erlbaum), 197–212.

—— (2000), "Patient arguments of causative verbs can be omitted: the role of information structure in argument distribution", *Language Sciences* 34: 503–24.

—— (2002), "Surface generalizations: an alternative to alternations", *Cognitive Linguistics* 13: 327–56.

—— (2003), "Words by default: inheritance and the Persian complex predicate construction", in E. Francis and L. Michaelis (eds.), *Mismatch: Form-Function Incongruity and the Architecture of Grammar* (Stanford, CA: CSLI Publications), 84–112.

—— (2004), "But do we need Universal Grammer?" *Cognition* 97: 77–84.

—— (2005), "Constructions, lexical semantics and the correspondence principle: accounting for generalizations and subregularities in the realization of arguments", in N. Erteschik-Shir and T. Rapoport (eds.), *The Syntax of Aspect* (Oxford: Oxford University Press).

—— and Ackerman, F. (2001), "The pragmatics of obligatory adjuncts", *Language* 77: 798–814.

—— and Casenhiser, D. (in prep.), "The role of type frequency in generalizations", Princeton University.

—— —— (forthcoming) in E. Clark and B. Kelly (eds.), *Constructions in Acquisition* (Stanford: CSLI Publications).

—— —— and Sethuraman, N. (2004), "Learning argument structure generalizations", *Cognitive Linguistics* 14: 289–316.

—— —— —— (2005), "The role of prediction in construction learning", *Journal of Child Language* 32(2) 407–426.

—— and Del Giudice, A. (2005), "Subject–auxiliary inversion: a natural category", *Linguistic Review* 22: 43–48.

—— and Jackendoff, R. (2004), "The resultative as a family of constructions", *Language* 80: 532–68.

Goldin-Meadow, S. (2005), "Watching language grow", *Proceedings of the National Academy of Sciences, USA* 10: 2271.

—— Yalakik, E., and Gershkoff-Stowe, L. (2000), "The resilience of ergative structure in language created by children and by adults', in J. C. Howell, J. A. Fish, and T. Keith-Lucas (eds.), *Proceedings of the 24th Annual Boston University Conference on Language Development*, Vol. 1 (Somerville, MA: Cascadilla Press), 343–53.

Gomez, R. (2002), "Variability and detection of invariant structure", *Psychological Science* 13: 431–6.

Gonzálvez-García, F. (2000), "'I found myself led into the path of constructions'", in L. G. Romero, M. M. Vazquez, B. R. Arrizabalaga, and P. R. Vaz (eds.), *Recent Approaches to English Grammar* (Grupo de Invetigacion Gramatica Contrastiva).

—— (2001), "Rethinking predicational *be*: from copula support to the construction of a lexical grammar of sentential complementation in English". Unpublished manuscript, Universidad de Almería, Spain.

Green, G. M. (1974), *Semantics and Syntactic Regularity* (Bloomington, Indiana University Press).

—— (1976), "Main clause phenomena in subordinate clauses", *Language* 52: 382–97.

—— (1985), "The description of inversions in generalized phrase structure grammar". Paper presented at the 11th Annual Meeting of the Berkeley Linguistics Society.

Greenberg, J. (1963), "Some universals of grammar with particular reference to the order of meaningful elements", in J. Greenberg (ed.), *Universals of Language* (Cambridge, MA: MIT Press), 58–90.

Grégoire, A. (1937), *L'apprentissage du Langage*, Vol. 1 (Paris: Droz).

Gregory, M. L. and Michaelis, L. A. (2004), "Topicalization and left dislocation: a functional opposition revisited", *Journal of Pragmatics* 33: 1665–706.

Grice, H. P. (1975), "Logic and conversation", in P. Cole and J. L. Morgan, *Syntax and Semantics, Vol. 3: Speech Acts* (New York: Academic Press), 41–58.

Gries, S. T. and Wulff, S. (2004), "Foreign language learners have constructions: evidence from sorting and corpora". Paper presented at the Third International Conference of Construction Grammar, Marseilles.

Griffin, Z. M. and Weinstein-Tull, J. (2003), "Conceptual structure modulates structural priming in the production of complex sentences", *Journal of Memory and Language* 49: 537–55.

Grimshaw, J. (1990), *Argument Structure* (Cambridge, MA: MIT Press).

Gropen, J., Epstein, T., and Schumacher, L. (1997), "Context-sensitive verb learning: children's ability to associate contextual information with the argument of a verb", *Cognitive Linguistics* 8: 137–82.

—— Pinker, S., Hollander, M., Goldberg, R., and Wilson, R. (1989), "The learnability and acquisition of the dative alternation in English", *Language* 65: 203–57.

—— Pinker, S., Hollander, M., and Goldberg, R. (1991), "Syntax and semantics in the acquisition of locative verbs", *Journal of Child Language* 18: 115–51.

Gross, M. (1975), "On the relations between syntax and structure", in E. L. Reenan (ed.), *Formal Semantics of Natural Language* (Cambridge: Cambridge University Press), 389–405.

Grosz, B., Joshi, A., and Weinstein, S. (1983), "Providing a unified account of definite noun phrases in discourse". Paper presented at the Proceedings of the 21st Annual Meeting of the Association for Computational Linguistics, Cambridge, MA.

—— —— —— (1995), "Centering: a framework for modeling the local coherence of discourse", *Computational Linguistics* 21: 203–25.

Gundel, J. K. (1985), "Shared knowledge and topicality", *Journal of Pragmatics* 9: 83–107.

—— (1998), "Centering theory and givenness hierarchy", in M. A. Walker, A. K. Joshi, and E. Prince (eds.), *Centering Theory in Discourse* (Oxford: Clarendon Press), 183–97.

Hagstrom, P. (forthcoming), "Particle movement in Sinhala and Japanese", in V. Dayal and A. Mahajan (eds.), *Clause Structure in South Asian Languages* (Dordrecht: Kluwer).

Haiman, J. (1983), "Iconic and economic motivation", *Language* 59: 781–819.

—— (1985), *Iconicity in Syntax* (Cambridge: Cambridge University Press).

Hale, K. and Keyser, J. (1997), "On the complex nature of simple predicators", in A. Alsina, J. Bresnan, and P. Sells (eds.), *Complex Predicates* (Stanford, CA: CSLI Publications), 29–65.

Halliday, A. K. (1967), "Notes on transitivity and theme in English. Part II", *Journal of Linguistics* 3: 199–244.

Hare, M. and Goldberg, A. E. (1999), "Structural priming: purely syntactic?" Paper presented at the Proceedings of the Cognitive Science Society.

—— McRae, K., and Elman, J. L. (2003), "Sense and structure: meaning as a determinant of verb subcategorization preferences", *Journal of Memory and Language* 48: 281–303.

—— —— —— (2004), "Admitting that admitting verb sense into corpus analyses makes sense", *Language and Cognitive Processes* 19: 181–224.

Harley, H. (2002), "Possession and the double object construction", *Linguistic Variation Yearbook* 2: 29–68.

Haspelmath, M. (1997), *Indefinite Pronouns* (Oxford: Clarendon Press).

—— (1999), "On the cross-linguistic distribution of same-subject and different-subject complement clauses: economic vs. iconic motivation". Paper presented at the International Cognitive Linguistics Association, Stockholm.

Hauser, M. D., Chomsky, N., and Fitch, W. T. (2002), "The faculty of language: what is it, who has it, and how did it evolve?" *Science* 298: 1569–79.

—— Newport, E. L., and Aslin, R. N. (2001), "Segmentation of the speech stream in a non-human primate: statistical learning in cotton-top tamarins", *Cognition* 78: B41–52.

Hawkins, J. A. (1979), "Implicational universals as predictors of word order change", *Language* 55: 618–48.

—— (1990), "A parsing theory of word order universals", *Linguistic Inquiry* 21: 223–61.

—— (1994), *A Performance Theory of Order and Constituency* (Cambridge: Cambridge University Press).

Healy, A. F. and Miller, G. A. (1970), "The verb as the main determinant of sentence meaning", *Psychonomic Science* 20: 372.

Heine, B. (1993), *Auxiliaries: Cognitive Forces and Grammaticalization* (New York: Oxford University Press).

Hintzman, D. L. (1986), "'Schema abstraction' in a multiple-trace memory model", *Psychological Review* 93: 1411–28 (American Psychological Association).

Hirsh-Pasek, K., Golinkoff, R. M., and Naigles, L. (1996), "Young children's use of syntactic frames to derive meaning", in K. Hirsh-Pasek and R. M. Golinkoff (eds.), *The Origins of Grammar: Evidence from Early Language Comprehension* (Cambridge, MA: MIT Press), 123–58.

Holland, J. H., Holyoak, K. J., Nisbett, R., and Thagard, R. E. R. (1989), *Induction: Processes of Inference, Learning and Discovery* (Cambridge, MA: MIT Press).

Homa, D., Dunbar, S., and Nohre, L. (1991), "Instance frequency, categorization, and the modulating effect of experience", *Journal of Experimental Psychology: Learning, Memory, and Cognition* 17: 444–58.

Homer, K. and Michaelis, L. A. (2005), *A Discourse Account of the That-Trace Effect and its Exceptions*. Unpublished manuscript, University of Colorado, Boulder.

Hook, P. E. (1983), "The English abstrument and rocking case relations", in *Papers from the 19th Regional Meeting of the Chicago Linguistics Society* (Chicago), 183–94.

Hooper, J. B. and Thompson, S. A. (1973), "On the applicability of root transformations", *Linguistic Inquiry* 4: 465–97.

Hopper, P. J. and Thompson, S. A. (1980), "Transitivity in grammar and discourse", *Language* 56: 251–99.

Horn, L. R. (1984), "Towards a new taxonomy for pragmatic inference: Q- and R-based implicature", in D. Schiffrin (ed.), *Meaning, Form, and Use in Context* (Washington, DC: Georgetown University Press), 11–42.

—— (1989), *A Natural History of Negation* (Chicago: University of Chicago Press).

Huang, C. (1982), *Logical Relations in Chinese and the Theory of Grammar* (Cambridge, MA: MIT Press).

Hudson Kam, C. L. and Newport, E. (1999), "Creolization: could adults really have done it all?" Paper presented at the Proceedings of the 23rd Annual Boston University Conference on Language Development, Boston.

—— —— (MS), "Getting it right by getting it wrong when do learners change languages?" Universty of California, Berkeley.

Hudson, R. (1990), *English Word Grammar* (Oxford: Blackwell).

Hunston, S. and Francis, G. (1999), *Pattern Grammar. A Corpus-Driven Approach to the Lexical Grammar of English*, Studies in Corpus Linguistics 4 (Amsterdam: John Benjamins), pp. xii, 289.

Ingram, D. and Thompson, W. (1996), "Early syntactic acquisition in German: evidence for the modal hypothesis", *Language* 72: 97–120.

Ioup, G. (1975), "Some universals of quantifier scope", in Kimball (ed.), *Syntax and Semantics*, Vol. 4 (New York: Academic Press), 37–58.

Israel, M. (1996), "The way constructions grow", in A. E. Goldberg (ed.), *Conceptual Structure, Discourse and Language* (Stanford, CA: CSLI Publications), 217–30.

—— (2002), "Consistency and creativity in first language acquisition", *Proceedings of the Berkeley Linguistic Society* 29.

Iwata, S. (2000). *Locative Alternation and Two Levels of Verb Meaning*. Unpublished manuscript, Gifu University, Japan.

Jackendoff, R. (1972), *Semantic Interpretation in Generative Grammer* (Cambridge, MA: MIT Press).

—— (1977), *X Syntax: A Study of Phrase Structure* (Cambridge, MA: MIT Press).

—— (1990), *Semantic Structures* (Cambridge, MA: MIT Press).

—— (1997a), *Architecture of the Language Faculty* (Cambridge, MA: MIT Press).

—— (1997b), "Twistin the night away", *Language* 73: 534–59.

—— (2002), *Foundations of Language* (Oxford: Oxford University Press).

James, D. (1972), "Some aspects of the syntax and semantics of interjections". Paper presented at the 8th Regional Meeting of the Chicago Linguistic Society, Chicago.

Janda, R. D. (1990), "Frequency, markedness and morphological change: on predicting the spread of noun-plural -s in Modern High German and West Germanic", *ESCOL* 7: 136–53.

Johnson-Laird, P. (1967), "Katz on analyticity", *Journal of Linguistics* 111: 82.

—— (1968), "The interpretation of the passive voice", *Quarterly Journal of Experimental Psychology* 20: 69–73.

Joshi, A. K., Levy, L. S., and Takahashi., M. (1975), "Tree adjunct grammars ", *Journal of the Computer and System Sciences* 10 (1): 136–63.

Jovanovic, B. et al. (forthcoming), "The role of effects for infants' perception of action goals", *Cognition*.

Jurafsky, D. (1996), "A probabilistic model of lexical and syntactic access and disambiguation", *Cognitive Science* 20: 137–94.

—— (forthcoming), "Probabilistic modeling in psycholinguistics: linguistic comprehension and production", in R. Bod, J. Hay, and S. Jannedy (eds.), *Probabilistic Linguistics* (Cambridge, MA: MIT Press).

—— Bell, A., Gregory, M., and Raymond, W. D. (2001), "Probabilistic relations between words: evidence from reduction in lexical production", in J. Bybee and P. Hopper (eds.), *Frequency and the Emergence of Linguistic Structure* (Amsterdam: John Benjamins), 229–54.

Just, M. A. and Carpenter, P. A. (1992), "A capacity theory of comprehension: individual differences in working memory", *Psychological Review* 98: 122–49.

Kaas, J. H. and Hackett, T. A. (1999), " 'What' and 'where' processing in auditory cortex", *Nature Neuroscience* 2: 1045–7.

Kadmon, N. (2001), *Formal Pragmatics* (Oxford: Oxford University Press).

Kako, E. (2005), "The semantics of syntactic frames", *Language and Cognitive Processes*.

Kaschak, M. P. and Glenberg, A. M. (2000), "Constructing meaning: the role of affordances and grammatical constructions in sentence comprehension", *Journal of Memory and Language* 43 (3): 508–29.

—— —— (2004), "This construction needs learned", *Journal of Experimental Psychology: General* 133: 450–67.

Kay, P. (1996). *Argument Structure: Causative ABC Constructions*. Unpublished manuscript, University of California, Berkeley.

—— (1997), "Notes on Argument Structure Constructions". Unpublished manuscript, University of California, Berkeley.

—— (2001), "Argument structure constructions and the argument-adjunct distinction". Unpublished manuscript, University of California, Berkeley.

—— (2002a), "English Subjectless Tagged Sentences", *Language*, 78 (3): 453–581.

—— (2002b), "An informal sketch of a formal architecture for construction grammar", *Grammars* 5: 1–19.

—— and Fillmore, C. J. (1999), "Grammatical constructions and linguistic generalizations: the what's X doing Y? construction", *Language* 75: 1–34.

Kayne, R. (1981), "On certain differences between French and English", *Linguistic Inquiry* 12: 349–71.

Keenan, E. L. (1976), "Towards a universal definition of 'subject'", in C. N. Li (ed.), *Subject and Topic* (New York: Academic Press), 303–34.

—— (1984), "Semantic correlates of the ergative/absolutive distinction", *Linguistics* 22: 197–223.

—— and Comrie, B. (1977), "Noun phrase accessibility and universal grammar", *Linguistic Inquiry* 8: 63–99.

Kemmer, S. and Verhagen, A. (2002), "The grammar of causatives and the conceptual structure of events", in *Mouton Classics: From Syntax to Cognition, from Phonology to Text* (Berlin: Mouton de Gruyter), 451–91.

Kempen, G. (1977), "Conceptualizing and formulating in sentence production", in S. Rosenberg (ed.), *Sentence Production: Developments in Research and Theory* (Hillsdale, NJ: Lawrence Erlbaum), 259–74.

Kersten, A. W. and Billman, D. (1997), "Event category learning", *Journal of Experimental Psychology: Learning, Memory, and Cognition* 23: 638–58.

Kidd, E., Lieven, E., and Tomasello, M. (2005), "Examining the contribution of lexical frequency and working memory to the acquisition of syntax". Unpublished manuscript, Max Planck Institute, Leipzig.

Kiparsky, P. (1973), "'Elsewhere' in phonology", in S. R. Anderson and P. Kiparsky (eds.), *A Festschrift for Morris Halle* (New York: Holt, Rinehart, and Winston), 93–106.

—— (1996), "Remarks on denominal verbs", in A. Alsina, J. Bresnan, and P. Sells (eds.), *Complex Predicates* (Stanford, CA: CLSI Publications), 473–500.

—— and Kiparsky, C. (1971), "Fact", in M. Bierwisch and K. Heidolph (eds.), *Semantics: An Interdisciplinary Reader in Philosophy, Linguistics and Psychology* (Cambridge: Cambridge University Press), 345–69.

Kitagawa, Y. and Fodor, J. D. (2003), "Default prosody explains neglected syntactic analyses in Japanese", in W. McClure (ed.), *Japanese/Korean Linguistics*, Vol. 12, (Stanford, CA: Center for the Study of Language and Information), 267–79.

Klein, D. E. and Murphy, G. L. (2002), "Paper has been my ruin: conceptual relations of polysemous senses", *Journal of Memory and Language* 47: 548–70.

Kluender, R. (1998), "On the distinction between strong and weak islands: a processing perspective", *Syntax and Semantics* 29: 241–79.

—— and Kutas, M. (1993), "Subjacency as a processing phenomenon", *Language and Cognitive Processes* 8: 573–633.

Koenig, J.-P. (1993), "Linking constructions vs. linking rules: evidence from French", *Proceedings of the 19th Meeting of the Berkeley Linguistics Society*, 217–31.

—— and Davis, A. (2001), "Sublexical modality and the structure of lexical semantic representations", *Linguistics and Philosophy* 24: 71–124.

Kruschke, J. K. (1996), "Base rates in category learning", *Journal of Experimental Psychology: Learning, Memory, and Cognition* 22: 3–26.

Kuno, S. (1972), "Functional sentence perspective: a case study from Japanese and English", *Linguistic Inquiry* 3: 269–320.

—— (1991), "Remarks on quantifier scope", in W. Winter (ed.), *Current English Linguistics in Japan* (New York: Mouton), 261–88.

Lakoff, G. (1970), *Irregularity in Syntax* (New York: Holt, Rinehart and Winston).

—— (1987), *Women, Fire, and Dangerous Things: What Categories Reveal About the Mind* (Chicago: University of Chicago Press).

—— and Brugman, C. (1987), "The semantics of aux-inversion and anaphora constraints", *13R Annual Meeting of the Berkeley Linguistics Society*, University of California, Berkeley, Feb. 14–16.

Lamb, S. M. (2002), "Learning syntax—a neurocognitive approach", in S. Niemeier, M. Putz, and R. Dirven (eds.), *Applied Cognitive Linguistics I: Theory and Language Acquisition* (New York: Mouton de Gruyter).

Lambrecht, K. (1990), "'What, me worry?' Mad magazine sentences revisited", *Proceedings of the 16th Annual Meeting of the Berkeley Linguistics Society* 215–28.

—— (1994), *Information Structure and Sentence Form* (Cambridge: Cambridge University Press).

—— (2004), "Focus-structure constructions and language typology: the case of spoken French". Paper presented at the Third International Conference on Construction Grammar, Marseilles, July.

—— and Polinsky, M. (1997), "Typological variation in sentence-focus constructions", *Papers from the Regional Meetings of the Chicago Linguistic Society* 33 (2): 189–206.

Landau, B. (2003), "Starting at the end: the importance of goals in spatial language and spatial cognition". Paper presented at the Conference on Spatial Language and Spatial Cognition, Baltimore, MD.

Langacker, R. W. (1987a), *Foundations of Cognitive Grammar*, Vol. 1 (Stanford, CA: Stanford University Press).

—— (1987b), "Nouns and verbs", *Language* 63: 53–94.

—— (1988), "A Usage-based model", in B. Rudzka-Ostyn (ed.), *Topics in Cognitive Linguistics*. (Philadelphia: John Benjamins), 127–61.

—— (1990), *Concept, Image, and Symbol: The Cognitive Basis of Grammar* (Berlin, New York: Mouton de Gruyter).

—— (1991), *Foundations of Cognitive Grammar*, Vol. 2 (Stanford, CA: Stanford University Press).

—— (1992), "Reference point constructions", *Cognitive Linguistics* 1–39.

—— (2003), "Construction grammars: cognitive, radical and less so". Paper presented at the International Cognitive Linguistics Conference, Logroño.

Larson, R. (1988), "On the double object construction", *Linguistic Inquiry* 19: 335–92.

—— (1990), "Double objects revisited: reply to Jackendoff", *Linguistic Inquiry* 21: 589–632.

Laughlin, R. B. (2005), *A Different Universe* (Philadelphia: Perseus Books).

—— and Pines, D. (2000), "The theory of everything", *Proceedings of the National Academy of Sciences* 97 (1): 28–31.

Leake, D. B. and Ram, A. (1995), "Learning, goals, and learning goals: a perspective on goal-driven learning", *Artificial Intelligence Review* 9: 387–422.

Leek, F. V. D. (1996), "Rigid syntax and flexible meaning: the case of the English ditransitive", in A. E. Goldberg (ed.), *Conceptual Structure, Discourse and Language* (Stanford, CA: CSLI Publications), 321–46.

Lees, R. B. (1960), *The Grammar of English Nominalizations* (The Hague: Mouton).

Lemmens, M. (1998), *Lexical Perspectives on Transitivity and Ergativity: Causative Constructions in English* (Philadelphia: John Benjamins).

Levelt, W. J. M. and Kelter, S. (1982), "Surface form and memory in question answering", *Cognitive Psychology* 14: 78–106.

Levin, B. (1993), *English Verb Classes and Alternations* (Chicago: Chicago University Press).

—— and Rappaport Hovav, M. (1993), "The dative alternation revisited". Paper presented at the workshop on verb classes and Alternations, Institut Für Linguistin/Anglistin, Universität Stuttgart, Jan. 10–11.

—— (1995), *Unaccusativity in the Syntax-Lexical Semantics Interface* (Cambridge, MA: MIT Press).

Levine, R. and Sag, I. A. (2003), "Some empirical issues in the grammar of extraction". Paper presented at the HPSG03 Conference, Michigan State University, East Lansing.

Levinson, S. C. (1983), *Pragmatics* (Cambridge: Cambridge University Press).

Liang, J. (2002), "Sentence comprehension by Chinese Korners of English: verb-centered or construction-based". Unpublished MA thesis, Guangdong University of Foreign Studies.

Lidz, J., Gleitman, H., and Gleitman, L. (2003), "Understanding how input matters: verb learning and the footprint of universal grammar", *Cognition* 87: 151–78.

—— and Gleitman, L. (2004), "Yes, we need universal grammar", *Cognition*, 94: 85–93.

Lieven, E. V. M., Pine, J. M., and Baldwin, G. (1997), "Lexically-based learning and early grammatical development", *Journal of Child Language* 24: 187–219.

Lindblom, B. (1990), "Explaining phonetic variation: a sketch of the H&H theory", in W. J. Hardcastle and A. Marchal (eds.), *Speech Production and Speech Modeling* (Boston: Kluwer Academics), 403–40.

Lindner, S. (1981), "A lexico-semantic analysis of verb-particle constructions with *up* and *out*". Unpublished dissertation, University of California, San Diego.

Loebell, H. and Bock, K. (2003), "Structural priming across languages", *Linguistics* 41–5: 791–824.

Losiewicz, B. L. (1992), "The Effect of Frequency on Linguistic Morphology". Unpublished Ph.D. dissertation, University of Texas, Austin.

MacDonald, M. C., Pearlmutter, N. J., and Seidenberg, M. S. (1994). "The Lexical Nature of Syntactic Ambiguity Resolution", *Psychological Review* 101(4): 676–703.

MacWhinney, B. (1977), "Starting points", *Language* 53: 152–68.

—— (1978), *The Acquisition of Morphophonology*, Vol. 43 (Chicago: University of Chicago Press).

—— (1982), "Basic syntactic processes", in S. Kuczaj (ed.), *Language Development*, *Vol. 1: Syntax and Semantics* (Hillsdale, NJ: Lawrence Erlbaum), 73–136.

—— (1995), *The Childes Project: Tools for Analyzing Talk* (2nd edn.) (Hillsdale, NJ: Lawrence Erlbaum).

—— (ed.), (1999), *The Emergence of Language* (Hillsdale, NJ: Lawrence Erlbaum).

—— (forthcoming), "Multiple solutions to the logical problem of language acquisition", *Journal of Child Language*.

Maddox, W. T. (1995), "Base-rate effects in multidimensional perceptual categorization", *Journal of Experimental Psychology: Learning, Memory and Cognition* 21: 288–301.

Manning, C. D. (1996), *Ergativity* (Stanford, CA: Center for the Study of Language and Information).

Marantz, A. (1997), "No escape from syntax: don't try morphological analysis in the privacy of your own lexicon", in A. Dimitriadis and L. Siegel (eds.), *University of Pennsylvania Working Papers in Linguistics*, Vol. 4.2 (Philadelphia), 201–25.

Maratsos, M., Gudeman, R., Gerard-Ngo, P., and Dehart, G. (1987), "A study in novel word learning: the productivity of the causative", in B. MacWhinney (ed.), *Mechanisms of Language Acquisition*. (Hillsdale, NJ: Lawrence Erlbaum).

Marcotte, J.-P. (2005), "Causative alternation errors and innate knowledge: consequences of the 'no negative evidence' fallacy", in E. V. Clark and B. F. Kelly (eds.), *Constructions in Acquisition* (Stanford, CA: Center for the Study of Language and Information).

Marcus, G. F., Brinkmann, U., Clahsen, H., Wiese, R., and Pinker, S. (1995), "German inflection: the exception that proves the rule", *Cognitive Psychology* 29: 189–256.

—— Vijayan, S., Bandi Rao, S., and Vishton, P. M. (1999), "Rule learning by seven-month-old-infants", *Science* 283: 77–80.

Markman, A. B., and Gentner, D. (1993), "Structural alignment during similarity comparisons", *Cognitive Psychology* 25: 431–67.

—— and Maddox, W. T. (2003), "Classification of exemplars with single and multiple-feature manifestations: the effects of relevant dimension variation and category structure", *Journal of Experimental Psychology: Learning, Memory and Cognition* 29: 107–17.

Matsumoto, Y. (1992), *Abstract Motion and English and Japanese Verbs*. Unpublished manuscript, Tokyo Christian University.

McCawley, J. D. (1978), "Conversational implicature and the lexicon", in P. Cole (ed.), *Syntax and Semantics 9: Pragmatics* (New York: Academic Press), 245–59.

Medin, D. L. and Edelson, S. M. (1988), "Problem structure and the use of base-rate information from experience", *Journal of Experimental Psychology: General* 117: 68–85.

Medin, D. L. and Schaffer, M. M. (1978), "Context theory of classification learning", *Psychological Review* 85: 207–38.

—— Wattenmaker, W. D., and Hampson, S. E. (1987), "Family resemblance conceptual cohesiveness, and category construction", *Cognitive Psychology* 12: 242–79.

Meir, R. and Rätsch, G. (2003), "An Introduction to Boosting and Leveraging", in S. Mendelson and A. J. Smola (eds.), *Advanced Lectures on Machine Learning: Machine Learning Summer School 2002, Camberra, Australia, Feb. 11–22, 2002. Revised Lectures* (Springer-Verlag), 118–83.

Menzel, R. and Giurfa, M. (2001), "Cognitive architecture of a mini-brain: the honeybee", *Trends in Cognitive Science* 5: 62–71.

Meyer, D. E. and Schvaneveldt, R. W. (1971), "Facilitation in recognizing pairs of words: evidence of a dependence between retrieval operations", *Journal of Experimental Psychology* 90: 227–34.

Michaelis, L. A. (1994), "A case of constructional polysemy in Latin", *Studies in Language* 18: 23–48.

—— (2001), "Exclamative constructions", in M. Haspelmath, E. König, W. Österreicher, and W. Raible (eds.), *Language Universals and Language Typology: An International Handbook* (Berlin: Walter de Gruyter), 1038–50.

—— (2004), "Implicit and explicit type-shifting in construction grammar", *Cognitive Linguistics* 14: 45–70.

—— and Francis, H. S. (forthcoming), "Lexical subjects and the conflation strategy", in N. Hedberg and R. Zacharski (eds.), *Topics in the Grammar-Pragmatics Interface: Papers in Honor of Jeanette K. Gundel* (Amsterdam: John Benjamins).

—— and Lambrecht, K. (1996a), "The exclamative sentence type in English", in A. E. Goldberg (ed.), *Conceptual Structure, Discourse and Language* (Stanford, CA: Center for the Study of Language and Information), 375–98.

—— —— (1996b), "Toward a construction-based model of language function: the case of nominal extraposition", *Language* 72: 215–47.

—— and Ruppenhofer, J. (2001), *Beyond Alternations: A Constructional Account of the Applicative Pattern in German* (Stanford, CA: Center for the Study of Language and Information).

Mithun, M. (1984), "The evolution of noun incorporation", *Language* 60: 847–94.

Monaghan, P., Onnis, L., Christiansen, M. H., and Chater, N. (2005), *The Importance of Being Variable: Learning Nonadjacent Dependencies in Speech Processing.* Unpublished manuscript, York University.

Moore, J. and Ackerman, F. (1999), *Proto-properties and Argument Encoding: a Correspondence Theory of Argument Selection* (Stanford, CA: CSLI Publications).

Morgan, J. L. (1975), "Some interactions of syntax and pragmatics", in P. Cole and J. L. Morgan (eds.), *Syntax and Semantics: Vol. 3: Speech Acts* (New York: Academic Press), 289–304.

Morris, W. C. and Cottrell, G. W. (1999), "The empirical acquisition of grammatical relations". Paper presented at the Proceedings of the Cognitive Science Society Meeting.

Mouner, G. and Koenig, J.-P. (2000), "Linguistic vs. conceptual sources of implicit agents in sentence comprehension", *Journal of Memory and Language* 43: 110–34.

Mughazy, M. (2002), "On the periphery of syntax: the N–P–N constructions in Egyptian Arabic". Paper presented at the Conceptual Structure, Discourse, and Language conference at Rice University.

Murphy, G. L. (1982), "Cue validity and levels of categorization", *Psychological Bulletin* 91: 174–7.

—— (2002), *The Big Book of Concepts* (Cambridge, MA: MIT Press).

Mussweiler, T. (2001), "The durability of anchoring effects", *European Journal of Social Psychology* 31: 431–42.

Naigles, L. (1990), "Children use syntax to learn verb meanings", *Journal of Child Language* 7: 357–74.

—— and Bavin, E. L. (2001), *Generalizing Novel Verbs to Different Structures: Evidence for the Early Distinction of Verbs and Frames.* Paper presented at the BU Conference of Language Acquisition, Boston.

—— Gleitman, H., and Gleitman, L. (1993), "Children acquire word meaning components from syntactic evidence", in E. Dromi (ed.), *Language and Cognition: A Developmental Perspective*, Vol. 5 (New Jersey: Ablex Publishing), 104–40.

—— and Hoff-Ginsberg, E. (1998), "Why are some verbs learned before other verbs? Effects of input frequency and structure on children's early verb use", *Journal of Child Language* 25: 95–120.

Nakajima, H. (2002), "Considering the basic assumptions of construction grammar", *The Rising Generation* CXLVII: 34–7. Translated for the author by Tsuguro Nakamura.

Nakamura, T. (1997), "Actions in motion: how languages express manners of motion", in M. Ukaji, T. Nakao, M. Kajita, and S. Chiba (eds.), *Studies in English Linguistics: A Festschrift for Akira Ota on the Occasion of His Eightieth Birthday* (Tokyo: Taishukan Publishing Company), 723–38.

Narasimhan, B. (1998), "The encoding of complex events in Hindi and English". Unpublished Ph.D. dissertation, Boston University.

Newmeyer, F. (2000), *Language Form and Language Function* (Cambridge, MA: MIT Press).

—— (2003), "Grammar is grammar and usage is usage", *Language* 79: 682–707.

—— (2003), "Theoretical implications of phrasal category–grammatical relations mismatches", in L. Michaelis and E. Francis (eds.), *Linguistic Mismatches* (Stanford, CA: CSLI Publications).

Nicol, J. L. (1996), "Syntactic priming", *Language and Cognitive Processes* 11: 675–9.

Nikolaeva, I. (1991), "Secondary topic as a relation in information structure", *Linguistics* 39: 1–49.

Ninio, A. (1999), "Pathbreaking verbs in syntactic development and the question of prototypical transitivity", *Journal of Child Language* 26: 619–53.

—— (2005), "Accelerated learning without semantic similarity: indirect objects", *Cognitive Linguistics* 16 3: 531–56.

Nosofsky, R. (1988), "Similarity, frequency and category representations", *Journal of Experimental Psychology: Learning, Memory, and Cognition* 14: 54–65.

Nunberg, G., Sag, I. A., and Wasow, T. (1994), "Idioms", *Language* 70: 491–538.

Oehrle, R. (1975), "Discourse constraints on dative movement", in *Syntax and Semantics* 12.

—— (1976), "The grammatical status of the English dative alternation". Unpublished Ph.D. dissertation, MIT, Boston.

Olguin, R. and Tomasello, M. (1993), "Twenty-five-month-old children do not have a grammatical category of verb", *Cognitive Development* 8: 245–72.

Osherson, D. N., Wilkie, O., Smith, E. E., Lopez, A., and Shafir, E. (1990), "Category-based induction", *Psychological Review* 97: 185–200.

Oshima, D. Y. (2005), *On Factive and Negative Islands: Discourse-Based Accounts.* Unpublished manuscript, Stanford University.

Park, T.-Z. (1977). *Emerging Language in Korean Children.* Unpublished manuscript, Institute of Psychology, Bern.

Partee, B. H. (1965/1979), *Subject and Object in Modern English* (New York: Garland).

Pawley, A. and Syder, F. H. (1983), "Two puzzles for linguistic theory", in J. Richards and R. Smith (eds.), *Language and Communication* (New York: Longmans).

Payne, D. L. (1997), "Argument structure and locs of affect in the Maasai external possession construction". *Proceedings of the 23rd Meeting of the Berkeley Linguistic Society: Special Session on Syntax and Semantics in Africa.*

Pearl, J. (1988), *Probabilistic Reasoning in Intelligent Systems: Networks of Plausible Inference* (San Mateo, CA: Morgan Kaufman).

—— (2000), *Causality: Models, Reasoning, and Inference* (Cambridge: Cambridge University Press).

Pesetsky, D. (1987), "Wh-*in-situ*: movement and unselective binding", in E. J. Reuland and A. G. B. ter Meulen (eds.), *The Representation of Indefiniteness* (Cambridge, MA: MIT Press), 98–129.

Peterson, R. R., Burgess, C., Dell, G. S., and Eberhard, K. (2001), "Dissociation between syntactic and semantic processing during idiom comprehension", *Journal of Experimental Psychology: Learning, Memory, and Cognition* 27: 1223–37.

Pierrehumbert, J. (2000), "What people know about sounds of language", *Studies in the Linguistic Sciences* 29: 111–20.

Pine, J., Lieven, E., and Rowland, C. F. (1998), "Comparing different models of the development of the English verb category", *Linguistics* 36 (4): 807–30.

Pinker, S. (1981), "Comments on the paper by Wexler", in C. L. Baker and J. J. McCarthy (eds.), *The Logical Problem of Language Acquisition* (Cambridge: MA: Harvard University Press), 53–63.

—— (1984), *Language Learnability and Language Development* (Cambridge, MA: Harvard University Press).

—— (1986), "Productivity and conservatism in language acquisition", in W. Demopoulos and A. Marras (eds.), *Language Learning and Concept Acquisition: Foundational Issues.* (New Jersey: Ablex).

—— (1989), *Learnability and Cognition: The Acquisition of Argument Structure* (Cambridge, MA: MIT Press/Bradford Books).

—— (1994), *The Language Instinct* (New York: William Morrow and Co.).

—— (1999), *Words and Rules: The Ingredients of Language* (New York: Basic Books).

—— and Jackendoff, R. (2005), "The faculty of language: what's special about it?" *Cognition* 95: 201–36.

Pizer, K. (1994), "Perception verb complementation. A construction-based account", *Chicago Linguistic Society* 30.

Plunkett, K. and Marchman, V. (1991), "U-shaped learning and frequency effects in a multilayered perceptron: implications for child language acquisition", *Cognition* 38: 43–102.

—— —— (1993), "From rote learning to system building: acquiring verb morphology in children and connectionist nets", *Cognition* 48: 21–69.

Polinsky, M. (1998), "A non-syntactic account of some asymmetries in the double object construction", in J.-P. Koenig (ed.), *Conceptual Structure and Language: Bridging the Gap* (Stanford, CA: CSLI Publications), 401–20.

—— and Kozinsky, I. (1992), "Ditransitive constructions in Kinyarwanda: coding conflict or syntactic doubling?" in C. Canakis, G. Chan, and J. Denton (eds.), *Papers from the 28th Regional Meeting of the Chicago Linguistic Society* (Chicago: Chicago Linguistic Society), 426–39.

—— and Potsdam, E. (2004), "Malagasy Control Constructions". Paper presented at the Berkeley Linguistic Society, Berkeley, CA, February 14.

Pollard, C. J. and Sag, I. A. (1987), *Information-Based Syntax and Semantics* (Stanford, CA: Center for the Study of Language and Information).

—— —— (1994), *Head-Driven Phrase Structure Grammar* (Stanford, CA: CSLI Publications).

Posner, M. I., Goldsmith, R., and Welton, K. E. J. (1967), "Perceived distance and the classification of distorted patterns", *Journal of Experimental Psychology: General* 73: 28–38.

—— and Keele, S. W. (1968), "On the genesis of abstract ideas", *Journal of Experimental Psychology* 77: 353–63.

Postal, P. (1998), *Three Investigations of Extraction* (Cambridge, MA: MIT Press).

Potter, M. C. and Lombardi, L. (1998), "Syntactic priming in immediate recall of sentences", *Journal of Memory and Language* 38: 265–82.

Pourcel, S. (2004), "What Makes Path of Motion Salient?" Paper presented at the Berkeley Linguistic Society, Berkeley, CA, February 14.

Prince, E. (1981), "Toward a taxonomy of given/new information", in P. Cole (ed.), *Radical Pragmatics* (New York: Academic Press), 223–54.

Prinz, W. (1990), "A common coding approach to perception and action", in O. Neumann and W. Prinz (eds.), *Relationships between Perception and Action: Current Approaches* (Berlin: Springer Verlag), 167–201.

—— (1997), "Perception and action planning", *European Journal of Cognitive Psychology* 9: 129–154.

Pullum, G. K. (1991), *The Great Eskimo Vocabulary Hoax* (Chicago: University of Chicago Press).

—— and Scholz, B. C. (2002), "Empirical assessment of stimulus poverty arguments", *Linguistic Review* 19: 9–50.

Pylkkanen, L. (2003), "Double objects and secondary predication". NYU presentation, New York.

—— and Murphy, G. (2004), "Sense competition and the representation of polysemy". Paper presented at the Linguistic Society of America, Boston.

Quiochi, V. (in prep.), "Argument structure frequencies in Italian". University of Pisa.

Rappaport Hovav, M. and Levin, B. (1985), *A Case Study in Locative Analysis: The Locative Alternation* Bar Illan and Stanford Universities.

—— —— (1988), "What to do with theta roles", in W. Wilkins (ed.), *Syntax and Semantics: Thematic Relations* (New York: Academic Press), 7–36.

—— —— (1998), "Building verb meanings", in M. Butt and W. Geuder (eds.), *The Projection of Arguments: Lexical and Compositional Factors* (Stanford, CA: CSLI Publications), 97–134.

Ratitamkul, T., Goldberg, A. E., and Fisher, C. (2005), "Discourse prominence and argument omission in Thai", *Child Language Research Forum* (Standord: CSLI Publications).

Reddy, M. (1979), "The conduit metaphor", in A. Ortony (ed.), *Metaphor and Thought* (Cambridge: Cambridge University Press), 284–324.

Regehr, G. and Brooks, L. R. (1995), "Category organization in free classification: the organizing effect of an array of stimuli", *Journal of Experimental Psychology: Learning, Memory, and Cognition* 21: 347–63.

Regier, T. (1996), *The Human Semantic Potential: Spatial Language and Constrained Connectionism* (Cambridge, MA: MIT Press).

—— and Zheng, M. (2003), "An attentional constraint on spatial meaning". Paper presented at the Proceedings of the 25th Annual Meeting of the Cognitive Science Society, Boston.

Reinhart, T. (1982), *Pragmatics and Linguistics: An Analysis of Sentence Topics* (Bloomington: Indiana University Linguistics Club).

Resnik, P. (1993), "Selection and information: a class-based approach to lexical relationships". Unpublished Ph.D. dissertation, University of Pennsylvania.

Riehemann, S. (1997), *Idiomatic Constructions in HPSG*. Unpublished manuscript, Stanford University.

Rips, L. J. (1989), "Similarity, typicality, and categorization", in S. Vosniadou and A. Ortony (eds.), *Similarity and Analogical Reasoning.* (Cambridge: Cambridge University Press), 21–59.

Robertson, S. S. and Suci, G. J. (1980), "Event perception in children in early stages of language production", *Child Development* 51(1): 89–96.

Roland, D. and Jurafsky, D. (forthcoming), "Verb sense and verb subcategorization probabilities", in S. Stevenson and P. Merlo (eds.), *Papers from the 1998 Cuny Sentence Processing Conference* (John Benjamins).

Rosch, E. and Mervis, C. B. (1975), "Family resemblances: studies in the internal structure of categories", *Cognitive Psychology* 7: 573–605.

Ross, B. H. and Makin, V. S. (1999), "Prototype versus exemplar models", in R. J. Sternberg (ed.), *The Nature of Cognition* (Cambridge, MA: MIT Press), 205–41.

—— Perkins, S. J., and Tenpenny, P. L. (1990), "Reminding-based category learning", *Cognitive Psychology* 22: 460–92.

Ross, J. R. (1967), "Constraints on Variables in Syntax". Unpublished Ph.D. dissertation, MIT. Published 1986 as *Infinite Syntax!* (Norwood, NJ: Ablex Publishing).

Rowlands, R. C. (2002), "Swarming with bees: property predication and the swarm alternation". Unpublished MA thesis, University of Canterbury.

Rudanko, R. (2002), *Complements and Constructions* (New York: University Press of America).

Ruppenhofer, J. K. (2004), "The Interaction of Valence and Information Structure". Unpublished Ph.D. dissertation. University of California, Berkeley.

Saffran, E. M. and Martin, N. (1997), "Effects of structural priming on sentence production in aphasics", *Language and Cognitive Processes* 12: 877–82.

Saffran, J. R. (2001a), "The use of predictive dependencies in language learning", *Journal of Memory and Language* 44: 493–515.

—— (2001b), "Words in a sea of sounds: the output of infant statistical learning", *Cognition* 81: 149–69.

—— Aslin, R., and Newport, E. (1996), "Statistical learning by 8-month-old infants", *Science* 274: 1926–8.

—— Johnson, E. K., Aslin, R. N., and Newport, E. L. (1999), "Statistical learning of tone sequences by human infants and adults", *Cognition* 70: 27–52.

—— and Wilson, D. P. (2003), "From syllabus to syntax: multilevel statistical learning by 12-month-old infants", *Infancy* 4: 273–84.

Sag, I. A. (1997), "English relative clause constructions", *Journal of Linguistics* 33: 431–84.

—— and Fodor, J. D. (1994), "Extraction without Traces", *WCCFL* 13 (West coast Conference on Formal Linguistics).

—— Wasow, T., and Bender, E. (2003), *Syntactic Theory: A Formal Introduction* (Stanford, CA: Center for the Study of Language Information Publications).

Sailer, M. (2002), *The German Incredulity Response Construction and the Hierarchical Organization of Constructions*. Handout at the 2nd International Conference on Construction Grammar, Helsinki.

Salkoff (1983), "Bees are swarming in the garden", *Language* 59: 288–346.

Sampson, G. (1997), *Educating Eve: The "Language Instinct" Debate* (New York: Cassell).

Sanches, M. (1978), *On the Emergence of Multi-Element Utterances in the Child's Japanese*. Unpublished manuscript, Austin, Texas.

Sandler, W., Meir, I., Padden, C., and Aronoff, M. (2005), "The emergence of grammar: systematic structure in a new language", *Proceedings of the National Academy of Science* 102: 2661–5.

Santorini, B. (2005), "(Un?)expected movement", <http://www.ling.upenn.edu/~beatrice/examples/movement.html>.

Saussure, F. D. (1916/1959), *Course in General Linguistics*, trans. by W. Baskin (New York: Philosophical Library).

Savage, C., Lieven, E., Theakston, A., and Tomasello, M. (2003), "Testing the abstractness of children's linguistic representations: lexical and structural priming of syntactic constructions in young children", *Developmental Science* 6: 557–67.

Schachter, P. (1977), "Reference-related and role-related properties of subjects", in P. Cole and J. Sadock (eds.), *Syntax and Semantics*, Vol. 8 (New York: Academic Press).

Schapire, R. (1990), "The strength of weak learnability", *Machine Learning* 5: 197–227.

Scheepers, C. (2003), "Syntactic priming of relative clause attachments: persistence of structural configuration in sentence production", *Cognition* 89: 179–205.

Scheibman, J. (2002), *Point of View and Grammar: Structural Patterns of Subjectivity in American English Conversation* (Amsterdam: John Benjamins).

Schlesinger, I. M. (1982), *Steps to Language: Toward a Theory of Language Acquisition* (Hillsdale, NJ: Lawrence Erlbaum).

Schmid, H. J. (2001), "Presupposition can be a bluff: how abstract nouns can be used as presupposition triggers", *Journal of Pragmatics* 33: 1529–52.

—— and Ungerer, F. (2002), "NP+Complement and NP+Be+Complement as Constructions". Paper presented at the 2nd International Conference on Construction Grammar, Helsinki.

Scholz, B. C. and Pullum, G. K. (2002), "Searching for arguments to support linguistic nativism", *Linguistic Review* 19: 185–224.

Schultze-Berndt, E. (1998), "Making sense of complex verbs: generic verb meaning and the argument structure of complex predicates in Jaminjung". Unpublished manuscript, Max Planck Institute, Nijmegen.

Searle, J. (1979), *Expression and Meaning: Studies in the Theory of Speech Acts* (New York: Cambridge University Press).

Seger, C. A. (1994), "Implicit learning", *Psychological Bulletin* 115: 163–96.

Sethuraman, N. (2002), *The Acquisition of Verbs and Argument Structure Constructions* (San Diego: UCSD).

—— Goldberg, A. E., and Goodman, J. (1997), "Using the semantics associated with syntactic frames for interpretation without the aid of non-linguistic context", in E. Clark (ed.), *Proceedings of the 27th Annual Child Language Research Forum* (Stanford, CA), 283–94.

—— and Goodman, J. (2004), "Children's monstery of the transitive construction". Paper presented at the Stanford Child Language Research Forum, Stanford, CA.

Shibatani, M. (1999), "Dative subject constructions 22 years later", *Studies in the Linguistic Sciences* 29: 45–76.

Siegel, L. (2000), "Semantic bootstrapping and ergativity". Paper presented at the Annual Meeting of the Linguistic Society of America, Chicago.

Silverstein, M. (1976), "Hierarchy of features and ergativity", in R. Dixon (ed.), *Grammatical Categories in Australian Languages* (New York: Humanities Press), 112–71.

Simpson, G. G. (1945), "The principles of classification and a classification of mammals", *Bulletin of the American Museum of Natural History*, Vol. 85 (New York), 1–350.

Slobin, D. I. (1985), "Crosslinguistic evidence for the language-making capacity", in D. I. Slobin (ed.), *A Crosslinguistic Study of Language Acquisition*, Vol. 2: *Theoretical Issues* (Hillsdale, NJ: Lawrence Erlbaum), 1157–256

Smith, L. B. (1981), "Importance of overall similarity of objects for adults" and children's classifications", *Journal of Experimental Psychology: Human Perception and Performance* 7: 811–24.

Smith, M. and Wheeldon, L. (2001), "Syntactic priming in spoken sentence production—an online study", *Cognition* 78: 123–64.

Sorace, A. (2000), "Gradients in auxiliary selection with intransitive verbs", *Language* 76: 859–90.

Spalding, T. L. and Ross, B. H. (1994), "Comparison-based learning: effects of comparing instances during category learning", *Journal of Experimental Psychology: Learning, Memory, and Cognition* 1251–63.

Spencer, A. (2001), "The word-and-paradigm approach to morphosyntax", *Transactions of the Philological Society* 99: 279–313.

Stefanowitsch, A. and Gries, S. T. (2003), "Collostructions: investigating the interaction between words and constructions", *International Journal of Corpus Linguistics* 8: 209–43.

Stowell, T. (1981), "Origins of Phrase Structure". Unpublished Ph.D. dissertation, MIT.

Strack, F. and Mussweiler, T. (1995), *The Enigmatic Anchoring Effect: A Pervasive Phenomenon in Search of a Viable Explanation.* Unpublished manuscript, University of Trier.

Strawson, P. (1964), "Identifying reference and truth values", *Theoria* 30: 96–118.

Sugisaki, K. and Snyder, W. (forthcoming), "Do parameters have default values? Evidence from the acquisition of English and Spanish", in Y. Otsu (ed.), *Proceedings of the Fourth Tokyo Conference on Psycholinguistics* (Tokyo: Hituzi Syobo).

Takami, K.-I. (1989), "Preposition stranding: arguments against syntactic analyses and an alternative functional explanation", *Lingua* 76: 299–335.

Talmy, L. (1976), "Semantic causative types", in M. Shibatani (ed.), *Syntax and Semantics, Vol. 6: The Grammar of Causative Constructions.* (New York: Academic Press), 43–116.

Tannen, D. (1987), "Repetition in conversation: toward a poetics of talk", *Language* 63: 574–605.

Taylor, J. (1995), *Linguistic Categorization* (Oxford: Oxford University Press).

Thompson, S. A. (1990), "Information flow and dative shift in English discourse", in J. Edmondson, K. Feagin, and P. Mühlhäusler (eds.), *Development and Diversity:*

Linguistic Variation across Time and Space (Summer Institute of Linguistics), 239–53.

—— and Fox, B. (2004), "Relative clauses in English conversation: relativizers, frequency and the notion of construction". Unpublished manuscript, University of California, Santa Barbara.

—— and Hopper, P. J. (2001), "Transitivity, clause structure and argument structure: evidence from conversation", in J. L. Bybee and P. J. Hopper (eds.), *Frequency and the Emergence of Linguistic Structure* (Amsterdam: John Benjamins), 27–60.

Toivonen, I. (2002), "The directed motion construction in Swedish", *Journal of Linguistics* 38(2).

Tomasello, M. (1992), *First Verbs: A Case Study of Early Grammatical Development* (Cambridge: Cambridge University Press).

—— (1999), *The Cultural Origins of Human Cognition* (Cambridge, MA: Harvard University Press).

—— (2000), "Do young children have adult syntactic competence?" *Cognition* 74: 209–53.

—— (2003), *Constructing a Language: A Usage-Based Theory of Language Acquisition* (Cambridge, MA: Harvard University Press).

—— (forthcoming), "Acquiring linguistic constructions", in R. Siegler and D. Kuhn (eds.), *Handbook of Child Psychology: Cognitive Development.*

—— Akhtar, N., Dodson, K., and Rekau, L. (1997), "Differential productivity in young children's use of nouns and verbs", *Journal of Child Language* 24: 373–87.

—— and Stahl, D. (2004), "Sampling children's spontaneous speech: how much is enough?" *Journal of Child Language*, 31: 101–21.

Trueswell, J. C., Tanenhaus, M. K., and Kello, C. (1993), "Verb-specific constraints in sentence processing: separating effects of lexical preference from garden paths", *Journal of Experimental Psychology: Learning, Memory, and Cognition* 19: 528–53.

Tversky, A. and Kahneman, D. (1974), "Judgment under uncertainty: heuristics and biases", *Science* 185: 1124–31.

Uziel-Karl, S. (1999), "Children's verb lexicon". Paper presented at the Stanford Child Language Research Forum, Stanford, CA.

—— and Berman, R. A. (2000), "Where's ellipsis? Whether and why there are missing arguments in Hebrew child language", *Linguistics* 38: 457–82.

Valian, V. and Coulson, S. (1988), "Anchor points in language learning: the role of marker frequency", *Journal of Memory and Language* 27: 71–86.

Vallduvi, E. (1993), "Information packaging: a survey". Technical Report, HCRC research paper RP-44.

Van Hoek, K. (1995), "Conceptual reference points: a cognitive grammar account of pronominal anaphora constraints", *Language* 71: 310–40.

Van Valin, R. D. J. (1990), "Semantic parameters of split intransitivity", *Language* 66: 221–60.

—— (1998), "The acquisition of wh-questions and the mechanisms of language acquisition", in M. Tomasello (ed.), *The New Psychology of Language: Cognitive and Functional Approaches to Language Structure* (Hillsdale, NJ: Lawrence Erlbaum), 221–49.

—— and LaPolla, R. J. (1997), *Syntax: Structure, Meaning, and Function* (Cambridge: Cambridge University Press).

Verhagen, A. (2002), "From parts to wholes and back again", *Cognitive Linguistics* 13: 403–39.

Wasow, T. (1977), "Transformations and the lexicon", in P. W. Culicover, T. Wasow, and A. Akmajian (eds.), *Formal Syntax* (New York: Academic Press), 327–60.

—— (2002), *Postverbal Behavior* (Stanford, CA: Center for Study of Language and Information).

Webelhuth, G. and Ackerman, F. (1998), *A Theory of Predicates* (Stanford, CA: CSLI Publications).

Weiner, E. and Labov, W. (1983), "Constraints on the agentless passive", *Journal of Linguistics* 19: 29–58.

Whittlesea, B. W. A. (1987), "Preservation of specific experiences in the representation of general knowledge", *Journal of Experimental Psychology: Learning, Memory, and Cognition* 13: 3–17.

Wierzbicka, A. (1988), *The Semantics of Grammar* (Amsterdam: John Benjamins).

Willems, D. (1997), "On linking semantics and syntax through the lexicon. A macro-lexical approach of French verbs". Presentation given at Stanford University.

Williams, E. (1980), "Predication", *Linguistic Inquiry* 11: 203–38.

—— (1991), "Meaning categories of NPs and Ss", *Linguistic Inquiry* 22: 584–7.

—— (1994), "Remarks on lexical knowledge", *Lingua* 92: 7–34.

Wilson, T. D., Houston, C. E., Etling, K. M., and Brekke, N. (1996), "A new look at anchoring effects: basic anchoring and its antecedents", *Journal of Experiment Psychology: General* 125: 387–402.

Wisniewski, E. J. (1995), "Prior knowledge and functionally relevant features in concept learning", *Memory and Cognition* 21: 449–68.

Woodward, A. L. (1998), "Infants selectively encode the goal object of an actor's reach", *Cognition* 69: 1–34.

—— (1999), "Infants" ability to distinguish between purposeful and non-purposeful behaviors", *Infant Behavior and Development* 22: 145–60.

Yamashita, H. and Chang, F. (2001), ""Long before short" preference in the production of a head-final language", *Cognition* 81: B45–55.

—— —— and Hirose, Y. (2003), "Pure order priming: structural priming in Japanese". Paper presented at the City University of New York.

Zadrozny, W. and Ramer, A. M. (1995), "Idioms as constructions and universal grammar". IBM T. J. Watson Research Center, Yorktown Heights, NY.

Zaenen, A. and Uszkoreit, H. (1996), "Language analysis and understanding", in J. Cole, R. A. Mariani, H. Uszkoreit, A. Zaenen, and V. Zue (eds.), *Survey of the State of the Art in Human Language Technology* (Cambridge: Cambridge University Press), ch. 3.

Zanuttini, R. and Portner, P. (2003), "Exclamative clauses: at the syntax-semantics interface", *Language* 79: 39–81.

Zhang, N. (1998), "The interactions between construction meaning and lexical meaning", *Linguistics* 36: 957–80.

Zipf, G. K. (1935), *The Psycho-Biology of Language* (Boston: Houghton Mifflin).

Zwicky, A. M. (1974), "Hey watsyourname!" *Chicago Linguistic Society* 10: 787–801.

—— (1994), "Dealing out meaning: fundamentals of syntactic constructions", *Berkeley Linguistics Society* 20: 611–25.

Author Index

Subject Index